THE PASSOVER PLOT

HUGH J. SCHONFIELD

THE PASSOVER PLOT

New Light on the History of Jesus

PUBLISHED BY

BERNARD GEIS ASSOCIATES

DISTRIBUTED BY RANDOM HOUSE

© Hugh Schonfield 1965

Manufactured in the United States of America

In Memoriam R. H. Strachan, D.D.

Contents

Introduction

THE PASSOVER PLOT is the outcome of an endeavour which has extended over forty years to discover the man Jesus Christ really was. The difficulties all the way have been formidable, and by no means confined to problems of research. By far the hardest part of the undertaking has been to free the mind from preconceived ideas and the effects of traditional Christian teaching. There had to be a readiness to entertain whatever might be revealed even if this meant differing from former judgements. Most books about him have been devotional, apologetic or polemical, and I wished mine to be none of these. What I aimed at was to shed all disposition to make use of Jesus and allow him from his own time to explain himself to me.

I was first charged with responsibility for the task now completed when I was a student at Glasgow University. We were visited by an eminent Scottish Professor of New Testament History and Literature, whom I, a Jewish boy, rather startled by my youthful arguments and familiarity with the ancient Christian authorities I had studied on my own initiative. Already at that time the person of Jesus greatly attracted me, and I wanted to find out what had been the convictions of his original Jewish followers who acknowledged him as the Messiah. I read widely both the Christian and Jewish interpretations, and it seemed to me that both were partly right and partly wrong. There was a mystery which called for further explanation. My enthusiasm impressed the Professor, and he invited me to his home in Edinburgh where we talked into the small hours. In the end I made him a promise, which I have only been able to honour long after his death.

Through the intervening years, however, I pursued my researches, exploring many aspects of the subject. I wrote a number of books as much for my own instruction as for the enlightenment of those who read them. Finally I found it necessary to make a fresh English translation of the Christian Scriptures accompanied by copious explanatory notes, published as *The Authentic New Testament*, the most consequential of all my literary labours.

I have frequently been urged by numerous readers to set down my convictions about Jesus. They were persuaded that, in my unusual position as a Jew who has devoted a lifetime to the sympathetic elucidation of Christian Origins and is not connected with any section of the Church, I ought to have seen things which have escaped the observation of those more directly involved. Some of these correspondents may merely have been curious, and others eager to obtain my endorsement of their own beliefs. But on the whole there has been certified to me from the letters I continually receive from many parts of the world that there is a widespread desire for a realistic rather than an idealised representation of Jesus. The traditional portraiture no longer satisfies: it is too baffling in its apparent contradiction of the terms of our earthly existence. The God-man of Christianity is increasingly incredible, yet it is not easy to break with centuries of authoritative instruction and devout faith, and there remains embedded deep in the sub-conscious a strong sense of the supernatural inherited from remote ages.

Jesus still counts for so much, and answers so much to human need, that we are anxious to believe that there must have been something special about him, something which eludes our rational grasp and keeps us in our thought of him hovering perilously on the brink of naked superstition. We find in him the symbol both of the martyrdom and the aspirations of man, and therefore we must cling to him as the embodiment of an assurance that our life has a meaning and a purpose. Quite apart from the intrusion into early Christianity of a pagan assessment of his worth in

terms of deity, which historically we have to admit, no interpretation of Jesus can content us which does not show that our
confidence has not been wholly misplaced. If he was not more
than man, he was at the very least a most exceptional man, who
placed his own indelible stamp on the story of human experience
and achievement.

So this remarkable Jew continues to intrigue and agitate us,
the more so perhaps as the old ties of a settled faith are loosened.
'Tell me more about Jesus,' says a well-known hymn. Yet many
are now half afraid that the telling will destroy an illusion, that
the man behind the myth will prove to be less alluring, less con-
soling and inspiring.

It has emerged from recent literature and broadcasts, and from
my personal contacts, that it is not practicable to invest the
theological Jesus with convincing historicity, for the theological
figure continually conditions consideration of almost everything
relating to the actual man. It is so much more familiar, and hard
to shake off. There is an attitude of reverence, which projects
itself in the transmutation of the character of Jesus, who, despite
the evidence of the Gospels, is made out to be all love and compassion, in the treatment of his every word as divine wisdom, in
the wish to explain away his mistakes and extenuate his faults. I
recall my discomfort, while I was translating the New Testament,
when a distinguished and pious Christian layman said to me, 'If
you can get round Jesus cursing the fig tree you will have done
us a great service.'

The only way in which we can hope to know the real Jesus is
by first becoming conscious of him as a man of his own time,
country and people, which necessitates an intimate acquaintance
with all three. We have resolutely to refuse to detach him from
his setting, and let the influences which played upon him play
upon us. We have to mark the traits in him which were personal,
individual, whether pleasing or unpleasing, which convey to us
the attributes and idiosyncrasies of a creature of flesh and blood.
Only when this Galilean Jew has made an impact upon us in the
cruder aspects of his mortality are we entitled to begin to cultivate

him and estimate his worth, allowing him to communicate to us
the imaginations of his mind and the motivation of his actions.
If, then, we perceive in him some spark of genius, some quality
of greatness and nobility of soul, we shall not incline to exagger-
ate or convert him impossibly into a paragon of all the virtues.
Such a man could have his godlike moments, but could never be
consistently a reflection of the Divine except for those whose
notion of deity would permit the gods to share our human
frailties.

The modern dilemma of Christianity is patent and stems from
a creed which down the centuries has so insisted on seeing God
in Jesus Christ that it is in danger, as is now evident, of being unable to apprehend the existence of God without him. Far too
many Christians do not know God in any other way than through
Jesus. Take away the deity of Jesus and their faith in God is im-
perilled or destroyed. The New Testament is not entirely to be
blamed for this. The major fault lies with those who have
pandered to the ignorance and superstition of the people in giving
them a God created in the image of man. Yet Jesus and his own
nation, differently taught, could love and worship God without
recourse to incarnation.

I have often asked my Christian friends, 'Is it not enough if
you believe in the One God, Lord of all spirits, and accept Jesus
as his messianic messenger?' But it seemed that the messiahship
of Jesus in their view had only to do with the Jews, and meant
nothing in their experience. Many were not even aware that Christ
was simply a Greek translation of the Hebrew title Messiah (the
Anointed One), and supposed that it had to do with the heavenly
nature of the Second Person of the Trinity. It took me a long time
to appreciate that when we talked of God we were not speaking
the same language, and that there was a serious problem of communication. Finally it dawned on me, and I have in honesty to
say this, that Christianity was still much too close to the paganism
over which it had scored a technical victory to be happy with a
faith in God as pure Spirit. There had never been in the Church
a complete conversion from heathenism. We might be living in

the second half of the twentieth century, but the Gentile need remained for a human embodiment of deity. God had still to be grasped through a physical kinship with man and his earthly concerns, and there yet lingered the sense of the efficacy of the substitutionary and propitiatory sacrifice of a choice victim. As a consequence, where there has been emancipation from this ancient heritage this has tended to produce not a purer religion but the natural reaction of atheism. The Church must be held to be a major cause of promoting what it wholeheartedly condemns.

However, it is not my intention to embark on a theological treatise, only to draw attention to what is the most powerful influence which bars the way to the truth about Jesus. No doubt much could stem from a re-exposition of religion in a modern idiom, which reconciled and reunited Christians and Jews, and moved on towards the realisation of the age-old vision of the Brotherhood of Man and the Kingdom of God on earth of which Jesus was such an electrifying exponent. But if this is to be effected there will be a great deal to unlearn and to relearn.

I have had to indicate my consciousness of the gulf to be bridged, because this has affected the manner in which my subject has been presented. I have been most anxious to avoid being too academic, so that the book may be read without difficulty by the non-specialist. But I have had to take account of the fact that there is much ignorance about conditions in Palestine at the time of Jesus and about how Christianity originated. Few people are informed about the character of the Gospel records, how they came into being, and what credence is to be placed in their testimony. If they depend entirely on the New Testament they cannot form a correct judgement of Jesus. They must be put in a position where they are able to test the validity of what they find there by bringing to bear a multiplicity of factors of which they may not previously have been aware.

I have therefore divided the book into two parts, which are complementary but differ considerably in style and content. Part One is an imaginative reconstruction of the personality, aims and activities of Jesus. This part is biographical, but does not include everything reported about him, and is not offered as a 'life' of Jesus. It does, however, face some of the greatest difficulties which are contained in certain features of his life, especially the birth and resurrection stories.

My interpretation is founded, securely as it seems to me, on the belief of Jesus that he was the expected Messiah of Israel. Any view of him which ignores or evades this definite and illuminating information is self-condemned—however attractive and enticing it may be—as alien not only to the evidence of the New Testament, and to the fact of a faith coming into existence which could be called Christian or Messianist, but also to the atmosphere prevailing in Palestine at the time which evoked the response Jesus made. Much has been written to illustrate what light this throws on the central figure of Christianity; but it is possible to see still more, because due to modern discoveries like the Dead Sea Scrolls we know more.

But what is known can only be applied constructively when we are uninhibited by a religious compulsion to assume that the records about Jesus were divinely inspired. We must hold that they rate no higher than what can be established as to their reliability. They do not pass the test very well, though they certainly incorporate a good deal which is of the utmost value. The authors had to write up their subject with rather meagre resources of documentation and living recollection. This was because of the Jewish revolt against Rome in A.D. 66 which resulted in the devastation of Palestine and Jerusalem and largely extinguished access to fuller information. Actually we are better placed now than they were. When the Gospels were composed, legend, special pleading, the new environment of Christianity after the war, and a changed view of the nature of Jesus, gave them a flavour of which we have to be fully conscious when we enlist their essential aid in the quest for the historical Jesus.

These matters, and others highly pertinent to the understanding of Jesus, are considered, together with the research material, in Part Two. Here will be found disquisitions on crucial issues with the latest information and some quite new arguments which the reader minded to go more deeply into the subject can explore at his leisure.

What I have wished to be appreciated is that this is not one of those books which appear from time to time offering some far-fetched and highly fictitious account of Jesus which has no real roots in the knowledge in our possession. Where I have offered a theory which in the nature of things cannot be established I have plainly stated this.

I also desire to make clear that the image of Jesus which emerges does not, when honestly examined, detract from his greatness and uniqueness. Rather does it confirm, quite over-whelmingly, the earliest Christian conviction, that awareness of being the Messiah meant everything to Jesus. In affirmation of that office, that peculiar and incredibly difficult function, he directed his life, anticipated his execution, and envisaged his resurrection. This book reveals him as a master of his destiny, expecting events to conform to the requirements of prophetic intimations, contriving those events when necessary, contending with friends and foes to ensure that the predictions would be ful-filled. Such strength of will founded on faith, such concentration of purpose, such astuteness in planning, such psychological in-sight as we find him displaying, marks him out as a dominant and dynamic personality, with a capacity for action which matched the greatness of his vision. He could be tender and compassionate, but he was no milk-and-water Messiah. He accepted that authority had been conferred upon him by God, and he exercised it with profound effect, whether favourable or unfavourable, on those who came in contact with him.

The Passover Plot tells the story of his high adventure, perhaps the strangest human enterprise in all recorded history, boldly and circumstantially. Hence the deliberately dramatic title, which strikes the keynote of the whole extraordinary undertaking to which Jesus committed himself.

In certain places in this book, for the sake of clarity, I have em-ployed my own translation of the Christian Scriptures, *The Authentic New Testament*, the accuracy of which is vouched for by

eminent scholars. This is available in Britain and the Common-
wealth in hardcover published by Dobson Books and in paperback by Panther Books, and in the United States in paperback
only, as yet, by the New American Library of Literature (Mentor
Books). Acknowledgment is accordingly made to these pub-
lishers.

I fully realise that my treatment of the subject may cause considerable debate and controversy. I cannot undertake to answer
all comments whether in personal letters or in the Press; but I
will welcome them, and if this is warranted I will do my best to
reply in a further book. Where I have had to challenge traditional
beliefs it has not been with any hostile intent, and I hope therefore
that criticism will be temperate and confined to persuasion on the
basis of evidence. If I have had an objective, other than patient
seeking after truth, it has been to be of helpful service in providing people today with a more correct understanding of
Christ, which they can live with and from which they can draw
courage and inspiration, especially those in adversity and despondency. If it can be shown that to follow Jesus means to imbibe
his spirit and seek his ends for mankind then these pages may have
made a timely and constructive contribution to one of the most
vital dialogues of this generation.

HUGH J. SCHONFIELD

PART ONE

The Man who believed
He was Messiah

I

The Last Times

CHRISTIANITY is rooted in Palestine in a Jewish environment and in the historical circumstances of a plainly dated period. This assuredly requires no argument. To this time and place we are therefore bound to go for the elucidation of Christian Origins.

But it is by no means easy to relate the life of Jesus and the activities of his original followers, known as Nazoreans (Nazarenes), to the contemporary situation. This is largely due to the character of the New Testament and the paucity of external evidences about the beginnings of Christianity. To reach conclusions which can fairly be regarded as corresponding as nearly as possible to the reality entails a vast amount of analysis and comparison, the patient piecing together of a host of hints and scraps of tradition, and in particular a sympathetic involvement in the affairs of the Jewish people and detachment from considerations of Christian theology.

Because of what the Church has taught for so many centuries it has been extremely difficult for Christian scholars to undertake such an investigation objectively. Those who have embarked upon it and produced most valuable results merit the highest praise. One pioneer, Professor F. C. Burkitt of Cambridge, whom the writer was privileged to know personally, advisedly used these cautionary words: 'We must be prepared to find the whole drama of the rise of Christianity more confused, more secular, in a word more appropriate to the limitations of its own age, than we should gather from the epic selectiveness of the Creeds and the theological manuals.'[1] Such language is necessary, and should be heeded by those theologians who feel quite at liberty to expound Christianity as if it owed little or nothing to its original background of thought. The Bishop of Woolwich, to quote a recent instance, can freely employ key words like Christ and Gospel without apparent concern for their primary meaning and implications.[2] Christ is the Greek translation of the Hebrew term Messiah, meaning the Anointed One, and the Gospel, from the Greek Evangel, translating the Hebrew word for Good News, was initially the information that the Messiah expected by the Jews had appeared.

It makes all the difference to our understanding of Christianity if we are enabled to apprehend that it did not begin as a new religion but as a movement of monotheistic Jews who held Jesus to be their God-sent king and deliverer. Here, in a sentence, is what it is imperative to know about the origins of Christianity. Here we have the essential clue to the activities of Jesus and his first followers which helps to compensate for many material facts which are beyond recovery. Armed with this information we can get Christianity in correct perspective, and trace clearly and simply in the light of what is ascertainable how it was transformed into what it afterwards became.

It is often said that Christianity is founded upon a person. That is true. But it is only part of the historical truth. What, so to speak, was the person founded upon? The answer is that he was founded upon an idea, a strange idea current among the Jews of his time, an idea alien to Western thought which many non-Jewish theologians still find very inconvenient, the idea of Messianism. It was Messianism which made the life of Jesus what it was and so brought Christianity into being. It was Messianism, as accepted by Gentile believers, which contributed towards making the deification of Jesus inevitable. It was Messianism which provided the spiritual impulse behind the Jewish war with Rome which broke out in A.D. 66, resulting in the destruction of much authoritative testimony about Jesus and the substantial separation of Gentile from Jewish Christianity.[3]

The fundamental teaching of Christianity, then, was that in Jesus the Messiah (the Christ) had come. There can be not the shadow of a doubt about this. It is the ultimate conviction on which the whole edifice of Christianity rests, the historical fact on which all the Gospels are agreed. This teaching was the gospel, underlying all the Gospels, the one thing which gave them the right to be so called. The faith of the earliest believers in Jesus was that which voiced itself in the declaration of Peter, as recorded in Mark, 'You are the Messiah',[4] simply this without any qualification. The persuasion they had was built upon what Jesus had said and done. It was he who had given them cause to conclude that he was the Messiah, and he had done so quite deliberately. But what the Gospels do not tell us is what in the first instance had persuaded *him*. Unless we can discover why Jesus held himself to be the Messiah, what current teaching about the Messiah he applied to himself, we are not in possession of the key to the mystery of his life and death.

We have no right to say that while Jesus accepted the designation of Messiah he did so in a sense quite different from any expectations entertained in his time. It would be unthinkable for him to do this, firstly because being the Messiah meant answering to certain prophetic requirements which for him were divinely inspired, and secondly because he would consciously have been depriving his people of any possibility of acknowledging him: he would be inviting them to reject him as a false Messiah.

We have to take the view that Jesus believed it to be his calling and destiny to fulfil the Messianic Hope, and to do so in a manner which would conform with the predictions he accepted as authoritative. Our business is to find out the conditions with which Jesus felt he had to comply, and on this basis to follow the course of his actions. Obviously we have to divorce the issue altogether from the paganised doctrine of the incarnation of the Godhead with which for Christians it has become intermingled, since expectation did not identify the Messiah with God, and, indeed, the nature of Jewish monotheism wholly excluded such an idea. Jesus as much as any other Jew would have regarded as blasphemous the manner in which he is depicted, for instance, in the Fourth Gospel.

Taking the Gospels together, and these are the chief source of our information about Jesus, we have in them an epitome of the process by which the traditions about him grew and expanded with the changing needs and fortunes of succeeding generations of believers, Jewish and Gentile, so that Jesus as he appears in them is a composite and somewhat contradictory figure. His image is like the idol of Nebuchadnezzar's dream in the book of Daniel, part gold, part silver, part bronze, part iron and part clay. The gold is there to be extracted, but we cannot take hold of it unalloyed without knowledge of the influences and circumstances to which Jesus himself had responded. It is not enough to look back to him through the minds of much later believers not of Jewish origin: we have imperatively to look forward to him through the pre-Christian development of Messianism.

The coming of the Messiah was not something fortuitous: it was closely linked with a period of history prophetically anticipated, the Last Times or End of the Days, which would precede the inauguration of the Kingdom of God. The Messiah could not appear at any time, but only at the End of the Days, at a time of testing and great tribulation for Israel.

The conception of the Last Times drew upon Biblical predictions relating to the Latter Days and the Day of the Lord, which became combined with Babylonian and Persian ideas of a succession of Ages. During the Ages the forces of Good and Evil would contend with one another, and the struggle would reach its climax in the penultimate Age, being followed by the final Age of peace and bliss, the Kingdom of God. The Last Times would thus be the closing period of the old order, when the assaults of Evil would reach their most malevolent intensity, bringing great misery to humanity and persecution and suffering to the Elect of Israel. When these signs appeared then the Messiah was to be expected.

According to those who studied these matters, it could not be known how long the Last Times would endure, but it could be known approximately when they would begin. For this a basis of calculation had to be available, and it was found in the book of Daniel in the prophecy of the Seventy Weeks,[5] later understood to mean seventy weeks of years (490 years). The Last Times could be expected to begin after the lapse of 490 years 'from the going forth of the commandment [of Cyrus] to restore and build Jerusalem', that is to say, after about 46 B.C. Those who believed in this interpretation, and were living in the reign of Herod the Great (37–4 B.C.), could accept that the Last Times had now begun, and that therefore before very long the coming of the Messiah was to be expected. This explains why a strong messianic excitement manifested itself among the Jews from this time onward, and why no one before this had claimed to be the Messiah.

The part of the book of Daniel in which the prophecy occurs has been dated about 164 B.C. The author is assuming the name of a man supposed to be living near the end of the sixth century B.C. From other visions of his he appears to have expected the Era of Righteousness would come not very long after his actual time. Some thought it had come in the reign of John Hyrcanus I (137–3 B.C.). We do not know much about earlier calculations, and the one to which we have referred was worked out later when the hopes entertained of the Hasmoneans had been grievously disappointed. It is after 100 B.C. that the literature we have reveals a mounting interest in the Last Times and in the advent of messianic personalities. By the first century of our era it had become quite feverish, and had engendered a state of near hysteria among the people. It was wholly in keeping with the circumstances that a figure like John the Baptist should now appear proclaiming that the Kingdom of God was at hand, and calling upon the people to repent and save themselves from the Wrath to Come. It was no less appropriate that a man like Jesus should be convinced he was the Messiah and announce that 'the Time is fulfilled'. The calculations of pious scribes confirmed the time, but what was more the conditions of the time reinforced the calculations.

Messianism was a product of the Jewish spirit. It was inspired by the Hebrew reading of the riddle of the creation and destiny of mankind. Though some of its features did not originate with the Hebrews, they absorbed them and brought them into relationship with a great vision of the ultimate Brotherhood of Man under the rule of the One God and Father of all men. The vision was not simply a cherished ideal: it was associated with a plan for its realisation. According to this plan God had chosen and set apart one nation among the nations of the world, neither numerous nor powerful, to be the recipient of his laws, and by observing them to offer a universal example. The Theocracy of Israel would be the persuasive illustration of a World Theocracy: it would be 'a kingdom of priests and a holy nation' witnessing to all nations. Manifestly, according to this view, the redemption of humanity waited upon the attainment by Israel of a state of perfect obedience to the will of God. By so much as Israel failed to meet the Divine requirements, by so much was the peace and well-being of mankind retarded.

The history of Israel, seen in this light, was a prolonged schooling, national disposition to go astray having to be corrected by the infliction of appropriate punishments, conquest and oppression by foreigners, pestilence and famine, exile. Internally much depended on the guidance of rulers, priests and kings. These too were judged by whether they 'did right in the sight of the Lord'. Their failures called for an additional activity by messengers of God in a succession of prophets.

Eventually, it began to be despaired of that the whole people could be brought to the necessary state of perfection. Hopes were pinned on an elect remnant of faithful souls, by whose obedience the redemption would be hastened. They would be the élite of the final World Order, entitled to its highest honours by their loyalty and by their sufferings in this present world. The Messianic Hope became concentrated upon the determined efforts of the pious, the Saints, to observe the Law, thus justifying God in acting speedily. If the time was greatly prolonged even the Elect might prove unequal to the strain. It was imperative for the pious themselves to search out what Divine guidance had been given to set a term to their endurance, what signs were to be expected to intimate that the End of the Days had arrived. The last stage of the evolution of the Messianic Hope envisaged the intervention of God by means of the Anointed Ones, ideal figures, a Prophet like Moses, a perfect Priest, a righteous King of the line of David. These would come in the End of the Days as God's highest appointed representatives to transform the whole world scene and usher in the Kingdom of God.

The scheme of the Messianic Hope, as outlined here, must be understood to be composite and not fully comprehensive. Many ingredients went into the framing of the Hope. Different aspects were emphasised at different times and by different groups. It was accentuated as certain historical situations arose, particularly after the return from the Babylonian Exile, and was not consciously present in the thinking of the Jewish people all the time. Concern with the coming of messianic persons was part of the later expression of the Hope, especially from the second century B.C. onward, though it was nourished on ideas and predictions hundreds of years older, not excluding popular folklore and mythology.

We may select three circumstances as contributing importantly to making the Messianic Hope the powerful influence it became in the first century B.C. One of these was a change in attitude towards the Bible. The Hebrew Bible consists of three divisions; the Law, the Prophets (Joshua to Malachi), and the Writings (beginning with the Psalms and including the book of Daniel). The divisions represent stages of acceptance into canonicity. The Law, as consisting of the five books of Moses, had binding force by the fifth century B.C., or not much later. The Prophets did not acquire their force until about the third century B.C. The Psalms and some other books soon formed the basis of the third division, which was finally settled at the end of the first century A.D. The effects of the recognition of the Law and the Prophets, with the Psalms, as a corpus of sacred Scriptures were far-reaching. It opened the way for a new development, the treatment of these books as the Oracles of God. They became subject to all kinds of interpretation to draw out of them hidden meanings and prognostications.

A second circumstance was the worst calamity which had befallen the Jews since the destruction of the Kingdom of Judah and the loss of the Temple at the beginning of the sixth century B.C. The new calamity was seen by pious Jews to be impending as a consequence of the attractions of Hellenism, which since the time of Alexander the Great had made increasing inroads into Jewish life and thought, fostering moral laxity and apostasy. The judgement of God must surely fall upon the nation as it had done in the past. It fully confirmed this opinion when the Seleucid king Antiochus Epiphanes (175–62 B.C.) decreed the abolition of the Jewish religion and converted the Temple at Jerusalem into a shrine of Zeus Olympius. Throughout the country there was great persecution, until resistance was organised by the sons of the aged priest Mattathias of Modim. One son, Judas Maccabaeus, led the revolt in the name of God, and after a series of remarkable successes cleansed and rededicated the defiled Temple. One of the products of this testing time was the book of Daniel. Its apocalyptic dreams and visions were to exercise a major influence on messianic thinking and prediction.

The third circumstance to which we must draw attention is Jewish sectarianism. The experiences of the nation in the time of Antiochus and his immediate successors had administered a severe shock. The people became much more devout. There was revived in them a sense of destiny, of belonging to God in a special way, which demanded faithfulness to the Law revealed to them through Moses. They saw in the victories of the Maccabees the hand of God, outstretched for their deliverance when they were obedient to his commandments. The Messianic Hope comes out strongly in Daniel, where the people of the Saints of the Most High (likened to a Son of Man compared with the Beast figures representing the predatory heathen Empires) are entrusted with God's everlasting kingdom, when all rulers will serve and obey him.[6] It began to matter very much to the more spiritually sensitive that the Divine laws should be observed meticulously, and this inevitably gave rise to sectarianism, to competition in holiness. From this period three ways of life in particular are made known to us, those of the Sadducees, Pharisees and Essenes. They were minority movements, numbering only a few thousands in each case, but they were nevertheless extremely influential and gave impetus to the exposition of the Messianic Hope. Unfortunately, as regards the first two, they were also involved in a power-struggle for control of the political affairs of the nation.

From 160 B.C. we are in a new age, an age of extraordinary fervour and religiosity, in which almost every event, political, social and economic, was seized upon, scrutinised and analysed, to discover how and in what way it represented a Sign of the Times and threw light on the approach of the End of the Days. The whole condition of the Jewish people was psychologically abnormal. The strangest tales and imaginings could find ready credence. A new pseudonymous literature came into being, part moral exhortation and part apocalyptic prophecy, a kind of messianic science-fiction. People were on edge, neurotic. There were hot disputes, rivalries and recriminations.

The essence of the Messianic Hope, as we have seen, was the establishment of the Kingdom of God on earth, for which the prerequisite was a righteous Israel, or at least a righteous remnant of Israel. There must be a return to the relationship with God initiated at the Covenant of Sinai. Of this the prophecies of Jeremiah spoke, when he had said:

'Behold, the days come, saith the Lord, that I will make a New Covenant with the house of Israel, and with the house of Judah ... After those days, saith the Lord, I will put my Law in their inward parts, and write it in their hearts; and will be their God, and they shall be my people. And they shall teach no more every man his neighbour, and every man his brother, saying, Know the Lord; for they shall all know me, from the least of them to the greatest of them, saith the Lord: for I will forgive their iniquity, and I will remember their sin no more.'[7]

Here it was promised that the spiritual infirmity of Israel would be helped by the intervention of God. To become worthy of this interposition was imperative. The three movements to which we have referred, and there were others, were fundamentally responses to this conviction. The Sadducees emphasised a strict and literal adherence to the Laws of Moses and the cultivation of ethics. The Pharisees aimed at the sanctification of the whole of daily life, and formulated new rules which extended the application of the Law to cover all contingencies. The Essenes, determined to be even more faultless, formed close communities from which contamination and impurity could be excluded, and where the utmost simplicity of living and rigid discipline could overcome material and fleshly temptations.

These movements reveal in themselves how deadly serious had become the desire to merit God's intervention. We should be out of tune with the temper of the time if we did not realise this. It was the study of the manner of the redemptive intervention which now accented the advent of messianic figures. The Sadducees, proving everything from express statements in the Law, looked for the coming of the Prophet like Moses.[8] The Pharisees and Essenes ranged more widely and brought into prominence the perpetual covenants with Levi and David. The prophecies of Jeremiah had further contained this promise:

'Behold, the days come, saith the Lord, that I will perform that good thing which I have promised unto the house of Israel and to the house of Judah. In those days, and at that time, will I cause the Branch of Righteousness to grow up unto David; and he shall execute judgement and righteousness in the land. In those days shall Judah be saved, and Jerusalem shall dwell safely . . . For thus saith the Lord; David shall never want a man to sit upon the throne of the house of Israel; neither shall the priests the Levites want a man to offer burnt offerings, and to kindle meat offerings, and to do sacrifice continually.'[9]

Therefore, it was held, God would intervene by means of Anointed Ones (Messiahs) of the tribes of Levi and Judah. One writer declares: 'And now, my children, obey Levi and Judah, and be not lifted up against these two tribes, for from them shall arise unto you the salvation of God. For the Lord shall raise up from Levi as it were a High Priest, and from Judah as it were a King: he shall save all the race of Israel.'[10]

For the Essenes the Priestly Messiah would be the superior of the Royal Messiah, while for the Pharisees, who became disillusioned with hierarchical government, the Messiah *par excellence* would be the ideal king of the line of David.[11] But they admitted the priority of a Levitical messianic personality to the extent that the Davidic Messiah would be preceded by a priestly forerunner in the form of the returned Prophet Elijah, whom they held to have been a priest.[12]

For a brief period in the latter part of the second century B.C. the greatest hopes were entertained as a result of the victories of the Hasmonean ruler John Hyrcanus I, under whom the Jews not only regained complete independence, but also a territory larger than any under Jewish rule since the reign of Solomon son of David. Not a few were ready to see in John one who combined all the messianic offices, being Prophet, Priest and King.[13] But John Hyrcanus was no paragon, and his successors proved to be thoroughly unsatisfactory rulers, despotic, ambitious and unjust. Instead of the Kingdom of God there was war in Israel, and the Essenes had justification for their view that Satan had been let loose on the country.

From this time national affairs played an increasing part in the exposition of the Messianic Hope. It acquired a more personal and political colouring. The cry was raised, 'Behold, O Lord, and raise up unto them their king, the Son of David, in the time which thou, O God, knowest, that he may reign over Israel thy servant; and gird him with strength that he may break in pieces them that rule unjustly.'[14]

The change of emphasis in messianic expectations caused much thought to be given to the conditions which the Scriptures indicated would prevail when the Messiah would be revealed. There would be wars and tumults, public strife and divided families, pestilence and famine, persecution of the saints, a host of tribulations. These would be the Woes of the Last Times, presaging the coming of the Messiah. As Jewish affairs went from bad to worse by so much more were messianic convictions intensified. Those who looked for signs could find them in abundance. In 63 B.C. the Romans were called upon to aid John Hyrcanus II against his ambitious brother Aristobulus. There was internecine conflict, the siege and capture of Jerusalem, with the Roman general Pompey committing the enormity of entering the Holy of Holies in the Temple. The Jews lost their brief independence, and their land became a vassal state of Rome. Once more Israel was subject to the heathen, and finally forced to accept at Roman hands a king, who, though he was a professing Jew, was of alien Idumean origin.

The reign of Herod the Great (37–4 B.C.) was from the beginning attended by disorders. Not only had he to preserve his throne by adroit manœuvre and political intrigue in relation to the struggle then going on in the Roman world, he had to govern a people intensely hostile to his regime, only too willing to see in him a manifestation of diabolical sovereignty.

Herod was an ambitious man and a clever one, brave, with regal bearing and qualities of leadership, but he was impulsive and had neurotic tendencies which the circumstances of his reign so aggravated as to convert him into something like the raging ruthless monster his apocalyptic-minded subjects believed him to be. With real and imagined plots against him he could not feel secure until he had destroyed the Hasmoneans around whom popular support could still gather. First to be got rid of was Antigonus, then the boy Aristobulus whom he had made high priest at the age of sixteen, and then the aged former high priest and king, the inoffensive Hyrcanus II. Later the Hasmonean princess Mariamne, whom he had married and genuinely loved, was executed, followed by her mother Alexandra; and to the end of his days the king's fears of conspiracy by family and friends led him on to the destruction even of his own children.

Successfully switching his allegiance from the vanquished Marc Antony to the victorious Octavian, afterwards the Emperor Augustus, Herod reached a height of political power and prestige.

But as the friend of Caesar, devoted to the Romans and to the Hellenic way of life, he made himself ever more noxious to his people, who would not be placated even by his grandiose rebuilding of the Temple. They hated and feared him, and were kept from revolt only by the strongly manned fortresses which Herod constructed at strategic points and by his conversion of the country into what we would now call a police state.[15] The pious attributed to the wrath of God the great earthquake in Judea in the seventh year of his reign and the persistent droughts followed by pestilence in the thirteenth year of his reign. Such calamities seemed like the plagues of Egypt, and Herod appeared as another Pharaoh of the Oppression.[16] The signs seemed certainly to confirm the current interpretation of the prophecies that the Last Times had begun.

For the extreme pietists these days were 'the Period of the Wrath'. Many abandoned the cities and took to the wilderness. Sectarian communities, like that at Qumran by the Dead Sea, flourished as fresh recruits joined them. Such communities had long existed on the eastern fringe of the country; but now they were multiplied and increased in variety, holding themselves to be the faithful Elect of the Last Times.[17]

Through the sources of information at our command we obtain a picture of the situation in Palestine towards the close of the first century B.C. which, if it could be put on canvas, would seem to be the work of a madman, or of a drug addict. A whole nation was in the grip of delirium. The king on this throne was a sick and gloomy tyrant. His embittered subjects feared and detested him to an extent that was almost maniacal. Religious fanatics fasted and prayed, and preached wrath and judgement. Obsessed with conviction that the Last Times had come, terror and superstition overcame all reason among the people. Self-recrimination accompanied messianic fervour. No wonder that when Herod died all hell was let loose.

At first a cry of relief went up throughout the land, and then in a moment all was tumult and disorder. Soldiers went on the rampage. Bands of brigands plundered. In the name of liberty

from Rome and the Herodians various leaders set themselves up
as king and readily got together a multitude of armed followers.
'And thus', writes Josephus, 'did a great and wild fury spread
itself over the nation, because they had no king to keep the
masses in good order; and because those foreigners, who came to
reduce the seditious to sobriety, did, on the contrary, set them
more in a flame, because of the injuries they offered them, and
the avaricious management of their affairs.'[18] In punitive actions
by the Romans thousands were killed in different parts of the
country, and at Jerusalem two thousand were crucified.

NOTES AND REFERENCES

1. F. C. Burkitt, *The Gospel History and its Transmission*, p. 29.
2. John A. T. Robinson, *Honest to God*.
3. See Part Two, Chapter 1, *Messianism and the Development of Christianity*.
4. Mk. viii. 29.
5. Dan. ix. 24–7.
6. Dan. vii. 26–7.
7. Jer. xxxi. 31–4.
8. Deut. xviii. 15.
9. Jer. xxxiii. 15–26.
10. *Test. Simeon*, vii. 1–2 (*Testaments of the XII Patriarchs*, edition Charles).
Cp. *Test. Naphtali*, viii. 2–3; *Test. Joseph*, xix. 11.
11. Isa. xi.
12. A late commentary on the Psalms illustrates the position taken by the
Pharisees. 'To that generation (in Egypt) thou didst send redemption through
two redeemers, as it is said (Ps. cv. 26), "He sent Moses his servant and Aaron
whom he had chosen." So also to this generation (of the Last Times) he sendeth
two, corresponding to those other two. "Send out thy light and thy truth" (Ps
xliii. 3). "Thy light", that is the Prophet Elijah of the house of Aaron . . . and
"Thy truth", that is Messiah ben David, as it is said (Ps. cxxxii. 11), "The
Lord hath sworn unto David (in) truth, he will not turn from it." And likewise
it is said (Isa. xlii. 1), "Behold my servant whom I uphold" ' (*Midrash Tehillim*,
xliii. 1.) The return of Elijah is predicted in Malachi iv. 5–6.
13. '(John Hyrcanus) was esteemed by God worthy of the three privileges, the
government of his nation, the dignity of the high priesthood, and prophecy;
for God was with him, and enabled him to know futurities' (Josephus, *Antiq.*
XIII. x. 7.)
14. *Psalms of Solomon*, xvii. 23–4.

15. 'At this time Herod released to his subjects the third part of their taxes, under pretence indeed of relieving them after the dearth they had had; but the main reason was, to recover their goodwill, which he now wanted; for they were uneasy at him, because of the innovations he had introduced in their practices to the dissolution of their religion, and the disuse of their own customs, and the people everywhere talked against him, like those that were still more provoked and disturbed at his procedure. Against which discontents he greatly guarded himself, and took away the opportunities they might have to disturb him, and enjoining them to be always at work; nor did he permit the citizens either to meet together, or to walk, or eat together, but watched everything they did, and when they were caught they were severely punished; and many there were who were brought to the citadel Hyrcania, both openly and secretly, and were there put to death. And there were spies set everywhere, both in the city and on the roads, who watched those that met together . . . and those that could be in no way reduced to acquiesce under his scheme of government, he persecuted them in all manner of ways' (Josephus, *Antiq*. XV. x. 4).

16. 'An insolent king [Herod] will succeed them [the Hasmoneans], who will not be of the race of the priests, a man bold and shameless, and he will judge them as they deserve. And he will cut off their chief men with the sword, and will destroy them in secret places, so that no one may know where their bodies are. He will slay the old and the young, and he will not spare. Then the fear of him will be bitter unto them in their land. And he will execute judgements on them as the Egyptians executed upon them, during thirty and four years, and he will punish them' (*Assumption of Moses*, vi. 2–6, edition Charles).

17. The *Manual of Discipline* from Qumran declares: 'And when these things shall come to pass to the Community of Israel, in these determined moments they shall separate themselves from the midst of the habitation of perverse men to take to the wilderness to prepare there the Way of Him as was written: "Prepare ye in the wilderness the Way of the Lord: make straight to the desert a highway for our God" (Isa. xl. 3). This Way is the study of the Law . . . so as to act according to all that was revealed time after time, and according to what the Prophets revealed by His Holy Spirit.'

18. Josephus, *Antiq*. XVII. x. 5.

2

He that should Come

THE circumstances we have outlined, which used, perhaps, to be more familiar to previous generations of Christians than they are today, have an obvious bearing on the understanding of the life of Jesus, and must be allowed their full weight in any attempt to comprehend him. We have seen what strange imaginings had gripped the Jewish people at this time, the time Jesus came into the world, fed by those who interpreted the Scriptures to them. According to many preachers, the eleventh hour had come, the Last Times had begun, the Kingdom of God was at hand. The world was on the eve of Wrath and Judgement. The Messiah would appear.

Christianity affirms that Jesus was this Messiah, whose advent fulfilled the prophecies, but singularly fails to concentrate on the implications as the effective means of becoming better acquainted with his character and activities. The Messiahship of Jesus is asserted, and then side-stepped in order to disclose him in a light more congenial to Hellenic rather than Jewish concepts. Quite commonly, for instance, quite apart from the claim that Jesus was God, the view is expressed that the Jews of the time of Jesus were expecting a Warrior Messiah, one who would win military victories over the enemies of Israel, and in this way accomplish the deliverance. The Jews rejected Jesus because he was a man of peace, who represented the love of God.

But what authority is there for such a view? Had this been the contemporary opinion of those who studied the Scriptures, certainly Jesus could never have thought of himself as the Messiah.

But in fact in references to the Messiah up to the time of Jesus the conception of a Warrior Messiah does not appear. Among the peasantry of Palestine many did entertain such a notion, because conditions were so bad that violence seemed to offer the natural remedy. Living under alien domination, oppressed and ill-used, who is to blame them if they did? To the desperate the niceties of prophecy mattered little. Anyone would serve as Messiah, whether descended from David or not, if he was bold, courageous, a leader of men. There were plenty of people with little to lose, who were ready for any adventure which promised food and drink, and the destruction of the enemies, and who often quite sincerely would believe themselves to be fighting the battles of God. Such people over a thousand years later joined the Crusades. But we must not judge the Messianic Hope by such as they. Those who took things into their own hands, the violent ones, who resorted to militancy, were strongly criticised and denounced by the Pharisees, who were the chief spiritual instructors of the masses.

Of the Branch of David for whom pious Jews waited it was written: 'With righteousness shall he judge the poor, and reprove with equity for the meek of the earth: and he shall smite the earth *with the rod of his mouth*, and *with the breath of his lips* shall he slay the wicked.'[1] The sharp two-edged sword of the Messiah would be no physical weapon, but justice and righteousness.

Dating from the first century B.C. we have an exposition of the kind of Messiah who was expected, based on the passage from Isaiah just quoted.

'And a righteous king and taught of God is he that reigneth over them: and there shall be no iniquity in his days in their midst, for all shall be holy and their king is the Lord Messiah. For he shall not put his trust in horse and rider and bow, nor shall he multiply unto himself gold and silver for war, nor by ships shall he gather confidence for the day of battle . . . For he shall smite the earth with the word of his mouth even for evermore . . . He himself also is pure from sin, so that he may rule a mighty people, and rebuke princes and overthrow sinners by the might of his word. And he shall not faint all his days, because he leaneth upon his God: for God shall cause him to be mighty through the spirit of holiness, and wise through the counsel of understanding, with might and righteousness.'[2]

The Son of David who was to come would be holy and just, 'the Messiah of righteousness', as he is called in the Dead Sea Scrolls, living in close communion with God and obedient to his will. It is by the word of truth that he will convict and defeat his adversaries.

That the Messiah should have such a character fully accords with what we have brought out about the nature of the Messianic Hope. The goal was the universal rule of God acknowledged by all men, when war, strife and wickedness should cease. To reach that goal it was required that Israel should be 'a kingdom of priests and a holy nation'. How much more must the Messiah, who would come in God's name, be the perfect Israelite? To him would apply the words of the Psalmist: 'Thou lovest righteousness, and hatest wickedness: therefore God, even thy God, hath anointed thee with the oil of gladness above thy fellows . . . Then said I, Lo I come: in the volume of the book it is written of me, I delight to do thy will, O my God: yea thy law is within my heart.'[3]

This was the likeness to which the Messiah was expected to conform, and this is what Christians should have been taught. It was said of him:

'And he shall gather together a holy people, whom he shall lead in righteousness: and shall judge the tribes of the people that hath been sanctified by the Lord his God. And he shall not suffer iniquity to lodge in their midst; and none that knoweth wickedness shall dwell with him. For he shall take knowledge of them that they be all sons of their God, and shall divide them upon the earth according to their tribes . . . He shall judge the nations and the peoples with the wisdom of his righteousness. Selah.'[4]

These things were expounded to the people in the synagogues by preachers who mainly belonged to the fraternity of the Pharisees. But not all the messianic mysteries were public property.

The extreme pietists who delved into such matters largely kept their knowledge to themselves, setting down some of their ideas in books only disclosed to the initiated. To supplement our knowledge we have to ferret out information to the extent that we have access to the internal literature of these groups, some of it, like the Dead Sea Scrolls, only recently available. Much material that would assist us has long been lost or destroyed, and we still know all too little about the tenets and distinguishing features of the groups in question.

The discovery of the Scrolls has turned scholarly attention again to the ancient references to the various Jewish and related sects and to those relics of them which have survived. Research in this field has now become one of the most promising developments for the illumination of Christian Origins. Here we can only touch on some aspects which have a bearing on the Messianic Hope and its interpretation by Jesus, and relate to the region in which he lived.

It used to be customary to think of Jesus as brought up in a Judaism which answered roughly to that of the second century A.D. and derived from that of the Pharisees, and which was much the same all over Palestine. This view is no longer tenable, though on the basis of it we have had a book by Robert Aron, entitled *Jesus of Nazareth: The Hidden Years,* which while colourful is largely erroneous. Certain scholars long ago apprehended from the rabbinical literature that the people of the north and south did not see eye to eye on many things. It was possible even to detect in Primitive Christianity the clash of Galilean and Jerusalem traditions. But only lately has it become appreciated that northern Palestine down to the time of Jesus had retained many features of the old religion of Israel, when it was separate from Judah, and this not only among the Samaritans.

In Galilee those who were of Hebrew stock could be called Jews in that they served the God of Israel, but they differed in many ways from the Judeans. Their Aramean speech was hard to follow because they slurred the gutturals, and in their customs and religious observances they were distinguished in a number of respects from the southerners. The Galileans were proud, independent and somewhat puritanical, more resentful of alien domination and infringements of their liberty. They were to be found in the forefront of the resistance movement to the Romans and to the Jewish authorities subservient to them. When the imperial capitation tax was levied on the Jews in A.D. 6–7, it was the rebel Judas of Galilee who raised again the battle-cry 'No Ruler but God'. It was with these stubborn, hardy and intensely patriotic folk that Jesus, himself a Galilean, had to deal.

In the spiritual sphere the Pharisees were not nearly so well entrenched in Galilee as they were in Judea. They had a following in the north because of their piety and because they represented themselves as the People's Party, but they had an uphill struggle to contend with the Galilean way of life. The Gospels indicate that to meet the challenge of the teaching of Jesus the local Pharisees found themselves in need of the help of experts from Jerusalem.[5] That the Galileans and Judeans were still affected by age-old antagonistic feelings is brought out by the Gospel of John. At Jerusalem there was opposition to the idea that the Prophet or the Messiah could possibly come from Galilee, and Jesus was taunted with being a demon-possessed Samaritan.[6] On the other hand his Galilean followers remonstrated with him for wanting to return to Judea where 'the Jews of late sought to stone thee'.[7] We are so familiar with the application of the term Jew to all persons of Jewish faith that we may not realise that in the New Testament the name is sometimes used in the narrower sense to mean Judeans, the inhabitants of Judea, compared with Galileans or Samaritans.

We have also to think of Galilee as part of a region in which sectarian communities flourished. Some of these, like the Rechabites and Kenites, had an ancient tribal history. The area in which they functioned was in the proximity of the Sea of Galilee, in the Decapolis, Gilead and Bashan, the Gaulan and Hauran, and towards Lebanon and Damascus.

The *Damascus Document* among the Dead Sea Scrolls tells how in the early history of the Community 'the Penitents of Israel went forth out of the land of Judea and sojourned in the land of Damascus'. There they entered into the New Covenant spoken of by Jeremiah the prophet, undertaking to separate themselves from all unrighteousness, not to rob the poor, the widow and the orphan, to distinguish between clean and unclean, sacred and profane, to keep the Sabbath strictly, also the festivals and the Day of Atonement, to love each one his brother as himself, and to care for the poor, the needy and the stranger. This indication of locality should be taken much more seriously and literally. Those who followed the restored Mosaism did not all gravitate towards Qumran. We have every reason to believe that many remained in the northern districts we have mentioned and founded settlements there. These 'Elect of Israel' of the Latter Days would encounter many kindred spirits in northern Palestine among groups carrying on the old ascetic Nazirite way of life, abstaining from animal food and intoxicants. The term Essean-Essene appears to have come from the northern Aramaic word *Chasya* (Greek *Hosios*) meaning Saint. It would seem that we have to treat the term as generic, covering a variety of loosely related groups. For the people 'the Saints' were the Jewish eclectic bodies, who also bore or were given descriptive names according to their affiliations or characteristics.

There has been emerging ever clearer evidence that in the Galilean region an ancient Israelitish type of religion persisted in the time of Jesus, defying Judean efforts to obliterate it. To an extent we have to think of him in the context of that northern faith which so strongly coloured and influenced those communities of 'the Saints' which were spread across this area, and which gave rise to some expressions of Messianism with which he was acquainted.[8] The Gospels identify him with the small Galilean town of Nazareth; but the name he bears, Jesus the Nazorean, has northern sectarian implications. United with the fact that he was of Davidic descent, the prophetic intimations could be seen to be fulfilled in him which spoke of the Messiah as the sprout (*nezer*) from the root of Jesse.[9]

In the north the messianic doctrine of the Righteous King could

join hands with the idea of a Suffering Just One and the conception of the Messiah as the ideal Israelite, the Son of Man. In the
book of Daniel, as we have seen (above p. 26), the Saints who are
to possess the kingdom are already likened to a Son of Man. These
Elect of the Last Times regarded themselves as performing an
atoning work by their sufferings. In the *Community Rule* from
Qumran it is said of the leaders of the Council.

'They shall preserve the Faith in the land with steadfastness
and meekness, and shall atone for sin by the practice of justice
and by suffering the sorrows of affliction . . . And they shall
be an agreeable offering, atoning for the land and determining
the judgement of wickedness, and there shall be no more
iniquity.'[10]

Since the Messiah was to be the Branch of Righteousness, the
holy one who would bring iniquity to an end and reign over a
redeemed people, it was not difficult to move from the Son of
Man (collective) to the Messiah as the Son of Man (singular),
from the Elect Ones of Israel to the Elect One. If the Saints
could achieve an atoning work by their sufferings, how much
more the Messiah himself. For Jesus, especially with his northern
associations, this emerged clearly, and governed the character
of his messianic mission. His blood would seal the New Covenant
spoken of by Jeremiah, and must be shed for many for the re-
mission of sins.[11] In other words attributed to him, 'Ought not
the Messiah to have suffered these things, and then enter into
his glory (as king)?'[12]

We can say, therefore, that at the time when Jesus lived not
only was there a widespread expectation that the Messiah would
shortly reveal himself, but also that in some of the current thinking about 'he that should come' there was nothing inconsistent
with the way in which Jesus understood the functions of the
Messiah.

In approaching the historical Jesus no question of his deity
arises, since before the paganising of Jewish belief in the development of Christianity no authority identified the Messiah with the
Logos, the eternal Word of God, or conceived the Messiah to be

an incarnation of God. The very term, the Anointed One, indicates a call to office. It was not the title of an aspect of the Godhead. We do not have to entertain at all the notion that Jesus or
any other claimant to be the Messiah in Palestine at this period
could suppose himself for one moment to be divine. In the early
history of Christianity it can be sufficiently seen how the doctrine
arose out of the impact of the Gospel on the Gentile world, and
in the circumstances was almost inevitable.[13] There are plenty of
instances still today of Christianity in many lands being coloured
by the polytheistic faiths the Church has conquered and absorbed.
Our concern must be to overcome this barrier to our comprehension of Jesus, and reaching back to the core of Christianity
to deal only with the requirements of the messiahship as he would
have known them.

What, then, of the term Son of God? The Messiah was not
directly so-called; yet he could be thought of as having a filial
relationship to God without any idea among Jews that such a
description implied deity, and this could happen in so far as the
Messiah appeared as the representative Israelite and as the preordained King of Israel.[14] Sonship of God meant something quite
different to the Jewish mind than to the Gentile mind.

The right understanding of Jesus commences with the realisation that he identified himself with the fulfilment of the Messianic
Hope. Only on this basis do the traditions about him become
wholly intelligible. He was no charlatan, wilfully and deliberately
misleading his people, well knowing that his posing as the Messiah
was fraudulent. There is not the slightest suspicion of pretence
on his part. On the contrary, no one could be more sure of his
vocation than was Jesus, and not even the threat of imminent
death by the horrible torture of crucifixion could make him deny
his messiahship.

We have to accept the absolute sincerity of Jesus. But this
does not require us to think of him as omniscient and infallible.
It is possible to hold that the Messianic Hope was not only a
justifiable but indeed an inspired conception, and yet in many
respects the predictions and expectations of the interpreters of

the Scriptures could be quite wrong. It is one thing to see visions
and dream dreams, and quite another when it is demanded that
such visions and dreams be acted out on the plane of history in all
their apocalyptic grandeur. How could Jesus soberly imagine that
this could and would be accomplished? He could do so because
he was a Jew, belonging to a people whose history, as they read
it, was a record of miracles wrought on their behalf and who believed in greater miracles to come. But what Jesus anticipated
would happen was no more likely to be correct than that of any
other interpreter of the prophetic legends. During his lifetime he
could to an astonishing extent because of his personal qualities
enact and obtain compliance with the messianic scheme as he
apprehended it. But he had no control over what lay beyond, and
in much that he anticipated he was mistaken. The Church had to
face before very long the acute problem of the postponement of
his expectations, and dealt with it rather lamely and unconvin-
cingly by largely spiritualising them. The dogma of his deity did
not allow it to be admitted that he had been in error.

The convictions Jesus had, as we must appreciate, rested on
the oracular treatment of the Old Testament. The Jewish circles
in which he moved were accustomed to applying the text of the
sacred books not only to the messianic figures, but to other
individuals concerned in the Cosmic Drama, and in general to
the circumstances of what they believed to be the Last Times.
Abundant illustrations of this kind of prophetic exegesis are furnished by the Dead Sea Scrolls and the apocalyptic literature. The
Bible had secrets to yield which could be extracted by the right
methods for the guidance and instruction of the Elect of the End
of the Days.

Christianity got going when the followers of Jesus started to
proclaim that in him the Messiah had come, and sought to prove
this in the only way which would carry conviction, by demonstrating from the Scriptures that all that had befallen him had
been foretold. There is now every reason to believe that the first
written presentation of the gospel took the form of a compendium of such Biblical *Testimonies*, a work which in its various

recensions underlies the canonical Gospels, and whose influence can be discerned on other parts of the New Testament and on much of the patristic literature.[15] We have evidence that some accounts of the activities of Jesus became coloured and elaborated by prophecies which it was deemed appropriate to identify with them. But the picture we have of the immediate and spontaneous association of prophecies with the experiences of Jesus argues strongly that his disciples were not initiating the process, but continuing one they had acquired from him.

The Gospels insist that Jesus had some foreknowledge of his fate which he had derived from the Scriptures. Significantly, he began to communicate this information only after he had elicited from Peter at Caesarea-Philippi the affirmation that he was the Messiah. 'From that time forth began Jesus to shew unto his disciples how that he must go unto Jerusalem, and suffer many things of the elders and chief priests and scribes, and be killed, and be raised again the third day.'[16] He declared this on the ground that these things were *written* concerning the Messiah.[17]

If Jesus exhibited such foreknowledge this would be nothing extraordinary if he had had access to some of the literature of 'the Saints', as seems to be indicated by his familiarity with the idea of a Suffering Just One and with a Son of Man christology. Josephus tells us of the Essenes: 'There are some among them who profess to foretell the future, being versed from their early years in holy books . . . and oracular utterances of prophets.'[18] In his writings he gives instances of their powers, and no doubt many in such circles did acquire remarkable insight and capacity for seership as a result of their training.

Believing himself to be the Messiah, it would not be surprising if Jesus should have sought to learn from 'the Saints' as much as he could of what was required of him and what would befall him. There is no novelty in the view that he believed it to be incumbent on him to fulfil the messianic predictions. The early Christians delighted to pursue the quest for such fulfilments in his life to the extent that, with the help of the Greek Bible, they could uncover allusions in the most unlikely texts, and even create incidents to conform with supposed prophetic necessities. Ephraem the Syrian, in the fourth century, declaims: 'Come hither thou troop of prophets, ye interpreters of verities. See ye the King hath not turned aside from the path ye trod out for him!'[19] But it is needful to emphasise that neither before nor since Jesus has there been anyone whose experiences from first to last have been so pin-pointed as tallying with what were held to be prophetic intimations concerning the Messiah. The nearest comparison available to us is that of the Teacher of Righteousness of the Dead Sea Scrolls. It is only recently, since this discovery, that we have become fully aware that before the time of Jesus the Old Testament was being interpreted oracularly in the same way as we find in the New Testament.

The logical deductions from this vital piece of information were partly seen even before the evidence derived from the Scrolls. We may take as an example the inquiry conducted by Sir Edwyn Hoskyns and Noel Davey, published in 1931, from which we may quote two brief excerpts.[20]

'Jesus acted as He did act and said what He did say because He was consciously fulfilling a necessity imposed upon Him by God through the demands of the Old Testament. He died in Jerusalem, not because the Jews hounded Him thither and did Him to death, but because He was persuaded that, as Messiah, He must journey to Jerusalem in order to be rejected and to die.'

'The Historian is dealing in the end with an historical Figure fully conscious of a task which had to be done, and fully conscious also that the only future which mattered for men and women depended upon what He said and did, and finally upon His death. This conscious purpose gave a clear unity to His words and actions, so that the actions interpret the words and the words the actions.'

But if this contention is true, as it is hard to doubt, it means that before Jesus embarked upon his ministry he was equipped with knowledge of what had to happen obtained from previous messianic researches. His public activities lasted, perhaps, little more than a year. Their demands called for continual movement and engagement. Jesus was rarely alone and often weary to the point of utter exhaustion: he had no leisure for quiet study or the slow formation of ideas. There is no indication whatever that he was simply leaving things to chance, and had no inkling of what to expect. From first to last his actions are marked by the utmost purposefulness, and he speaks with an authority which made a profound impression on all who came in contact with him. He is revealed as a man who knows exactly what he is doing, and why. More than once in respect of his end he is reported to have said: 'My hour is not yet come.'[21]

What we have adduced leads up to a crucial question. If Jesus believed that a series of experiences would happen to him in accordance with prophetic requirements, did he, as Hoskyns and Davey suggest, *consciously* proceed to speak and act in accordance with them? It rather looks as if these scholars realised the implications of what they were saying, and being orthodox Christians they shied away from them, for at the end of their book we read:

'Thus far it might be argued that the evidence points to a strange human act of will by which Jesus determined to obey the will of God as He had extracted the knowledge of it from a persistent study of the Old Testament Scriptures. . . . But this is not the truth. No New Testament writer could think of Jesus as the Greeks thought of Prometheus. We must therefore conclude that Jesus Himself did not think of His Life and Death as a human achievement at all. Language descriptive of human heroism is entirely foreign to the New Testament. The Event of the Life and Death of Jesus was not thought of as a human act, but as an act of God wrought out in human flesh and blood, which is a very different matter.'[22]

This is not a conclusion on the plane of historical inquiry. It transfers judgement to the New Testament, whose views reflecting subsequent Christian opinion we are invited to endorse as the truth. If the evidence points to 'a strange human act of will' on the part of Jesus why should we be afraid to accept that as the truth? Why should we not conclude, historically, that, before his baptism by John, Jesus had succeeded in producing a kind of

blueprint of the Messiah's mission with the prophetic requirements organised to show a progressive programme of events
having their climax at Jerusalem when he would suffer at the hands
of the authorities?

Here could be the explanation of much that is mysterious in
the Gospel story. Reading the story in this messianic light could
make it possible to know, much more clearly, accurately and
decisively, the real Jesus. In making the attempt to do so we shall
chiefly be concerned with the way in which he prepared for and
carried out what he believed to be his messianic task, emphasising
in particular to an extent not previously brought out the manner
in which he sought to attain his objectives so as to compel circumstances to comply with what for him were the imperative requirements of the prophecies.

For the man who embarked on this formidable and fantastic
undertaking this was no game he was playing. He was in deadly
earnest. As he saw it in his own time and setting, with its strange
obsessions, tremendous issues depended on the measure of his
faithfulness to unalterable divine decrees. He had need of all
those qualities of mind and character which had been promised
to the Messiah to enable him to succeed.

NOTES AND REFERENCES

1. Isa. xi. 4.
2. *Psalms of Solomon*, xvii. 35–42.
3. Ps. xlv. 7 xl. 7–8.
4. *Psalms of Solomon*, xvii. 28–31.
5. Mk. iii. 22, vii. 1.
6. Jn. vii. 40–3, 51–2, viii. 48.
7. Jn. xi. 7–8.
8. See Part Two, Chapter 2, *North Palestinean Sectarians and Christian Origins*.
9. Isa. xi. 1; Mt. ii. 23.
10. *The Community Rule*, viii. *The Dead Sea Scrolls in English*, Tr. Vermes.
11. Mt. xxvi. 28; Isa. liii. 11.
12. Lk. xxiv. 26, and see Part Two, Chapter 3, *The Suffering Just One and the Son of Man*.

13. See Part Two, Chapter 1, *Messianism and the Development of Christianity.*

14. Israel is called the Son of God, the Firstborn, the Only-begotten and Dearly Beloved One, and Solomon son of David and by interpretation the Messiah is brought into a filial relationship with God (see Part Two, Chapter 1). But this Sonship only meant close association in representing God and carrying out his will.

15. See Part Two, Chapter 4, *Gospels in the Making.*

16. Mt. xvi. 21. At intervals Jesus repeated his prediction (Mt. xvii. 22–3, xx. 17, xxvi. 2).

17. See Mk. ix. 12; Jn. v. 46; Mk. xiv. 21; Lk. xxiv. 44–7.

18. Josephus, *Wars* II. viii. 6.

19. *Rhythm against the Jews,* a Sermon delivered on Palm Sunday. We may cite here Stather Hunt, 'It is significant that both ancient and modern scholars should, apparently quite independently, come to the same conclusion, that the Gospels are almost entirely testimony matter put into narrative form' (*Primitive Gospel Sources,* p. 236).

20. *The Riddle of the New Testament,* pp. 160 and 250.

21. See Jn. ii. 4, vii. 6–8, xii. 27; Mk. xiv. 41.

22. *The Riddle of the New Testament,* p. 254.

3

A Child is Born

THE mysteries about the birth of Jesus are mainly prosaic, where and when he was born. The choice for the first lies between Nazareth in Galilee and Bethlehem in Judea, and for the second between about 6 B.C. or about A.D. 6.[1] But certainly from infancy his environment was Galilean.

This child, however, the first-born of a Jewish artisan named Joseph and his wife Miriam, was to prove to be no ordinary boy, for he was destined to play a unique part in history. He drew to himself the dreams and visions of his people, and so clothed his life in them that he procured for himself immortality and gave rise to a faith which identified him among many Jews as the Messiah and among many Gentiles as the Divine Saviour of the world. Within a century of his birth stories relating to the circumstances of his nativity appropriate to the dignity in which he was held were in circulation among his following.

These stories, simply and beautifully told, still have a strong emotional appeal, since they enshrine deep-seated human hopes and longings. They bring us back again and again to that sacred place of childhood's imagination where there is no barrier to the commerce between heaven and earth. In this respect they are a fitting tribute to the man who had so great a faith that he succeeded in lighting up the darkness of mundane experience with the joyous effulgence of fairyland. Here was his genius, and this is how we must understand him, as the one above all others who showed mankind how to make their dreams come true.

With the birth stories of Jesus, and of John the Baptist also, we pass directly from the world of sober reality into the world of fairy-tale. It has the appearance of being the same world with which we are familiar. There are the same kind of people in it and certain matching events take place. But we are instantly aware that we are in a very different atmosphere, and that extraordinary things are going on which everyone seems to accept as perfectly normal. Our minds are confused by the matter of fact manner of narration of the strangest circumstances in which heavenly beings appear to and converse with mortals, and we do not know what to believe.

The presentation of what takes place does not distinguish at all between the factual and the legendary, and no criteria are provided to enable us to separate the one from the other. We feel this to be grossly unfair, an imposition on our credulity. If we entered this other world through any other volume than the Bible we should not have this distress, because we should employ standards of judgement which took account of what was characteristic of the people who produced the literature. But we have been persuaded, quite wrongly and in complete disregard of the nature of spiritual folklore, that what is set down in the Bible is to be received as true in the literal and absolute sense of being the very word of God. We have been induced to credit that it is not we who have entered into a world of imagination in which all things are possible, but that such a world has entered ours and has become one with it to the extent that its miraculous features have operated under our conditions, in our time, space and history. All we need is the application to our eyes of the fairy dust called faith to enable us to see and acknowledge this.

This insistence—and it is Religion which requires it—is not to be rejected as wholly fanciful and devoid of reality. We need to be sensitive to intimations of the existence of much beyond our finite grasp. But we also have to be safeguarded against the follies of the narrow traditionalists. The Bible has to be treated through and through intelligently, by applying to its understanding knowledge of the ways and ideas of those who had a hand in its composition in their various periods. To withhold or ignore vital information is a spiritual crime.

With the nativity stories it should have been taught by the Church that they are deliberate idealisations, that intentionally they mingle the legends of the heroes of Israel and of Hellas, and draw upon these legends for their basic ingredients. How should it be known by the unscholarly that the stories are of the same order as those marvels with which Jews of the time had enriched and expanded the Biblical accounts of the births of Noah, Abraham and Moses?[2] And as to the non-Jewish element relating to the divine origin of Jesus, why not refer, as Justin Martyr did in the second century,[3] to the divine birth of Perseus from the virgin Danae, and relate what was told of the heavenly nativity of a world ruler like Alexander the Great and of a sage like Apollonius of Tyana?[4]

What our Gospel stories so engagingly offer is a tribute typical of the thinking and literary expression of the world of nineteen centuries ago, couched in language which Christianity had derived from its Jewish inspiration. This is what the advent of Jesus had come to mean to those who came after him and believed in him; and this is how they suitably adorned and compensated for the meagre facts at their disposal.

There was nothing peculiar about the birth of Jesus. He was not God incarnate and no Virgin Mother bore him. The Church in its ancient zeal fathered a myth and became bound to it as dogma. Since Christians largely continue to suppose that their faith stands or falls by the doctrine of the deity of Christ the dogma goes on being sustained to the detriment of what is really significant about the person and contribution of Jesus. It is pathetic to have theologians, whether orthodox or liberal, trying to save themselves and the credit of the Church's teaching by questing for terms which will enable them to retain what they should have outgrown.

Men in all ages according to their lights have sincerely subscribed to erroneous notions, and no one who has ever lived has been exempt from error. There is no call to perpetuate such

notions or to regard them as in some special or mysterious sense
true just because they have been conserved by a priesthood, or are
found in the Bible, or in any other work held to be sacred or inspired. Neither is it legitimate to employ different standards of
judgement in testing validity or veracity because one set of records
is regarded with greater reverence than another. In all cases it is
incumbent upon us to reach conclusions and get at results in
the first instance by the same methods. There must be an honest
foundation for the acknowledgment of the presence of factors to
which these methods are inapplicable, and we must exercise the
utmost care not to mislead ourselves, and not to miss those considerations which suggest that a rational explanation of circumstances exists, even if it is not readily apparent. It is an obligation
to quest for and sift all relevant evidence, and by no means to
neglect or to suppress what may help to clear up a mystery.

With the consideration of Jesus, it is incumbent upon us before
reaching convictions about him to endeavour to dispel, so far as
this is practicable, the mists through which his figure much larger
than life looms before us in the Gospels. The view of him which
we are communicating here has been arrived at by such prior
investigation, and is represented in its main essentials in the
notes provided and in Part Two of this book. It does not matter
if we cannot furnish all the answers, and due to the circumstances
brought to the reader's notice it would be quite impossible to do
so. The initial word does not lie within the province of the
theologian, but of the historian and the psychologist. If what is
discoverable should seem to demand an interpretation which the
theologian is best qualified to supply he will be placed in a
stronger position to make it afterwards for our benefit.

Facing first, then, the origins of Jesus, his advent at such a
crucial period may ultimately be regarded as an act of God, if
we should believe with the Jews in the movement of God in
history. But apprehending both the heroic and the theological
intentions of the nativity stories there is no call whatever to
suppose that his arrival in this world of ours was in any way
exceptional or attended by any supernatural occurrences. He was

as completely human as every baby, the eldest child, as we have said, of a Jewish artisan named Joseph and his wife Miriam (Mary), inheriting his form from their stock and his portion of their character and disposition.

The nativity stories add very little of substance to the slender information otherwise at our disposal. They are late introductory compositions, ranking with the poetic prologue to the Fourth Gospel in putting the finishing touches to convictions about Jesus as these had become defined in the various Christian circles.[5] We already know from the main stream of Christian tradition that the family to which Jesus belonged was settled in Galilee, and could trace its descent from the house of David from which the Messiah was expected to come. We know the names of the parents of Jesus, and that his father was by trade a carpenter. We know that he was their first-born, and that he had four younger brothers and at least two sisters.[6] We can judge that they were pious people, and that the atmosphere of the home was strongly religious.

We do not have to see any peculiar significance in the fact that the eldest child of Joseph and Miriam was named Joshua (Jesus), any more than that they called their other sons Jacob (James), Joseph, Simeon and Judah. All are good Biblical names and were in common use. When Jesus was accepted as Messiah by a Jewish following it did mean much to them that he bore the name of the appointed successor of Moses who led Israel into the Promised Land, a name that spoke of God's salvation, just as those who followed John the Baptist found it fitting that his Hebrew name Johanan should have reference to the Lord's favour.

It is purely speculative whether the parents of Jesus entertained a secret hope that their first-born would prove to be the Messiah, being of the line of David and being born at a time when messianic fervour was rampant. It is equally speculative whether the thought came in childhood to Jesus himself, and if so, whether this was through any external circumstance. We cannot completely dismiss the possibility, conveyed in Luke by the prognostications attributed to the aged Simeon and the prophetess Hannah, that someone who saw the boy in infancy or later made some laudatory remark about his future. Josephus records that when Herod was a child and had no prospect whatever of royal dignity he was encountered one day on his way to school by the Essene Menahem, who clapped him on the bottom and told him that he would become king of the Jews.[7]

Whether through some such experience, or as the outcome of his own imaginings, the seed of identification of himself with the Messiah was planted in the mind of Jesus, and it is quite possible that he was of tender years when this happened. Children are highly impressionable, and readily see themselves playing the part of heroes. The land in which the boy Jesus lived had rung with the exploits of the patriot leader Judas of Galilee. It was told how he had opposed paying tribute to Caesar, proclaiming that Jews had no ruler but God. It was told how with great daring he and his men had broken into the heavily fortified Galilean city of Sepphoris and had got away with weapons and money belonging to the government. In Galilee there was hatred of the heathen Romans and their Herodian minions who controlled the country, and ostracism of Jews who sold their souls to serve them. Preachers in the synagogues urged the people to repent that God might intervene on their behalf and send the Messiah:[8] they expounded the Scriptures of consolation and hope. There was much to make any sensitive Jewish lad conscious of strange and momentous events in store, events with which he might be intimately associated.

Except for a single story, related exclusively by Luke, the Gospels pass over in complete silence the whole life of Jesus prior to the short final period of his public ministry. Of the circumstances of what Luke says was nearly thirty years[9] they tell us nothing directly, and evidently tradition had furnished no information. Yet it is about those years that we particularly need to be informed, for they were the years in which Jesus became the man of the brief Gospel history, the years of preparation for the purposeful climax of his career. As we have already pointed out

(above p. 44) the major features of what he had to do were clear
to Jesus before he went to be baptised by John, and he set himself
deliberately to carry out the programme which he believed to be
incumbent on him in the character of Messiah. To understand the
behaviour of Jesus during his public ministry we have to have
some insight into what had gone before. Consequently we have
to wrestle with the Gospels to obtain from them not simply
those things which they are most concerned to bring to our
attention and place so to speak under our noses, things on which
interest is commonly concentrated. Rather do we have to labour
to extract what they incidentally and unconsciously reveal, information which bears the impress of truth just because it was not
felt to be significant. Certain inferences and deductions cannot
positively be confirmed, but on the principle that the child is
father of the man what is reported of the man can be made to
illuminate with the help of external evidences a good deal that
has not been narrated about the child.

The one incident cited by Luke is an attempt to break the
silence by laying the foundation for the qualities exhibited by
Jesus. It is supposed to have occurred when his hero was twelve
years of age. According to Luke, Jesus had accompanied his
parents, no doubt for the first time, on the pilgrimage to Jerusalem
for the Passover festival. At the close of the celebration, when the
party left the city to travel home, the boy quietly absented himself, and when he was missed he was finally discovered by his
anxious parents in the Temple listening to the religious teachers
and asking them questions. Those present were amazed at his
intelligence. His mother said to him: 'Why have you treated us
like this, boy? Here have your father and I been searching
anxiously for you.' To this Jesus is said to have replied: 'Why
did you search for me? Didn't you know I was bound to be
occupied with my father's affairs?' His parents could make no
sense of this reply.

Obviously we are meant by Luke to understand that Jesus
was referring to his heavenly Father, in accordance with the
evangelist's previous statement that he would be called 'Son of

the Most High'.[10] We would naturally expect the story to reflect
the belief of Christians around the end of the first century A.D.
when the Gospel was composed, and there is no need therefore
to labour the point that Jesus is made here in childhood to express
consciousness of a special relationship to God. Something strange-
ly like this story, without this element, was told by Josephus
in his autobiography about his own boyhood, and the author of
Luke–Acts was indebted to that contemporary historian in a
number of respects.[11]

Whether the story owed its inspiration to Josephus, with or
without some foundation in tradition, Luke at any rate has
detected a characteristic of Jesus which comes out in the Gospel
records of the ministry. There we find Jesus after his baptism
going off quietly into the wilderness to struggle with biddings
which come to tempt him. Then at Capernaum, where he has
been healing the sick, he rises before dawn and without a word to
his disciples goes out to a solitary place to pray. At another time,
associated with the feeding of the five thousand, he sends away
the people and his disciples and departs by himself to a mountain
to pray. Almost at the last, at Gethsemane, he similarly seeks
solitude to commune with God.[12] So it can be inferred that such
wandering off alone was typical of him, and Luke may well be
correct in making him act in this way in his youth.

It is a fair deduction about the young Jesus that he was inclined
to be introspective, closely guarding his secret thoughts even
from those nearest and dearest to him. At times he felt strongly
the need to be alone, to meditate and seek guidance in prayer.
At others he would seize opportunity to obtain answers from
those best qualified to inform him to questions with which his
young mind was struggling, and which were of the utmost consequence to him. On these occasions he would quietly disappear
without saying where he was going. One of the things he told
his followers was that when they prayed they should go to their
room, close the door, and pray to their Father who is in secret;
and he taught them to pray as he must often have prayed fervently
himself.[13] It can be seen from the Gospels that it was not

uncommon with Jesus to be withdrawn. His disciples became familiar with his spells of silence which they feared to break. They would be walking with him, talking animatedly among themselves, even arguing heatedly, virtually ignoring his presence. Suddenly he would say something, either at the time or later, which showed that he was not wholly inattentive, and had heard at least a part of their conversation. We may assume that he was like this as a child.

So the picture we can form of the young Jesus is of a quiet, dutiful, watchful individual, with an inner life of his own and a deep-seated faith. He had a bright intelligence and was by no means aloof from his surroundings, yet was prone to detach himself from them. He was not at all uncommunicative when it came to finding out what he wished to know; but he was rather a strange boy and something of a puzzle to his parents, not readily drawing attention to himself, and inwardly busy with tremendous imaginings which it was impossible for him to reveal. What some of his cherished thoughts were about we may hazard a confident guess: they were about the world, about God's dealings with Israel, and about the deliverer who had been promised to his people.

NOTES AND REFERENCES

1. Jesus was born at Bethlehem according to the nativity stories, because it was the city of David, and because of the prediction in Micah v. 2; but some doubt about this is expressed in Jn. vii. 41–2. On the chronological problem, see Part Two, Chapter 6, *Some Gospel Mysteries*.

2. In the *Genesis Apocryphon* found among the Dead Sea Scrolls the lost opening apparently told of the miraculous birth of Noah, and the text begins with the suspicion of his father Lamech that his wife had been made pregnant by an angel and therefore had been unfaithful to him. She repudiates this. (See Vermes, *The Dead Sea Scrolls in English*.) Of Abraham it was told that when he was born a star appeared in the east and moved across the heavens. The wise men went to King Nimrod and informed him that this meant the birth of a child destined to be great. Terror seized the king and he sent for his councillors, who advised him to kill the son of Terah. The king sent his soldiers to slay the child, but God protected him by dispatching the angel Gabriel to conceal him by clouds and mists. Afterwards Terah, fearing for the boy's life, fled secretly

from the country. (See *Book of Jashar* and *Maase Abraham*.) Concerning the birth of Moses the legends tell that Pharaoh decreed the death of the Israelite male children because of a dream which the magicians interpreted to mean that by an Israelite child Egypt would be destroyed. Amram, whose wife was pregnant, was alarmed by the decree; but God spoke to him in a dream and told him that the child to be born to him would be the one whom the Egyptians dreaded. He would, however, be concealed from those who would destroy him (Moses) and become the deliverer of the Hebrews. (See *Targum of Palestine* and Josephus, *Antiq.* II. ix. 3–4.)

3. Justin Martyr, *First Apology*, xxi–xxii.

4. According to one story Olympias before her marriage to Philip of Macedon dreamt that a thunderbolt fell from heaven kindling a fire in her belly, thus indicating the heavenly origin of her son Alexander. Another story tells of a serpent which kept company with Olympias while she slept. Philip saw this and consulted the Delphic Oracle, which informed him that the god Jupiter Ammon had consorted with his wife in the form of a serpent. Alexander was the offspring of this union. (See Plutarch, *Life of Alexander the Great*.) In the case of Apollonius, the famous sage who flourished in the second half of the first century A.D., it was related that the god Proteus appeared to his mother before his birth. She was not afraid, but asked him what sort of child she would bear. 'Myself,' he replied. 'And who are you?' she inquired. 'I am Proteus the god of Egypt,' he told her. (See Philostratus, *Life of Apollonius of Tyana*.)

5. See Part Two, Chapter 5, *The Second Phase*.

6. Roman Catholics, because of the doctrine of the perpetual virginity of Mary, are obliged to hold that the brothers and sisters of Jesus were the children of Joseph by a former wife. The Gospels give no warrant for this teaching, since it is stated that Joseph had intercourse with Mary after the birth of Jesus, who was her first-born son (Mt. i. 25). The other children of the family are described as the brothers and sisters of Jesus in the Gospels without any qualification, and nothing is said of Joseph having been previously married.

7. Josephus, *Antiq.* XV. x. 5.

8. Jesus himself preached frequently in the synagogues of Galilee.

9. See Part Two, Chapter 6, *Some Gospel Mysteries*.

10. Lk. i. 32, 35.

11. See Part Two, Chapter 5, *The Second Phase*. Josephus tells (*Life* ii) that he was noted as a boy for his learning, and when he was only fourteen was often consulted by the chief priests and doctors of Jerusalem.

12. Mk. i. 12–13, 35, vi. 45–6, xiv. 32–5.

13. Mt. vi. 6–13.

4

The Formative Years

WHAT transpired during what are commonly called the Silent Years of the life of Jesus is not for us an interest dictated by idle curiosity. We require to know to the fullest extent possible the man we are dealing with if we are to interpret correctly what has been handed down concerning him. We are persuaded that the documents we possess, when we understand their character and how they came into being, are able to yield a straightforward and sensible answer to the question of the natives of Nazareth, 'Whence hath this man these things?'

It is certified to us that Jesus was the eldest of a fairly large family brought up in humble circumstances. Poverty was widespread at this period, due to taxation, political disorganisation and the effects of famine and civil strife. The household at Nazareth was accustomed to frugal living. Things that Jesus said point to personal experience of economic stringency, which his associations converted into a philosophy of life. He was assured that in God's providence there would be enough for simple necessities, enough to manage on, and one should not be anxious about tomorrow. 'Sufficient unto the day is the evil thereof.'

Memories doubtless spoke in such teaching, and we can fathom what some of these may have been. While still a youth Jesus would appear to have lost his father, the breadwinner of the family. After the incident when Jesus was twelve, as reported by Luke, Joseph disappears from the story. At the marriage in Cana of Galilee it is the mother of Jesus who is there, not both his parents,[1] and elsewhere in the accounts of the public ministry it is only his mother and brothers who play a part. Jesus does not directly refer to his father, but we find him showing concern for the lot of the poor widow and tenderness towards little children and the orphan.

Jesus is said to have followed his father's trade, but we may infer that temperamentally he was not well suited to assume responsibilities as head of the family, which made demands upon him at variance with his need for solitude and opportunity to pursue the matters with which his mind was burdened. His mother may not have taken too kindly to his inwardness and habit of going off alone. His family should be his first consideration. It was not easy, even with care and scrimping, to provide for so many mouths, to save for the dowries of the girls. Jesus may have had a recollection of his mother in mind when he told of the woman who had lost a small silver coin, and who lit a lamp and swept the house through until she found it. His stories were often based on real life as he had known and observed it.

If this was the position, it would not be surprising if Mary was disturbed about Jesus. When he embarked on his public activities it would seem all wrong that he should turn his back on his family to go off preaching. She loved her eldest son, and perhaps thought of him as in some ways so like his father, but she could not pretend to understand him. His kinsfolk went further. They decided that he must be out of his mind and attempted to take control of him. His mother and brothers sought access to him, and we are left in doubt whether he received them.[2] When Jesus is found addressing his mother it is with respect and sympathy, but not in terms that suggest there was a close bond between them.

With the father of Jesus it had been different. We may judge from his references to fatherhood that Jesus had adored Joseph and that this feeling was reciprocated. Joseph had taught his son his trade, and inevitably they must have been constantly together. To the boy God was conceived in his father's image, and when Joseph was taken away the intensity with which Jesus turned to

God as the Father in Heaven is eloquent of how greatly he had
loved and felt the loss of his earthly parent. Today it would probably be said that he had a father fixation. The unexpected death
of Joseph when Jesus was still at a most impressionable age may
well have been an important factor in convincing him of his
messianic destiny. Had not God said of the son of David, 'I
will be his father, and he shall be my son'.[3] By taking Joseph was
not God signifying the fulfilment of the messianic promise of the
Psalmist?[4] This is brought out in the Gospel account of the baptism of Jesus, representing his authorisation to take up his work
as Messiah. The words that came to him then seem to echo
not only the Psalmist's language, but the affectionate encourage-
ment his father had given him in childhood in the carpenter's
shop, 'You are my dear son: I am very pleased with you.'

We must not minimise the struggle which Jesus underwent,
his self-examination and mental anguish, before he could accept
for himself that he had been chosen to be the Messiah. It was a
conclusion he had to reach without the help of any human being
in whom he could confide. No wonder if he should often wish to
be alone and pour out his soul to the One who was now the only
father he had. When he turned over again and again those prophecies held to relate to the Messiah he must have stood aghast
at what was involved of wisdom and perfection of character.
Who could measure up to such a standard? The worst thing to
contend with was the temptation to the sins of pride and power-
seeking and self-sufficiency. Once youthful dreams were submitted to more mature judgements such temptations must have
weighed heavily upon him, long before they were finally resisted
and put to flight in the contest which tradition reports took place
in the wilderness after his baptism. 'Lead us not into temptation,
but deliver us from the Evil One!'

It may never previously have occurred to us what a tremendous
and heart-searching thing it was for Jesus to own himself as the
man his people awaited. The Christian will have supposed that
in some sense even as a boy he was conscious of deity within
him, and that accordingly he accepted that he was the Messiah

without qualm or misgiving. All he did, on this view, was effectively and for almost the whole of his life to conceal his divine nature from everyone he met, suppressing the revelation of his powers, performing no miracles, healing no sick, so that the people of Nazareth had no inkling of his quality, and not even a demon had the temerity to identify him. Such a view, apart from its intrinsic improbability, does not correspond with the picture of Jesus in the Gospels as a man who readily responded with the capacities in him to the call of human need. If he was the same before his baptism as he was afterwards this could hardly fail to be manifest in his earlier years. After Jesus had been accepted as God it did not take Christians very long to appreciate this difficulty, and they produced a number of books purporting to relate authentically the prodigies he had performed as a boy, and which may be read in M. R. James's *Apocryphal New Testament*. But quite evidently there had been no such exploits, and nothing to indicate that the young Jesus son of Joseph was other than he seemed.

We may not underrate how much the true understanding of the Jesus of the Gospels depends upon what preceded and led up to his public activities. We have to realise that for him the prospect of being the Messiah must have been in certain respects quite terrifying. How could he obtain full knowledge of all that was involved and what he would be required to do? How should he prepare himself? It was conceivable that he might even be deluding himself about his vocation. He had no experience of government or anything to do with the exercise of authority. The life to which he was accustomed was relatively uncomplicated, village life among ordinary people. But he could not deny that a fire burned within him, as it had burned within the prophets of old, most of whom like himself were persons of no eminence, and yet they had spoken the word of the Lord to princes.

It was essential for Jesus to acquire more insight into the messianic interpretation of the Scriptures, more ability to comprehend the will of God. The messianic import of a number of passages he well knew from what he had heard in the synagogue, and perhaps from what his father and others had told him. But since no one had had to face the fulfilling of the prophecies there existed no systematic presentation of what should befall the Messiah. This had to be discovered and worked out. A clear pattern had to emerge. Though Jesus may have believed that he would be guided aright when the time came, he still had to visualise the mission of the Messiah more concretely and relate it to contemporary conditions and circumstances.

Even with the responsibilities at home which Jesus was obliged to discharge, especially while his younger brothers and sisters were growing up, there was the possibility to learn much, and it is clear that he availed himself of it to the full. While he would often seek solitude, he did not lock himself away in a private world of his own. He became a keen student of life and human character. Very little escaped his penetrating notice. The man we meet in the Gospels is one who knows the countryside of Galilee intimately, its flowers and trees, fields and orchards, the activities of the people in work and worship, in their social, spiritual, political and economic affairs. The things he teaches and the realistic tales he tells to illustrate his teaching, are proof of how much he has absorbed. Such a store of information could only have been the outcome of prolonged and acute observation. There had been nothing somnambulistic in his walks abroad. He had deemed it to be vital to his equipment that he should have first-hand knowledge of the ways of the world.

There is no need to imagine, as some writers have done, that Jesus travelled to other lands such as Egypt and even Tibet in order to learn from the Masters there. He exhibits no familiarity at all with any foreign country, and refers to the outside world only in the most general terms. The only country he knew was Palestine. But it is no less negatived that nothing whatever had been shaping itself in the mind of Jesus concerning the demands of the messiahship, and that illumination and all that went with it came to him suddenly out of the void when he was baptised by John. Everything we read in the Gospels is against such a view.

The Jesus of the Gospels alludes to himself from the beginning as the Son of Man, a northern messianic title.[5] He speaks clearly and positively on a wide range of themes. He appears to know exactly what he has to do and why, and all this from the outset of his brief ministry. When tempted to take another course than that which he has determined in advance is right he rejects it out of hand. He is so familiar with the Scriptures and their implication that he seems to carry the whole Bible in his head. What he had succeeded in mastering surprised the doctors of Jerusalem, so that they could say of him, 'How is he acquainted with learning, never having studied?'

But though Jesus was no 'disciple of the wise' as understood by the Pharisees, he could well have had access to other sources of knowledge. It would be natural for him to seek out those who could further enlighten him on messianic matters. Among them in Galilee would have been groups of those whom the people revered as 'the Saints'. There were many such 'Essenes' in the region, varying in their antecedents. It is suggested by the Gospels that Jesus had imbibed a good many of their notions, and his younger brother James was strongly attracted to the nazirite ascetic way of life. Jesus was not himself an Essene, as has often been asserted, but it seems fairly certain that he must have consorted with such sectaries, and was familiar with some of their literature and teaching.[6] He accepted some of their tenets and recognised the existence of an 'Elect of Israel', but he also repudiated much that they represented, their asceticism, secretiveness, rigidity of discipline, harsh judgements and uncompromising attitudes. He could not go all the way with them, any more than he could with the Pharisees.

It would not have been difficult in later years for Jesus to be away from home for protracted periods in an endeavour to learn what 'the Saints' could teach him. His domestic responsibilities would have diminished considerably once his younger brothers could earn a living and one or more of his sisters had married. We know that some of his trade were itinerant, going from village to village like gipsy tinkers giving the services of their craft. This possibility has been explored by Robert Eisler in his work *The Messiah Jesus and John the Baptist*, where he regards the pre-Christian Nazoreans as having an affinity with the ancient sectarian migrant tribes of Rechabites and Kenites, as more recently does Matthew Black, many of whom followed the calling of smiths and carpenters. Eisler compares them with the still-existing bedouin Sleb of Syria, a tribe of itinerant craftsmen whose name derives from the cross-mark they put on their foreheads. These people have little use for money and are often ready to accept grain or dates in payment for their work. Eisler draws attention to the Essene-like position of Jesus in respect of wealth and possessions, and his instructions to his apostles when he sent them out. Jesus declared that no man could serve God and Mammon. Men should not lay up treasure on earth. It was easier for a camel to go through the eye of a needle than for a rich man to enter the Kingdom of Heaven. We must therefore regard it as highly probable that for a time Jesus attached himself to a travelling body of sectarian craftsmen, and thereby came to be known as the Nazorean.

Naturally such thinking is speculative in the absence of direct evidence. But the indirect evidence which has accumulated is very impressive.

Whatever Jesus learnt, however, and in whatever way he obtained his knowledge, including elements of the healing art cultivated and practised by the communities of 'the Saints', there was always before him the destiny for which he prepared. In the last resort, he alone, earnestly soliciting the help of the Heavenly Father, must penetrate to the inner recesses of the sacred writings and marshal in order the intimations of the Divine Oracles. The novel achievement of Jesus was to mark out clearly the path the Messiah would have to tread. *Thus it was written.*

What is so striking in the Gospels, as scholars have noted, is the dynamic purposefulness of Jesus. He proceeds methodically to carry out certain actions calculated to have particular effects and leading up to a predetermined conclusion. It is as if he was a chemist in a laboratory confidently following a formula set down

in an authoritative textbook. There is scarcely a hint of hesitation
or indecision. He is like a chess player with a master plan, who has
anticipated and knows how to counter the moves of his opponents, and indeed to make them serve the ends of his design. He
says and does things quite unexpected by his intimate associates,
which take them by surprise or which they are unable to fathom.
They may like to think they are wholly in his confidence, and
even that he will do what they have in mind for him. But he
baffles and defeats them, and makes arrangements of which they
have not been cognisant to secure his objectives.

The man of the Gospels is clearly putting into operation a
programme which was the outcome of his prior messianic investigations in the years before his baptism, with absolute conviction of the validity of his findings. What God had spoken by
the mouth of his prophets must surely and inevitably come to
pass down to the last jot and tittle. So informed is he that he is
readily able to take his cue from situations as they arise, and
actively assist in shaping them so that they will make their foreordained contribution. He does not, of course, know beforehand
to what extent and in what manner they will play their part, but
with the help of his sources and his knowledge of contemporary
affairs he can discern that certain categories of persons will be
involved.

We might well be sceptical that Jesus could do this, or imagine
that if he did he must have been superhuman, were it not for the
information we possess, notably since the discovery of the Dead
Sea Scrolls. But now we have ample confirmation of the oracular
treatment of the Scriptures at the time of Jesus, whereby it was
elicited from them what would happen in the Last Times to
nations, groups and individuals, often in some detail. We are
still ignorant of the methods employed, but we have before our
eyes some of the results of the curious science of the Elect. It
is plainly disclosed that the anticipations of Jesus, allowing for
exaggerations in the Gospel tradition, could have been reached
by the methods which were in use.

From caves near Qumran have come manuscripts, some two

thousand years old, which show how the books of the Bible were prophetically interpreted in an extraordinary manner to make them relate to the fortunes of the Elect and the persecution of the Teacher of Righteousness, to the punishment of the Wicked Priest and the other chief priests of Jerusalem.[7] When we read these strange documents it is not difficult to understand how Jesus could have arrived at comprehension of what the Messiah would experience. He evidently accepted that assured results were obtainable in the ways which were in vogue,[8] and a prophetic blueprint of the Days of the Messiah was the outcome of his investigations. The Scriptures thus disclosed to him the character of his mission, how his message would be received, his fate, and his subsequent appearance in glory as king and judge of the nations. The nearest individual approach to the achievement of Jesus is the prophetic and didactic power which the Essenes associated with the unnamed Teacher of Righteousness.[9]

We must dare to be honest about Jesus, and ready to take advantage of every circumstance which may help to throw light on his personality and the working of his mind. The faith he had in God is fully in keeping with a type of mystical Jewish piety, by no means extinct, in which there is a liberal mixture of superstition. He was oriental in his poetry, his pictorialism, his addiction to aphorisms and inclination to invective. He had the bright intelligence of his race, vivid imagination and great strength of will. It was in his nature to scheme and plan, and patiently and stubbornly to pursue a chosen course to the end. He had what is called in Jewish jargon a *yiddishe hertz*, a Jewish warmth of benevolent affection. He was highly sensitive and a shrewd judge of people. In his make-up there was no ambition of self-aggrandisement: his recognition of himself as the Messiah-designate cannot be attributed to megalomania. He saw himself as the Servant.

It is not within the province of this book, or the competence of its author, to provide a psychoanalytical study of Jesus. But it is necessary with what help we can obtain from the idealised records, supplemented by other knowledge which can be brought to bear on the subject, to have some insight into the character of the man we are dealing with. Only so can we apprehend that certain implications of the narratives are in keeping with that character, when they reveal how Jesus converted his convictions into actions and set out deliberately to bring upon himself those consequences which, according to his interpretation, the prophecies had predetermined.

The motives of Jesus must be sought in the land where he was born and the times in which he lived. On his own showing, he was not sent except to the lost sheep of the house of Israel. They were oppressed. Their country was controlled by a powerful heathen people, governed by its officials and their representatives. They suffered. They were in dread. They sinned and were wretched, angry and anxious. Yet upon their redemption there waited the peace and happiness of the whole world, which should arise from Israel's return to the Lord, when the worship of the One God and Father would be extended to all the children of men. The Scribes instructed in the Kingdom of God had made known that the Last Times of the old order had come, that the Messiah would speedily be revealed as the instrument of the great change, the Regeneration. But the transition would not be accomplished without sorrows and judgements, conflicts and calamities on an unprecedented scale. The Shepherd himself would be required to give his life for the sheep. All this Jesus saw and believed, and found in his heart a great love and compassion for his people, the flooding into his soul of a prompting to respond at whatever cost to the cry which he both felt and heard going up to heaven.

If he was a strange man it was because he was the product of a strange people with a strange faith that they were chosen of God to lead all nations to him, so that justice, righteousness and peace might reign on earth. It was a strange country, a holy land, in which Jesus was born and grew up. It was a strange period, the End of the Days, of which holy men of long ago had written. The most dramatic moment in human history was now believed to be imminent, and the signs of its arrival were multiplying.

This was the heritage, and these were the circumstances, which explain Jesus to us far more intelligibly than the quasi-pagan interpretation to which Christianity still largely subscribes under compulsion of its traditions and inclinations.

We may consider that Jesus had a strong sense of the dramatic, which not only brought home to him acutely the character and implications of his people's history, but led him to see himself as the embodiment of their hopes. In his own person he dramatised their dreams and saw himself acting out the prophecies. We may hold that this is how he came to marshall the messianic predictions in order as no one else had done so that they acquired the form of a drama developing to its appointed climax. His visualisation of the role of the Messiah was highly theatrical, and he played out the part like an actor with careful timing and appreciation of what every act called for. His calculated moves, his symbolic actions such as the forty days in the wilderness and the choice of twelve apostles, his staging of the triumphal entry into Jerusalem and the Last Supper, all testify to his dramatic consciousness, as do many of his gestures and declamations. Only one who possessed such a consciousness could have conceived, contrived and carried out the Passover Plot so masterfully and so superbly. But the portrayal of the Messiah's tragedy, and the anticipation of the happy ending, was utterly sincere. This was reality not make-believe.

For Jesus it was of the essence of his faith that God in his mysterious ways had made choice of him, a descendant of David, as the means of fulfilling those purposes which from age to age the Lord had inspired his messengers to proclaim. It was a knowledge which he could not communicate to anyone, could not even hint at before his call came. He could only prepare himself, and wait.

The effects of all he may be imagined to have endured, as he contemplated what was to come and dare not betray his secret, were bound to take their toll and show themselves in his physical appearance. It is conveyed by John's Gospel that he looked considerably older than his years.[10] He was approaching thirty, according to Luke, when at last the news came which told him that his long and exacting probation was at an end.

NOTES AND REFERENCES

1. Jn. ii. 1.
2. Mk. iii. 21, 31–5.
3. II. Sam. vii. 14.
4. Ps. ii. 7.
5. See Part Two, Chapter 2, *North Palestinean Sectarians and Christian Origins.*
6. See Part Two, Chapter 2.
7. The Biblical Commentaries from Qumran are extremly revealing, and may readily be consulted in the translation of G. Vermes, *The Dead Sea Scrolls in English* (Penguin Books). Special attention is drawn to the *Commentary on Habakkuk* and that on Psalm xxxvii. A specimen from each is given here by way of illustration. Square brackets indicate words restored where the manuscripts are defective.

Commentary on Habakkuk.
  [*For the violence done to Lebanon shall overwhelm you, and the destruction o, the beasts*] *shall terrify you, because of the blood of men and the violence done to the land, the city, and all its inhabitants* (Hab. ii. 17).
  Interpreted, this saying concerns the Wicked Priest, inasmuch as he shall be paid the reward which he himself tendered to the Poor. For *Lebanon* is the Council of the Community; and the *beasts* are the Simple of Judah who keep the Law. As he himself plotted the destruction of the Poor, so will God condemn him to destruction. As for that which he said, *Because of the blood of the city and the violence done to the land:* interpreted, *the city* is Jerusalem where the Wicked Priest committed abominable deeds and defiled the Temple of God. *The violence done to the land:* these are the cities of Judah where he robbed the poor of their possessions.

Commentary on Psalm xxxvii.
  The Wicked draw the sword and bend their bow to bring down the poor and needy and to slay the upright of way. Their sword shall enter into their own heart and their bow shall be broken (14–15).
  Interpreted, this concerns the wicked of Ephraim and Manasseh, who shall seek to lay hands on the Priest (i.e. the Teacher of Righteousness) and the men of his Council at the time of trial which shall come upon them. But God will redeem them from out of their hand. And afterwards, they (i.e. the wicked) shall be delivered into the hand of the violent among the nations for judgement...

8. James the brother of Jesus utilised this technique to confirm that the Gentiles would respond to the Gospel (Acts xv. 14–18), and the Pharisee Johanan son

of Zaccai also did so to foretell the destruction of the Temple which took place in A.D. 70.

9. In the Habakkuk Commentary he is called 'the Priest [in whose heart] God set [understanding] that he might interpret all the words of his servants the Prophets, through whom He foretold all that would happen to His people and [His land]' (II). He is also called the 'Teacher of Righteousness, to whom God made known all the mysteries of the words of His servants the Prophets' (VII).

10. Jn. viii. 57.

5

The Anointing

THERE could be no beginning of the work of the Messiah until the coming of the Prophet Elijah. That he would return before the Day of the Lord had been declared by the last of the prophets of old. The expectation became linked with the hope of a Priestly Messiah, so that Elijah began to be thought of as a priest. He would reveal and anoint the Messiah of Israel, the Son of David. The Scribes allowed their fancy to play around the prophecy of Elijah's advent, associating with it all kinds of quaint notions. No one knew how he would appear, and make himself known. He might arrive on the clouds of heaven, or suddenly be present and announce himself. Some, holding the doctrine of the transmigration of souls, supposed that the soul of Elijah would enter the body of a boy who should be born at the predestined time. Others considered that the spirit of Elijah would come upon someone as anciently it had done on his disciple Elisha. But we get the impression that many took the promise of Elijah's return only half seriously, as they did the coming of Doomsday and of the Messiah himself. It was a long time since there had been a prophet in Israel, and it seemed only remotely probable that another would arise. The common people clung to the belief, however, and so did the pious and earnest men who pored over the prophecies and sought to read the Signs of the Times.

Jesus, for one, was in no doubt at all. He had absolute faith in the fulfilment of the prophecies, and was as sure about the coming of Elijah as he was that he was destined to be the Messiah. We are compelled by the evidence at our command, which we have already presented and built upon in the previous chapters, to think of him as a man with very definite spiritual convictions who treated the Bible as the incontrovertible Word of God and interpreted it in the oracular manner of the fringe sects of pietistic Judaism.

It chimed therefore with the expectations of Jesus when news reached him in Galilee that a strange antique figure had suddenly emerged from the Wilderness of Judea and was now standing on the banks of the Jordan, preaching to the people and dipping them in the river. This wild man, as report had it, wore the hair garment characteristic of the ancient prophets, bound with a leather girdle like the Prophet Elijah.[1] The name he bore was Johanan (John) son of Zechariah. He was of priestly stock, as it was currently said Elijah had been. It was from the banks of Jordan that Elijah had been taken up to heaven,[2] and now in the guise of John, as it could be thought, he had come back as foretold.

We cannot know, of course, how Jesus reacted to the news about John, but we can guess at his excitement. A sense of enormous relief would be mingled with feelings of deep solemnity. At long last, as it seemed, there was amazing external confirmation that what he believed about himself was true. He had not been wrong: his inner vision had not lied, and he had been guided aright in all that he had seen and worked out of his messianic vocation. He must go to the Jordan to John, listen and judge for himself. But already in his heart any lingering traces of doubt were dispersing like mists before the sun. The trying years of waiting were over.

There is considerable mystery about John. Little is known of his antecedents except that he was the son of a priest called Zechariah of the priestly course of Abijah, and that his mother's name was Elisheba (Elizabeth). The late Christian story, told only by Luke, has it that John's mother was a kinswoman of Mary the mother of Jesus, and that John was only six months older than Jesus. Luke's account of John's nativity probably depends in large part on material produced by Baptist sectaries, which has been adapted and enlisted to support the superiority of Jesus without detracting from the prophetic significance of John.[3] The blood relationship between them is therefore unlikely, and other indications are that John was very much older than Jesus. Matthew is vague about when the Baptist's ministry began, but he may be understood to date it in the reign of Archelaus, successor to Herod the Great,[4] in which it is also placed by the Slavonic version of Josephus' *Jewish War*.[5] It is entirely possible that John had made a brief public appearance at that time, which being so long ago Jesus may not have heard about it. In any case the dramatic quality of John's present activities and the impression they created was not affected.

Jesus was by no means alone in supposing that John was Elijah returned. Others wondered if he could be the Messiah or the Prophet like Moses. In the Gospels the prophecy of the Messenger is applied to him, linked with that of the voice crying in the wilderness, 'Prepare ye the way of the Lord.'[6] John's concern, we are told, was with the urgent call to repentance he had been mandated by God to deliver in these Last Days, and he may well have believed himself to be the forerunner of the Messiah. A hermit-like denizen of the waste lands, a long-haired Nazirite, he was a weird embodiment of the apocalyptic sensationalism of his time, delivering his exhortations with all the fire and assurance of the old prophets of Israel. He declared that the Kingdom of God was at hand, and urged the people to save themselves from the Wrath to Come. At his hands they were dipped in the sacred river to cleanse them from their defilement, as Elisha, the follower of Elijah, had instructed the leprosy-stricken Naaman the Syrian.[7] To be Children of Abraham, John proclaimed, offered no guarantee of salvation. The people must amend their ways, and wash away their sins, as did the Gentile in abandoning idolatry and seeking admission into the community of Israel. Then only would they be worthy to share in the great Deliverance.

The commanding uncompromising voice of John struck terror into the hearts of multitudes who heard it. Everywhere there was talk of this extraordinary portent, which not a few were ready to interpret as signifying that the Romans would soon be driven out of Palestine and their Jewish minions in high places would meet their just doom. From all parts the crowds flocked to John to be baptised. The scenes on the banks of the Jordan were fantastic.

What did Jesus think would happen when he went to the Jordan? Did he anticipate that John would recognise and identify him as the Messiah? It would be natural for him to expect some experience which would certify to him that his call had come, that he was anointed for his office. The prophecies required that when that time arrived he would undergo a profound change: he would be invested with powers which would qualify him for the exacting part he would have to play. It was written: 'And the Spirit of the Lord shall rest upon him, the spirit of wisdom and understanding, the spirit of counsel and might, the spirit of knowledge and of fear of the Lord. . . .'[8]

The Gospels clearly regard the baptism of Jesus as the effective beginning of his ministry, the moment of his designation as king of Israel, when God made acknowledgement of him as his messianic son and representative. What underlies their testimony is the original Jewish-Christian doctrine which has been termed Adoptionist, because in keeping with the Scriptures[9] it held that Jesus on that occasion had been received into sonship of God. This teaching became overlaid in Gentile-Christianity by the concept of the Incarnation, which asserted in pagan fashion that Jesus had been born Son of God by a spiritual act of fatherhood on God's part which fertilised the womb of the Virgin Mary, and then went on to claim by an elaboration and partial misunderstanding of Pauline theology that the Son of God had eternally pre-existed and was manifested on earth in Jesus, who thus from birth was God dwelling in a human body by a hypostatic union of the two natures. The Gospels, the later ones especially, naturally bring the pristine faith of the followers of Jesus into line with the prevailing ideas. They are also inevitably concerned to combat the view that Jesus in being baptised by John was admitting himself to be a sinner and the inferior of the Baptist. So in Matthew's Gospel John is made to say that it is he who should be baptised by Jesus, and Jesus explains why he submits. The Fourth Gospel also stresses the inferiority of John and offers his reiterated witness to this effect. The early Christians had to meet a strong challenge from the sect which adhered to John as the Messiah. The literature preserved by the Mandaeans of the Lower Euphrates, which honours John to this day, excuses him for having baptised in Jesus a false Messiah.[10] Luke, as we have seen, emphasises the superiority of Jesus in the nativity stories. In the more primitive Markan tradition of the Baptism John does not recognise Jesus, and the psychic experience Jesus has as he comes up out of the water is confined to himself.

The conclusion to which we are led is that Jesus did have an experience. He was confident that he would have it, and that the Spirit of God would be poured upon him. Everything was there, as we can gather from the Gospel descriptions of the crowds which flocked excitedly to the Jordan to hear John and be baptised, to intensify the emotions of Jesus. When he saw John there was no doubt in his mind that Elijah had indeed come.

Never had Jesus witnessed such a scene or listened to such words. Truly here was a prophet who spoke with the voice of God, spoke in language that united with all he had thought and believed! He stepped into the chill stream, and the hairy hand of John was upon him, sending him down, down into the depths. Jesus prayed. Slowly he rose up out of the water; and then he had the experience. Tradition says that he heard a Voice from heaven, and that the Spirit of God descended upon him like a dove, or in the likeness of a dove, and entered into him, thus signifying that he was the Messiah. Whatever the actual experience of Jesus was, the tradition certainly conveys appositely and graphically what it meant to him.

There are conflicting accounts of what followed the baptism. The synoptic Gospels say that the Spirit of God drove Jesus into the wilderness to undergo a critical test. For forty days, a symbolic period, he was alone with his thoughts, wrestling with a satanic temptation to misuse his new powers and seek a short cut to the Throne which would eliminate any necessity for his suffering. These urges he triumphantly conquered. He would adhere firmly to the path God had marked out for him in the prophecies. Only after an interval did he return to Galilee.

The Gospel of John has no reference to the Temptation in the Wilderness. Instead, it makes Jesus linger by the Jordan, where John in the presence of two of his disciples points him out as the Lamb of God. Those disciples follow Jesus, and they spend a night with him. One of them is Andrew, brother of Simon afterwards called Peter. They are convinced that he is the Messiah, and the outcome is that Jesus gains his first followers, Andrew, Simon, Philip and Nathanael, and the unnamed disciple whose memories are reflected in this Gospel. All but he are Galileans, and they set out immediately for Galilee.

Not long after this the Baptist was arrested by order of Herod Antipas and incarcerated in the fortress of Machaerus in Perea east of the Dead Sea. He had been at liberty just long enough for Jesus to see him and be baptised by him. Already things were beginning to happen as ordained.

At this time Herod was threatened with war by the king of Arabia, whose daughter had been Herod's wife and whom he had discarded for Herodias, former wife of his brother Philip. John had denounced the marriage as illegal, but over and above he was in our parlance a security risk. With the people, many of them subjects of Herod, ready to take any action the Baptist might command, or even take their cue from his condemnation of Herod, there was grave danger of a revolt in Galilee which would force the tetrarch to fight on two fronts. This could be the end of his government and might cost him his life. In any case the Emperor Tiberius would be angered, and might order the Roman legate of Syria to send forces and depose him. He could count on no sympathy from Pontius Pilate, the present governor of Judea, who already had his difficulties because of his high-handed flouting of Jewish religious sentiment.

From now on Jesus was called upon to make good the work of the Messiah. As a result of the spiritual 'anointing' he expected to be different; and he was different. The prophecies had said that the Messiah would receive from God wisdom and insight, the power to heal and to subjugate evil. The faith of Jesus was so strong that he did not question that these capacities had now been conferred upon him. He believed it implicitly, and proceeded to act accordingly. He spoke positively and with the authority of his position: '*I* say unto you.' He moved on his appointed way with assurance and masterly skill. The sense of his dynamic power awed his humble followers. He dealt with human disorders as entitled to dominate and control them, and evoked a responsive faith in a multitude of sufferers. His own townsfolk were astounded at the tremendous change in him. This was not the retiring and rather inconspicuous Jesus with whom they had been acquainted, who did not talk very much and seemed moody and often remote. This was another man, outspoken and decisive.

Rapidly his fame spread far and wide, and his name became a legend overnight. Nothing was too impossible to be credited to him. There were those, on the other hand, who were scandalised by his teaching and behaviour, particularly members of the Pharisee fraternity who considered themselves to be the custodians of the nation's morals and spiritual instruction. The more strait-laced of them winced at some of the things he said and were offended by the freedom of his conduct. His autocratic attitude roused them to fury. Since initially he made no declaration of his identity, they were not to know that he spoke as the Messiah when he told a man his sins were forgiven. For them he was a religious upstart and demagogue. They did not deny that he wrought cures, as did many of the Essenes and the Pharisees themselves. But in his case they spitefully attributed his successes to possession by the prince of the demons. Jesus retorted that such an accusation was blasphemy of the Spirit of God which was in him, an unforgivable sin now and hereafter.

The alteration in Jesus was real enough. His absolute conviction that he had been owned by God as the Messiah had brought out and intensified certain of his natural qualities. Like a man who has experienced what is called conversion he felt in himself that he was a new being, and this feeling would have been stimulated by his sudden emancipation from the tension engendered by the long years of waiting, by the knowledge that he had liberty to speak and act now instead of having everything pent up inside him. He had not to quest around for what to do, how to begin. He did not fumble or hesitate. The course to be pursued was already mapped out in its essentials. He had only to take the right decisions and make the right arrangements to reach the positions which were progressively indicated. He had the agility of mind and the strength of purpose to attain these objectives.

NOTES AND REFERENCES

1. Zech. xiii. 4; II. Ki. i. 8.

2. II. Ki. ii. 8.

3. See Schonfield, *The Lost Book of the Nativity of John*.

4. Mt. ii. 23, iii. 1.

5. The text is given in the Appendix to *The Jewish War* in Thackeray's translation of Josephus (Loeb Classical Library). In the Slavonic version the Baptist is brought before Archelaus and the doctors of the Law, threatened with punishment and released.

6. Mal. iii. 1; Isa. xl. iii.

7. II. Ki. v. 10.

8. Isa. xi. 2–4.

9. II. Sam. vii. 14; Ps. ii. 7.

10. In the Mandaean records Jesus seeks to be baptised by John and is at first refused as a deceiver. John finally gives way because of a message he receives. The passage is in the *Sidra d'Yahya* (Book of John), section 30. A translation is given by G. R. S. Mead, *The Gnostic Baptizer*, pp. 48–51.

6

Attempt and Failure

WE ARE now standing with Jesus on the threshold of his ministry, as he began to follow that course of action which should
accomplish what the will of God, as revealed to him from the
Scriptures, demanded as the first phase of the work of the Messiah.
In this phase he was called to function as the Teacher of Righteousness of the Last Days, as the Prophet like Moses, to preach
repentance to Israel and reveal the character of the Kingdom of
God in which the redeemed would participate. Elijah had come in
John the Baptist to present him with the very words to signal
the opening of his campaign, 'Repent, for the Kingdom of Heaven
is at hand.'

The Gospels look back on the activities of Jesus with the help
afforded by the prophetic testimonies which the Nazoreans had
zealously assembled as proof that he was the Messiah, while we
with Jesus are seeking to look forward. The positions are not
wholly different, because many of the same testimonies, we may
be confident, had long been present to the mind of Jesus and
directed his planning. His followers, afterwards, could see a
prophetic significance in almost everything he did, and find texts
to fit it: they could even by this means heighten estimation of the
quality of Jesus by the introduction of miracles and marvels.[1]
But we may consider that his own findings related to passages
which could be understood to have a more direct and less imaginative bearing upon the Messiah's work and experiences.

As an indication of his immediate function Jesus could use the
word of Isaiah, 'The Spirit of the Lord God is upon me; because

the Lord hath anointed me to preach good tidings unto the meek; he hath sent me to bind up the brokenhearted, to proclaim liberty to the captives, and the opening of the prison to them that are bound; to proclaim the acceptable year of the Lord. ...'[2] But the compilers of the testimonies could go much further. When Jesus abandoned Nazareth and made his headquarters at Capernaum by the Sea of Galilee, this for them was a fulfilment of the prophecy: 'The land of Zebulon and the land of Naphtali ... the way of the sea, beyond Jordan, in Galilee of the Gentiles. The people that walked in darkness have seen a great light: they that dwell in the land of the shadow of death, upon them hath the light shined.'[3] Similarly, when Jesus addressed the crowds in parables, this was seen to fulfil what the psalmist had said, 'I will open my mouth in parables: I will utter dark sayings of old.'[4] Yet these measures on the part of Jesus were dictated by other necessities, as we can appreciate.

The region in which Jesus began to proclaim his message was in his native Galilee, among people of strongly independent spirit, whose faith and love of liberty made it hard for them to stomach the heathen domination of Rome and the immediate government of Antipas, son of their old enemy King Herod. Galileans were in the forefront of rebellious movements, and though at this time the zealots among them were relatively quiescent, they were ever ready to demonstrate passionately whenever a situation outraged their sentiments, and to resort to armed violence. If at this stage of his mission Jesus let it be known in Galilee that he was the Messiah the consequences could well be disastrous. To be the Messiah the Son of David, we must remember, meant that he was the legitimate king of Israel, to whom the militant elements would readily have rallied. He would openly be committing an act of treasonable sedition which would not be tolerated by Rome and its representatives. However peaceful were his intentions, there would be outbreaks of violence. He would be hunted down by the Government forces, and either killed or seized and crucified. Even if by luck he managed to make his escape abroad the result would still have been complete failure.

He would have been Messiah for a day, and patently a false Messiah into the bargain.

All this had long been known to Jesus, though most Christians even today have never given serious thought to the situation he faced. They simply have not realised the political implications, and how explosive the conditions were. But Jesus was well aware of them and proceeded circumspectly. He chose as his headquarters a small town on the shores of the Sea of Galilee which was essentially a commercial centre with a fairly mixed population, including Roman and Jewish government officials. Capernaum was not the sort of place where the disaffected and those zealous for the Law of Moses congregated, which a conspirator would be likely to use as his base. When Jesus travelled round the country preaching on the highly political as well as spiritual theme of the Kingdom of God he spoke in parables, so that the spies and informers who made it their business to be present wherever crowds gathered round a public speaker would be unable to detect anything subversive or inflammatory in what he said. He conveyed that he was speaking cryptically in his parables by adding, 'He who hath an ear to hear, let him hear,' in other words, 'He who can catch my meaning, let him do so.'

Jesus was not interfered with at this time because so far as the State was concerned he gave the impression of being a harmless religious enthusiast. Some of his sayings, indeed, would meet with the full approval of the authorities. His instructions were excellent for these stubborn rebellious Galileans, and might help to keep them in order. 'Resist not evil,' the preacher declared, 'and whosoever shall smite thee on the right cheek, turn to him the other also. And whosoever shall force thee to go a mile, go with him two.' This was with reference to the *angaria*, military requisitioning of labour and transport. 'Love your enemies, bless them that curse you, do good to them that hate you, and pray for them which despitefully use you, and persecute you.'

But Jesus was not acting as an unpaid Government agent, though he was intentionally warning the people against taking the law into their own hands and retaliating. If they resorted to

violence, if they even nourished hatred in their hearts, not only
would they be playing into the hands of their enemies to their
own undoing, they would be abandoning the path God had
marked out for them as a 'kingdom of priests and a holy nation'
to win the heathen to God. They would be behaving like the
rest of the nations, and would be unworthy to share in the Kingdom of God. Many of the Pharisees taught in the same vein.

While his call to repentance was going out to the lost sheep of
the house of Israel, Jesus had to take double precautions. He had
to prevent the abrupt interruption of his activities, as those of
John the Baptist had been cut short, by getting himself arrested
and imprisoned as a menace to public security. He had also to
guard against some ill-advised contrivance by his followers, or
spontaneous outburst by the people, to acclaim him as king. He
was to meet with narrow escapes in this connection. In the early
part of his ministry, when anyone most unwisely hailed him as
Son of David, he silenced him immediately. He was in any case
walking on a knife-edge by creating faith in his powers of healing.
What he was doing could not fail to cause excited speculation
about who he was. The people were expecting a deliverer, and
flocked to anyone who might be the medium of the fulfilment
of their hopes. Jesus denounced the hypocrites and false prophets, and the false Messiahs as well, as much as he did the men of
violence. All were misleading the nation and diverting it from
carrying out the will of God, trading on the people's emotions
and longings. 'Wide is the gate, and broad is the way, that leadeth
to destruction, and many there be which go in thereat. But narrow
is the gate and constricted the way, which leadeth unto life, and
few there be that find it.'

Jesus chose to refer to himself as the Son of Man (i.e. the Man),
a term which gave him external anonymity without having to deny
his true identity. Only to the communities of the Saints, who were
no danger to him, did the description have messianic significance. Many might be intrigued and ask, 'Who is this Son of
Man?' But comparatively few, and these not communicative, could
answer, 'He is the Messiah.' Otherwise, as in his reply to the

emissaries of John the Baptist,[5] Jesus left it to those who knew the prophecies to infer who he was from his activities.

Another step Jesus took was to enlist a small band of close disciples. The first group were fishermen from the lakeside township of Bethsaida. We do not know for certain whether Jesus was previously acquainted with some of them, though this is stated in the Fourth Gospel. Men like the brothers Simon and Andrew, James and John, were valuable recruits. They were patriotic and had a simple direct faith: they were physically strong and their personal loyalty could be counted on. Jesus nicknamed Simon 'the Rock' (*Kepha*, Peter), and James and John 'the Stormy Ones' (*Boane-ragsha*, Boanerges). They would make a useful bodyguard. They also had boats; so that if danger threatened, or the attentions of the crowds became too overwhelming, a line of escape or retreat was open across the lake to the independent territory of the Decapolis, a league of ten self-governing mainly Greek cities.

By these various devices and tactics Jesus assured for himself, so far as he could, safety and freedom of movement, and opportunity to deliver his message without hindrance. Already he was proving, and we should remark this, a skilful strategist and planner, alert and resourceful. He could be very gentle, but there was nothing meek about him. He is revealed as a man of inflexible determination and keen perception with all the qualities of the born leader. The glimpse we have here of his character shows him to be one who was fully capable of conceiving and carrying out, as will be demonstrated later, what we have termed the Passover Plot.

There was one thing, however, which Jesus may not sufficiently have taken into account, the extent of his fame as a wonderworker. As the days passed into weeks it speedily became evident that his mission was being gravely hampered by the multitudes who thronged to him, not primarily to listen to his teaching, but to be cured of their complaints or bring their relations for healing. Sometimes he had the utmost difficulty in getting about because of the press of people. He was aware that the time available to

him was short, and at his present rate of progress the ground he
would be able to cover would be very limited.

Some of the things Jesus had to say in defence of his conduct
were beginning to antagonise a small but influential section of
his audience, the local Pharisees. At great pains this fraternity of
devout Jews had laboured for upwards of a century to promote
a stricter obedience to the Law (the *Torah*) among the people, so
that they might merit God's favour and salvation. It was uphill
work because there was an ingrained resistance, especially in
Galilee, to being told what to do and what not to do. Like the
Essenes, the Pharisees among other things regarded the rigid
keeping of the Sabbath as imperative, for it was a divine institution marking the difference between the holy and the profane,
between Israel and the nations. It was written: 'If thou call the
Sabbath a delight, the holy day of the Lord, honourable; and
shalt honour him, not doing thine own ways, nor finding thine
own pleasure, nor speaking thine own words; then . . . I will
cause thee to ride upon the high places of the earth, and feed
thee with the heritage of Jacob thy father: for the mouth of the
Lord hath spoken it.'[6] The Essenes had abandoned all present
hope of converting the people to the exact performance of the
requirements of the Torah, and had withdrawn into their own
disciplined camps and communities. But the Pharisees struggled
gamely on with their missionary and educational work. Sometimes in their zeal, as is often the way, they lost sight of the spirit
of an institution in stressing its strict observance; but their intentions were good.

Now here was this teacher, who had the ear of the multitude,
undermining their efforts, casting off the yoke of the commandments as they had carefully defined them, violating their Sabbath
injunctions, eating with defiled hands and with publicans and
sinners, setting the worst possible example. How could his influence be checked? How could he be got out of the way? These
were two different propositions, and initially only the first was
considered. Jesus was repeatedly challenged, and when this
proved unavailing learned Scribes from Jerusalem were sent for.

As we have seen, when they arrived they pronounced Jesus to be demon-possessed: but this did not stop the people coming to him for cures, and Jesus took prompt action to quash the accusation. How could Satan cast out Satan? Were the Pharisees also demon-possessed when they like himself cured the sick? Let them be their own judges. Some of them felt driven to take a graver step. They had no love for the Jewishly lax Government, but now, we are told, they conferred with the Herodians. If what Jesus said could be construed to indicate that he had subversive or seditious intentions he would be arrested. Spies listened acutely to catch some incautious words; but Jesus was on his guard, and, again as we have seen, they were defeated by his circumspection and parabolic teaching. We must not suppose that these more hostile Pharisees, contrary to all their principles, were plotting the death of Jesus. They simply wanted him locked up and out of commission, like John the Baptist, another thorn in their flesh. In fact, they greatly overestimated the effects of the teaching of Jesus. The people listened gladly, but only a meagre handful responded. But Jesus was now plainly warned.

The essential problem which Jesus had to overcome was the difficulty created by the crowds which everywhere surrounded him and besought his help, and made it hard for him to extend quickly enough the areas in which he could hope to deliver his message personally. What with teaching and healing, and people struggling frantically to reach him, to touch even the sacred fringe of his robe as he passed, by the end of most days he was utterly exhausted. At one time by the lake to gain freedom to speak he used a boat moored off-shore as his pulpit. He even crossed to the other side for a brief respite. But the people ran round the coast to meet him as he landed, or followed in other boats. He could not get away.

The decision Jesus took was to appoint twelve of his more intimate followers as envoys (apostles). Their number was symbolic of the twelve tribes of Israel. They were to travel through the country on his behalf. He gave them precise instructions. They were to confine their mission to Israelites, and not visit

Gentile territory or enter any city of the Samaritans. They were to travel light and in poverty, as the Essenes did. They were to stay where they were welcomed, but only long enough to deliver their message. Where they were not received they were not to delay, but shake the dust of that house or city from their feet. 'I tell you positively,' he said, 'it shall be more tolerable for the land of Sodom and Gomorrah in the Day of Judgement than for that city.' They must exercise the utmost care in their speech and conduct. 'Behold, I send you forth as sheep in the midst of wolves: be ye therefore wise as serpents, and harmless as doves.'

This action on the part of Jesus reveals his recognition of the urgency of his task and that the time available to him was short. Despite these endeavours to make every minute work, however, he had soon to admit to himself that his message had largely fallen on deaf ears. The apostles when they reported back told of demons being subject to them, but not of any other success. It was evident that the call to repentance had largely gone unheeded. By failing in Galilee, his own land, Jesus had lost the whole country.

According to the Fourth Gospel Jesus made one or two early incursions into Judea at festival seasons, the Passover and probably Pentecost. John claims that he taught and performed cures on these occasions. The synoptic tradition says nothing of these visits, and it is likely that John has overemphasised their significance in his endeavour to establish that Jesus had made his messiahship evident from the beginning. But between Pentecost in May and Tabernacles in October there is no indication that Jesus went up to Jerusalem, and this is the period with which we are at present concerned.

Through his study of the Scriptures Jesus must have believed that his message would probably be rejected.[7] But he was in duty bound to proclaim it. There was always the hope of a miracle. He spoke more than once of the Prophet Jonah, born at Gath-Hepher in Galilee not very far from Nazareth, whose tomb was a place of pilgrimage. Though God had declared by Jonah that in forty days Nineveh would be overthrown, yet the people repented and turned from their evil way; and God had spared

Nineveh and the prophecy did not come to pass. The same thing could happen again.

But it was not to be. Nevertheless Jesus was deeply moved and hurt at his failure, even though it had not really looked as if he would succeed. And being human he was angry too, angry at the stupidity, the senseless waste, the awful suffering that was bound to come upon his nation. Contemplating this fearful prospect the certainty now of his own fate paled into insignificance. Inwardly, through his distress, he could even welcome it; for if God would accept his suffering as an atonement for the sins of his people he would give his life gladly. And if they would then heed, the worst that was in store for them might not happen. It was written: 'All we like sheep have gone astray; we have turned every one to his own way; and the Lord hath laid on him the iniquity of us all . . .'[8]

Jesus found vent for his feelings in bitter and scathing words. Momentous matters were being side-tracked by petty disputes, and the situation was deteriorating into a slanging-match.

'O generation of vipers, how can ye, being evil, speak good things?

'An evil and adulterous generation seeketh after a sign; and there shall no sign be given to it, but the sign of the prophet Jonah. For as Jonah was a sign unto the Ninevites, so shall also the Son of Man be to this generation. The queen of the south shall rise up in the Judgement with this generation, and shall condemn it: for she came from the uttermost parts of the earth to hear the wisdom of Solomon; and, behold, what is greater than Solomon is here. The men of Nineveh shall rise up in the Judgement with this generation, and shall condemn it: because they repented at the preaching of Jonah; and, behold, what is greater than Jonah is here.

'Woe unto thee, Chorazin! woe unto thee, Bethsaida! for if the mighty works, which were done in you, had been done in Tyre and Sidon, they would have repented long ago in sackcloth and ashes. But I say unto you, It shall be more tolerable for Tyre and Sidon in the Day of Judgement, than for you. And thou, Capernaum, which art exalted unto heaven, shall be brought down to hell: for if the mighty works, which have been done in thee, had been done in Sodom, it would have remained until this day. But I say unto you, that it shall be more tolerable for the land of Sodom in the Day of Judgement than for thee.

'Whereunto shall I liken this generation? It is like children sitting in the markets, and calling unto their fellows, and saying, We have piped unto you, and ye have not danced; we have mourned unto you, and ye have not lamented. For John came neither eating nor drinking, and they say, He hath a devil. The Son of Man came eating and drinking, and they say, Behold a man gluttonous, and a wine-bibber, a friend of tax collectors and sinners. But wisdom is justified of her children.'[9]

Yet it was of no avail for Jesus to be searingly reproachful, and useless to repine. Luke alone reports a final effort in sending out seventy disciples to preach as previously he had sent out the twelve; but we have to treat this as an intentional duplication by the author to foreshadow the calling of the Gentiles, since the world was supposed to consist of seventy nations. The fact had to be faced that the first phase of the work of Jesus was finished. The Teacher of Righteousness had been rejected. Unhappily it had come to pass as foretold, 'By hearing ye shall hear, and shall not understand; and seeing ye shall see, and shall not perceive: for this people's heart is waxed gross, and their ears are dull of hearing, and their eyes they have closed; lest at any time they should see with their eyes, and hear with their ears, and should understand with their heart, and should turn again, and I should heal them.'[10]

Now, as the prophecies had indicated to Jesus, the second phase of the work of the Messiah would come into operation. There was no time to be wasted in vain regrets. Sadly but resolutely he braced himself to face the future, and carry out God's will to the end. Did people think he was harsh when he refused one would-be follower's request to be permitted first to bury his father, and another's to take leave of his family? The words were drawn from an aching heart when he said, 'Leave the dead to bury their dead,' and, 'No man, having put his hand to the plough, and looking back, is fit for the Kingdom of God.'

NOTES AND REFERENCES

1. See Part Two, Chapter 6, *Some Gospel Mysteries*.

2. Isa. lxi. 1–2.

3. Isa. ix. 1–2.

4. Ps. lxxviii. 2.

5. Mt. xi. 2–6.

6. Isa. lviii. 13–14.

7. Several passages in the Prophets seemed to foreshadow such rejection of the call to repentance. Cp. Isa. vi. 9–10, quoted in the text at the end of the present chapter.

8. Isa. liii. 6.

9. See Mt. xi. 16–19, 21–3, xii. 39–42, Lk. x. 13–15, xi. 29–32.

10. Isa. vi. 9–10; Mt. xiii. 13–15.

7

The Disclosure

IF ANYTHING further was needed to convince Jesus that he could no longer delay to get ready for the tremendous test awaiting him it was the news which reached him of the execution of John the Baptist. That burning and shining light had suddenly been extinguished, a sign as sure as his own calling at Jordan. He must therefore begin to take his chosen twelve disciples more fully into his confidence, identify himself plainly to them as the Messiah, which in their hearts some of them already believed him to be, and prepare their minds for what was in store for him.

The Gospels are unable to provide us with any reliable scheme of the ministry, so that we have events and teaching in their actual chronological order. The information at their disposal made this impossible. Early tradition had furnished an outline of major events and trends into which they had to fit to the best of their ability the oral and written material available to them.[1] But there are sufficient clues to enable us to follow developments in the policy and planning of Jesus, and to detect what he was seeking progressively to achieve. Certain landmarks appear to guide our steps and apprise us of our position. One of these is the tradition that the disclosure by Jesus of the violent end he would meet at the hands of the authorities came after he was informed of the death of John the Baptist, and was made in connection with the acknowledgement of his messiahship. From now on it was demanded that to comply with the conditions of his fate he must increasingly reveal himself as the Messiah and abandon his incognito.

We learn that Herod Antipas, tetrarch of Galilee and Perea, had been greatly affected by reports of the activities of Jesus. As we have pointed out previously, Herod at this time was faced with the prospect of war with the king of Arabia whose daughter had been his wife, and whom he had insulted by marrying Herodias, formerly the wife of his half-brother Philip. He had imprisoned John in his Perean fortress of Machaerus, his present head-quarters, for denouncing this union, and because the Baptist might provoke a rebellion among his subjects when he needed his forces to meet the Arabian threat. According to the Gospel account, Herodias was determined that John should die, and found an occasion to force her husband's hand and procure the execution of the prophet. Now Herod heard with dismay that another preacher was operating in Galilee and drawing large crowds, giving out the same message as John. It was as if the Baptist had risen from the dead to mock and defeat him. Here was a new menace, and for the first time Jesus was in physical danger.

An incident reported only by Luke appears to relate to these circumstances. 'The same day', we read, 'there came to Jesus certain of the Pharisees, saying unto him, Get thee out and depart hence: for Herod will kill thee. And Jesus said unto them, Go ye, and tell that fox, Behold, I cast out demons, and I perform cures today and tomorrow, and the third day I shall be perfected. Nevertheless I must walk today and tomorrow, and the day fol-lowing: for it cannot be that a prophet perish out of Jerusalem.'[2] The passage is interesting because it shows a section of the Phari-sees doing their utmost to save the life of Jesus. There were two schools of thought among them, the one following the precepts of the gentle Hillel, and the other the severer teaching of Sham-mai. The latter would have been far more offended by the conduct of Jesus, and wish to see him discredited and even imprisoned, if that was the only way to stop his activities. But there were plenty of milder Pharisees well disposed towards him, who welcomed him into their homes.

The reply of Jesus to the friendly warning was defiant. It was the first occasion he had spoken disparagingly of a ruler; and he could commit this indiscretion because his mind was now set on his ordeal at Jerusalem, where—and nowhere else—he must fulfil his destiny. As Jesus viewed the situation he was not in imminent peril, since Herod was too heavily engaged to proceed against him at present. However, he did not completely disregard the risk he was running, and prudently withdrew to the north of the Sea of Galilee into the territory which had belonged to Philip.

It was in the region of Caesarea-Philippi that Jesus asked his disciples what people were saying about him, whom they thought he was. They told him that opinion differed. Some supposed he was John the Baptist, Elijah, Jeremiah, or another of the old prophets returned to earth. 'And what do you say?' Boldly Simon spoke for them all, 'You are the Messiah,' and so earned the nickname Peter (Rock). Jesus rejoiced that the truth had been revealed to them. It was a heartening confirmation of his status; but he ordered them to keep his identity secret. It was still too soon to make the fact generally known. That time would come when he went to Jerusalem for the last trials which as Messiah he must undergo.

The words Jesus used to convey to his disciples what was in store for him are momentous. They may be said to initiate the second phase of his ministry. Never before had he spoken about his end, but the death of John the Baptist made it essential that he should now do so. We cannot be certain of the language, though the sense is doubtless there. We seem to be reading the introductory paragraph to the Passion section of the primitive Testimony Book, and something of the kind did perhaps preface the Oracles setting out the Messiah's rejection, execution and resurrection. The announcement as it is first made in Mark's Gospel reads: 'And he began to teach them, that the Son of Man must suffer many things, and be rejected of the elders, and of the chief priests, and scribes, and be killed, and after three days rise again.'[3] Thereafter, with slight variations, it is repeated at intervals like a refrain.[4] In these statements Jesus is able already to specify who will act against him. The elders, chief priests and scribes can only mean the Sanhedrin, the Council for Jewish Affairs at Jerusalem, while the Gentiles, introduced on another occasion, must be the Romans represented by the Procurator of Judea.

Jesus could make such a deduction only by interpreting the Scriptures in the manner of the Essenes. Following the commentaries of the Dead Sea Scrolls we can create for ourselves an apposite *pesher* (oracular explanation) of the opening of the second Psalm.[5]

'*Why do the heathen rage, and the people meditate a vain thing? The kings of the earth set themselves, and the rulers take counsel together, against the Lord, and against his anointed.*' The explanation is, that in the Last Times the wicked will conspire against the Messiah of Righteousness to destroy him; but in the end their design will come to nothing, for the Lord will deliver him out of the hands of his enemies. *The kings of the earth*, these are the Kittim (synonym for Romans in the Scrolls) who rule over many nations. The *rulers*, these are the elders and priests of Jerusalem who govern Israel through their evil Council.

What Jesus had done in his earlier years was to see the Messiah in the different stages of his manifestation as one of the great objects of prophecy. He had gathered to himself the sufferings and the faith in survival of the righteous, which had poured itself out in poem and prediction. He had applied to himself what was written by his ancestor David as an outlaw hunted by the king, but whom God had chosen to rule his people Israel, and what was written concerning the persecuted servant of God as of those messengers whom kings and priests had mocked and condemned. All these Scriptures, and many others, pointed towards and would find their expression in the experiences of the Messiah, all the tears and ultimately the triumph.

When the Nazoreans looked back on the dramatic climax of the life of the Messiah, as many of us still do through the libretto to Handel's Oratorio, they were overwhelmingly impressed by the appositeness of so many passages to what had transpired.

Having to establish both for themselves and for Jewish audiences
that what had taken place was in accordance with the Scriptures,
they were able to build up a formidable array of testimonies. In
their zeal they even amplified and supplemented the account of
his experiences, as certain texts appeared to require additional
incidents which would fulfil them. Almost insensibly teaching was
converted into fact, and individuals could claim that they had
heard such things from someone, who had heard them from one
of the apostles. Thus the legend grew from story to testimony
to embellished story.[6] We have to be fully conscious of this
process of gilding the lily in studying the Gospels and the early
patristic literature.

The feat of Jesus was far more extraordinary, because he was
looking forward into the unknown, seeking to determine the
shape of things to come as a guide to his own actions. It was his
achievement to have extracted from the Oracles so clear a picture,
and to have been so assured of its reliability, that he could follow
it like a star which charted his course, and commit himself to
certain positive predictions of what would take place. The
achievement was particularly remarkable because it transcended
the relative vagueness of contemporary Messianism, and brought
its ideas into a sharper and indeed a singular focus. There were
strands of different colours held to mark the role of distinct
messianic personalities, the Prophet like Moses, the Suffering
Just One, the Son of David, the apocalyptic Son of Man. Jesus
wove them into one. No wonder what he disclosed to his un-
tutored disciples with their popular notion of the Messiah only
as the royal heir of David surprised and shocked them, and
brought an instantaneous protest from the outspoken Peter.
How could Jesus utter such words of ill-omen! But Jesus was
not being in the least morbid. As a Scribe instructed in the affairs
of the Kingdom of God, who had brought out new things as well
as old, he was simply stating what to him was plain and incontrovertible.

To get behind the statement of Jesus we must ourselves make
an excursion into Testimony Land. We must set out at least a

section of those Scriptures that for many years had been the meat and drink of the soul of Jesus, marshall them in order, and savour them in their bitterness and in their sweetness. We are not pretending to reproduce with assurance the very passages which informed him of what would befall in his time of testing; but in the fashion of the Nazorean compilers of testimonies we can demonstrate the effect of the conjunction of some of the things that were written.

OPPOSITION AND REJECTION

'The kings of the earth set themselves, and the rulers take counsel together, against the Lord, and against his anointed.' 'He is despised and rejected of men; a man of sorrows, and acquainted with grief: and we hid as it were our faces from him; he was despised and we esteemed him not.' 'The stone which the builders rejected is become the head of the corner.' 'Mine enemies speak evil of me, When shall he die, and his name perish? . . . All that hate me whisper together against me: against me do they devise my hurt.' 'And one shall say unto him, What are these wounds in thine hands? Then shall he answer, Those with which I was wounded in the house of my friends. Awake, O sword, against my shepherd . . . Smite the shepherd and the sheep shall be scattered.' 'The mouth of the wicked and the mouth of the deceitful are opened against me: they have spoken against me with a lying tongue. They compassed me about with words of hatred; and fought against me without a cause. For my love they are my adversaries . . .'[7]

ILL-TREATMENT AND EXECUTION

'I gave my back to the smiters, and my cheeks to them that plucked off the hair: I hid not my face from shame and spitting.' 'He was oppressed, and he was afflicted, yet he opened not his mouth: he is brought as a lamb to the slaughter . . . He was taken from prison and from judgement: and who shall declare his generation? for he was cut off out of the land of the living: for the transgression of my people was he stricken.' 'I am a worm and no man; a reproach to men, and despised of the people. All they that see me laugh me to scorn: they shoot out the lip, they shake the head, saying, He trusted in the Lord that he would deliver him: let him deliver him, seeing he delighted in him ... I am poured out like water, and all my bones are out of joint: my heart is like wax, it is melted in the midst of my bowels. My strength is dried up like a potsherd; and my tongue cleaveth to my jaws; thou hast brought me into the dust of death. For dogs have compassed me; the assembly of the wicked have enclosed me; like a lion they are at my hands and my feet. I will tell all my bones: they look and stare upon me. They part my garments among them, and cast lots upon my vesture.' 'Reproach hath broken my heart; and I am full of heaviness: and I looked for some to take pity, but there was none; and for comforters, but I found none. They gave me also gall for my meat; and in my thirst they gave me vinegar to drink ... For they persecute him whom thou hast smitten; and they talk to the grief of those whom thou hast wounded.' 'They shall look upon me whom they have pierced and they shall mourn for him, as one mourneth for his only son, and shall be in bitterness for him, as one that is in bitterness for his firstborn.'[8]

SALVATION AND RESURRECTION

'Though I walk in the midst of trouble, thou wilt revive me: thou shalt stretch forth thine hand against the wrath of mine enemies, and thy right hand shall save me. The Lord will perfect that which concerneth me.' 'The bands of the grave compassed me about: the snares of death prevented me. In my distress I called upon the Lord, and cried unto my God: he heard my voice, out of his temple, and my cry came before him, even into his ears. Then the earth shook and trembled; the foundations of the hills moved and were shaken ... He sent from above, he took me, he drew me out of great waters. He delivered me from my strong enemy.' 'Come, and let us return to the Lord: for he hath torn, and he will heal us; he hath smitten, and he will bind us up. After two days will he revive us: and on the third day he will raise us up, and we shall live in his sight.' 'I have set the Lord always before me: because he is at my right hand, I shall not be moved. Therefore my heart is glad, and my glory rejoiceth: my flesh also shall rest in hope. For thou will not leave my soul in the grave; neither wilt thou suffer thy holy one to see corruption. Thou wilt show me the path of life; in thy presence is fulness of joy: at thy right hand there are pleasures for evermore.' 'God will redeem my soul from the grasp of the grave: for he shall receive me.' 'The king shall joy in thy strength, O Lord; and in thy salvation how greatly shall he rejoice! . . . Thou settest a crown of pure gold on his head. He asked life of thee, and thou gavest it him, even length of days for ever and ever. His glory is great in thy salvation: honour and majesty hast thou laid upon him.'[9]

What we have done here is to string together in the ancient fashion some of the Biblical texts regarded as affording messianic testimonies, and the impression they create is both moving and eloquent. We can appreciate the influence they exercised on the early Christians in moulding and shaping the account of the Messiah's Passion so that it was brought into conformity with the Oracles. This is why we cannot accept as historical certain features of the narratives of the Passion as reported in the Gospels. The testimonies come between the reality and the later descriptions. But we are not entitled to jettison the whole story. There is much in it that rests on reliable tradition, and fortunately the Christian records furnish some evidence of which the authors did not realise the worth or importance. We therefore have to examine the Gospels closely for the elements of truth.

But while we must hold that the Nazoreans inspired by the Scriptures historicised in retrospect matters which they found in them, the same sources could and did to an extent inform Jesus in prospect. Accepting that their oracular message concerned the Last Times, and believing that many of the passages were thus to be applied to himself as the Messiah, he could—like the Essenes—bring their implications into relationship with contemporary conditions in Palestine, and plan accordingly. We are to think in terms of his Jewish faith and ideas of an apocalyptic order, strange and even incredible as they may appear to us. Our alien concepts are useless as a standard by which to judge the workings of his mind. They can never give the real sense and feel of him, though it may satisfy us to fashion him in a likeness which we find more acceptable.

With the help of the Oracles Jesus had deduced that he was required to suffer ignominiously at the hands of the rulers at Jerusalem. As self-confessed Messiah this stood to reason also. Under Tiberius no king of the Jews could exist who had not been approved by Caesar and confirmed by the Roman Senate, and it was the business of the authorities in Palestine, Jewish and Roman, acting for Caesar, to apprehend anyone claiming to be king. In the case of one who was not of the Roman nobility nor a Roman citizen he would be condemned to death, if found guilty, death by crucifixion, the barbarous punishment the Romans meted out for highway robbery, mutiny, high treason and rebellion. That Jesus was aware of this is shown by the words he used just after he had privately and under pledge of strict secrecy admitted to the twelve that he was the Messiah. 'And when he had called the people unto him with his disciples also, he said unto them, Whosoever will come after me, let him deny himself, and take up his cross, and follow me. For whosoever will save his life shall lose it; but whosoever shall lose his life for my sake and the good news, the same shall save it.' He could not yet state openly that he was the Messiah, but he could warn that anyone associating with him from now on should know what the penalty was likely to be. Yet if they suffered with the Messiah, they would also reign with him.

The reactions of the disciples to the disclosure of the fate awaiting him, and their behaviour thereafter, certified to Jesus that he could not take them fully into his confidence. They seem quickly to have dismissed his words as a mystery which they could not fathom, and perhaps thought that he had been made melancholy by the death of John the Baptist. They were more concerned with the material rewards expected when the kingdom of Jesus was established, and squabbled among themselves as to which of them should have the highest positions.

Jesus had now to prepare for the most difficult and dangerous part of his present mission, which demanded the utmost caution, and the most careful organisation and timing. He could not look to his disciples to assist him directly in the arrangements for his coming ordeal. He could not even trust them not to work against him if he told them too much; and they might easily ruin everything which he had to contrive. They were devoted to him, and loyal in their own way, but of limited intelligence, simple Galileans for the most part, who would not be at all at home in the sophisticated atmosphere of Jerusalem. What Jesus had need of now for the furtherance of his designs were dependable friends in Judea.

We have allowed that the Fourth Gospel may possibly be right that Jesus at the outset of his ministry had gone up to Jerusalem for the spring festivals of Passover and Pentecost; but it would be quite inconsistent with his policy to have staged any premature demonstration there, like the cleansing of the Temple, or indulged in debate of a character which could not fail to provoke summary action against him, which he would have richly deserved if he had spoken as the Fourth Gospel makes him speak. The Greek author of this Gospel, as we have it, has effectively buried the Jesus of history and substituted his own theological notion of the Son of God, a posturing polemical figure with a streak of antisemitism, wholly incompatible with the Messiah of apostolic tradition. It is not to the credit of the Church that it has taken this presentation of a pathological egoist to its bosom as the veritable Jesus. We have to dismiss it as accurate portraiture, while recognising that the author of it had access to some genuine unpublished reminiscences of the unnamed Beloved Disciple, which he has freely employed as it suited him to lend verisimilitude to his otherwise impossible creation.[10] It is difficult to free the gold from the dross; but we catch a gleam here and there which makes us thankful for the book's preservation. Without the Fourth Gospel we might never have heard of Nicodemus or of Lazarus of Bethany, and we would be quite unfamiliar with the part played by the Beloved Disciple himself.

The synoptic tradition, which seems in this respect to be much more in keeping with the probabilities, requires us to believe that Jesus most carefully concealed his identity as the Messiah in the early part of his ministry, and never at any time claimed to be other than human. If this were not the case the ministry would have had an even shorter duration, and Jesus would not have been crucified as king of the Jews. We must never let theology entice us away from the historical circumstances, so that we lose contact with the factors which Jesus had to take into account. He turned towards the south now, because there were things to set in train there if the Scriptures were to be fulfilled. He had to achieve mastery over the conditions, that they might serve the ends of God, and not of man.

NOTES AND REFERENCES

1. See Part Two, Chapter 4, *Gospels in the Making*.
2. Lk. xiii. 31–3.
3. Mk. viii. 31.
4. Mk. ix. 3, x. 32–4.
5. Ps. ii. 1–2.
6. See Part Two, Chapter 6, *Some Gospel Mysteries*.
7. Ps. ii. 2; Isa. liii. 3; Ps. cxviii. 22; Ps. xli. 5–7; Zech. xiii. 6–7; Ps. cix. 2–4.
8. Isa. l. 6; Isa. liii. 7–8; Ps. xxii. 6–18; Ps. lxix. 20–6; Zech. xii. 10.
9. Ps. cxxxviii. 7–8; Ps. xviii. 5–7, 16–17; Hos. vi. 1–2; Ps. xvi. 8–11; Ps. xlix. 15; Ps. xxi. 1–5.
10. See Part Two, Chapter 4, *Gospels in the Making*.

8

Setting the Stage

'JESUS steadfastly set his face to go to Jerusalem.' These words in
Luke are well chosen. They mark the purposefulness with which
the gallant Galilean now proceeded towards the spiritual and
political capital of the Jewish nation. Here, and here alone, the
messianic drama must be acted out. The city was by no means
unfamiliar to Jesus; but for him it was not merely a busy metro-
polis with crowded noisy streets, with men and merchandise
from many lands, magnificent buildings and squalid hovels: it
was the Holy City, the place of God's House, the preordained
centre of the Kingdom of God reaching out to redeem and bless
all nations. Jerusalem and the Messiah, both were the subjects
of mighty prophecies and inspired visions. Their destinies were
interwoven while the earth endured, until all things that were
written should be accomplished.

Today Jerusalem was under a cloud. The heathen ruled there.
Roman troops in Fort Antonia kept surveillance over the Temple
courts. There was unseemly haggling and huckstering in the
sacred enclosure, and evil was wrought in high places. Unless
there was a penitent turning to the Lord from the highest to the
lowest the present city would perish in anguish. The suffering
which the Messiah was required to undergo at Jerusalem would be
infinitely multiplied in the doom which would overtake the city.
But Jerusalem, like the Messiah, would rise again in newness
of life as the City of God where his anointed king would reign in
peace and in righteousness. At the first there would be the

Passover: at the last there would be Tabernacles, the feast of ingathering.

It was the season of Tabernacles now, in the fall of the year, an opportunity to make a bid to reclaim the soul of Israel before it should be too late. If this failed, then . . . 'Jesus steadfastly set his face to go to Jerusalem.' His mission there was to occupy three months from October to January. A parable quoted only by Luke comes in aptly in this connection.

'A man had a fig tree growing in his vineyard, and he came in quest of fruit on it, but found none. "For three years now," he told the gardener, "I have come in quest of fruit on this fig tree, but I have never found any. Cut it down. Why should it take up ground-space?" "Let it be for this year, sir," replied the gardener, "to give me a chance to dig round it and manure it. If it should bear fruit next year—well, you can still cut it down if it doesn't." '

Jesus followed a route from Galilee which would take him through Samaria. The Samaritans, to whom the Temple at Jerusalem was a false sanctuary, the true one where they worshipped being on Mount Gerizim, were hostile to Jews from the north passing through their territory on the way to Jerusalem for the festivals, and sometimes attacked them. But Jesus must have felt that the risk just now was considerably less than if he travelled by the alternative route through Perea on the east of the Jordan, where he was liable to encounter the forces of Herod Antipas. He had no intention of falling into the hands of 'that fox'.

Luke's narrative seems to tie in here with John's report of the secret journey of Jesus to Jerusalem at the time of the feast of Tabernacles.[1] According to the Fourth Gospel, Jesus had been challenged by his sceptical brothers to go up to Jerusalem for the festival and bring himself to public attention. He had refused to join the Galilean caravan, which would be taking the Perean road, because of the world's (Herod's?) enmity towards him. 'Go ye up unto this feast,' he told his brothers. 'I go not up yet unto this feast; for my time is not yet full come.' Jesus stayed on in Galilee, 'but when his brethren were gone up, then went he also up unto the feast, not openly, but as it were in secret'.

We have to be very guarded in our use of the Fourth Gospel because what is left in it of the reminiscences of the unnamed Judean disciple whom Jesus loved has been so overworked, strained and subordinated to the theological interests of the Greek elder at Ephesus who fathered the Gospel in support of his own ideas. But to pursue the activities of Jesus in the south at this period we have largely to utilise this Gospel since, except in some matters introduced by Luke, the Markan (Galilean) tradition does not deal with the Judean ministry. It is not difficult to understand this omission, as we shall see; but it is most unfortunate. It is also unfortunate that we do not have the unnamed disciple's evidence intact. However, as regards the movements of Jesus during the Judean ministry and certain other features which reflect local conditions and circumstances it is probable that the Greek author has retained a good deal of what was in his source.

The movements of Jesus may then be traced approximately as follows. He arrived at Jerusalem in October during the feast of Tabernacles, and remained there for about three months, until shortly after the feast of Dedication in late December.[2] Then he went east to the Jordan to the ford of the river (Beth-abara), not far north of its exit into the Dead Sea, where John had preached.[3] He returned hastily to Bethany near Jerusalem on learning of the serious illness of his friend Lazarus. After this he retired again to a Judean town called Ephraim at the edge of the wilderness near the Jordan a good many miles north-east of Jerusalem.[4] Mark, followed by Matthew, omits altogether the stay of Jesus at Jerusalem and the visit to Bethabara, but possibly jumps to his sojourn at Ephraim, when it is said: 'And he arose from thence, and cometh into the coasts of Judea by the farther side of Jordan.'[5] Luke, as we have indicated, preserves some trace of the beginning of the Judean ministry, since he makes Jesus set out for Jerusalem via Samaria, and his next point of locality is the arrival of Jesus at a certain village (Bethany) where he is welcomed by

a woman called Martha, who had a sister Mary.[6] Luke does not
mention their brother Lazarus, though he makes Jesus tell a story
of the death of a beggar of that name which may have a connection with the tradition peculiar to John of the raising of Lazarus.[7]
Luke too has no reference to the activities of Jesus in Jerusalem,
but he brings in uniquely how Jesus was informed of Pilate's
slaughter of Galileans in the city. But these omissions of the first
three Gospels do not mean that the tradition behind Mark was
altogether ignorant of the ministry of Jesus at Jerusalem. When
Jesus was arrested in Gethsemane we have the saying; 'I was
daily with you in the Temple teaching, and ye took me not.'[8]
This would hardly refer to the day or two when Jesus was in
the Temple in Passion week, but rather to his daily teaching in
the previous autumn, when, as the Fourth Gospel states, attempts
were made to take him, 'but no man laid hands on him'.

Briefly here we should consider the reasons why a consequential part of the life of Jesus is passed over by the synoptic Gospels.
In the first place these Gospels are related to the early Christian
Testimony Book, where the prophecies from the Old Testament
were most heavily massed at the climax of the story which was
the hardest to explain to Jewish audiences. There was a leading
up to the moment when Jesus entered Jerusalem as the King
Messiah, and from then on the testimonies dealt with his rejection, betrayal, suffering and resurrection. The Testimony Book
was not a biography, though it offered a roughly biographical
outline of the ministry. It was not concerned, therefore, with any
experiences of Jesus in Jerusalem before Palm Sunday. It was only
needed to bring him to Jerusalem for the events of Passion Week.
When Mark was composed the narrative was fitted to the testimony outline, followed in turn by Matthew and Luke, though
with greater difficulty because of their additional material, especially the teaching document 'Q'.[9] An account of the three
months Jesus spent at Jerusalem could have got into Mark, if the
Petrine tradition had spoken of it. But evidently it did not. The
Galilean disciples of Jesus were not at home or happy in the
atmosphere of Judea and Jerusalem, where their provincialisms

of speech and manners caused comment, and where they felt their intimacy with Jesus weakened by his friendship and regard for others, notably Lazarus and the unnamed Beloved Disciple. There is no direct reference to either in the synoptic Gospels.

Without the Fourth Gospel we could not know that Peter was not only well acquainted with the unnamed disciple, but was also jealous of the affection Jesus had for him. Their first meeting was perhaps after the baptism of Jesus. The Gospel speaks of two disciples of John the Baptist who followed Jesus. One of them was Andrew, Peter's brother, and it is to be inferred that the other was the Beloved Disciple, who there is reason to believe was a young Jewish priest from Jerusalem.[10] He would have met Peter when Andrew brought his brother to Jesus. We do not encounter the young man again until the scene shifts to Jerusalem in Passion Week. But unless he was often in the company of Jesus during the three months with which we are at present concerned there would have been almost no record of this period at all. Four times we find him linked with Peter. At the Last Supper he occupies a place of honour, leaning on the breast of Jesus, and Peter invites him to ask Jesus to identify the one who will betray him. After the arrest of Jesus the disciple effects Peter's entry into the palace of Annas where Jesus had first been taken. When it is reported that the body of Jesus has been removed from the tomb, the disciple runs with Peter to the sepulchre and outdistances him. The final reference is where Peter asks the risen Jesus about the young man's future rôle, and exhibits jealousy of him. In the circumstances we would hardly expect the devoted Peter to be forthcoming about the part played by the Judean disciple who was so close to Jesus.

This digression has been necessary to explain the silence of the synoptic Gospels concerning the activities of Jesus at Jerusalem at the close of the year before his death. We can forgive the author of the Fourth Gospel a great deal in our gratitude to him for having preserved information which is vital to our understanding of how Jesus laid his plans. Unwittingly this Gospel furnishes the key to what transpired in Passion Week. It does not simply supplement the story of the first three Gospels: it compels us to read that story quite differently and in a much more revealing light.

The events of Passion Week, still some months away, had their origin in what happened now in Jerusalem. Jesus had three things to accomplish, first to deliver his prophetic call to national repentance in the very heart of Jewish life and worship where it would reach the greatest number and command the most attention, second to bring himself personally to the notice of the highest Jewish authorities, who previously had only certain reports of his activities in Galilee, and third, with the help of his friends, to set the stage for the revelation of himself as the Messiah and the accomplishment of his destiny. Jesus had to an extent discerned how the prophecies would have their fulfilment; but he did not imagine that everything would come about automatically at a time and in a manner unknown to him. To the contrary, he appreciated fully that what must come to pass would demand of him the most careful timing, planning and organisation. Throughout his ministry he had acted purposefully and with decision, in conscious command of his affairs and exhibiting remarkable capacity for exploiting situations. It is quite unthinkable that at this advanced and crucial stage of his mission he was proposing to play a passive part and leave everything to fate.

In going up to Jerusalem Jesus was deliberately embarking on the most difficult and dangerous of all his enterprises, where a false move could wreck everything. He was not among his own Galileans now, but in more critical Judea, where even his accent was against him. Who would heed a prophet who spoke the outlandish tongue of the north? Many would make fun of him or treat him as a madman. Moreover, he would have to contend with powers and forces alien to his experience. Never before had he had to pit his wits against the subtle political brains of the supreme Jewish and Roman authorities. Yet he was quite sure he would not fail, because the Spirit of God was working in him and through him. But this would be the supreme test of his faith, and the ultimate proof that he was indeed the Messiah.

Whatever view we may take of the chronology of the life of Jesus, it is not to be doubted that the atmosphere in Jerusalem at this time was tense and anxious, though on the surface things might appear fairly normal. The Roman governor Pontius Pilate was detested, and the lordly family of Annas, which held the sacred office of high priest in fee with gold from its well-filled coffers, was feared and resented. But lately the ire both of the Sanhedrin and the people had been concentrated on the blundering and high-handed Pilate, who had laid impious hands on the dedicated treasure of the Temple (the Corban) to construct a conduit to bring additional water to the city. There had been a demonstration against him, which the governor broke up by dressing a number of his soldiers in civilian clothes, but carrying weapons under their cloaks, who at a given signal fell upon the crowd and killed and wounded many. The populace may have been more threatening than the first-century Jewish historian Josephus reports, and some may have risen in arms and struck back. Luke refers to Galileans whose blood Pilate had mingled with their sacrifices, and Mark speaks of a certain Barabbas and others with him held prisoners for their part in the insurrection.[11]

The chief priests, as a consequence of the outbreak, were at this juncture in no enviable position. Antagonistic to Pilate, they had to dissimulate and maintain courteous diplomatic relations with him as Caesar's representative, while scheming to get him so discredited that Tiberius would be forced to recall him. If they were to succeed, it was imperative that there should be no further anti-Roman riots in Jerusalem, which would only play into the governor's hands, and enable him to plead complete justification for his actions on the ground of the continual rebelliousness of the Jews. What the chief priests wanted to show was that while they were loyal to the emperor, Pilate's personal conduct was fomenting disaffection by wilful aggression and violation of legitimate religious customs.

With this top-level struggle in progress, a struggle on the Jewish side for the survival of what was left of spiritual and political autonomy, Jesus by his coming to Jerusalem was adding a fresh complication. The last thing that was wanted by the Sanhedrin at the moment was the appearance of a would-be prophet, especially one of those fiery and unpredictable Galileans, capable of rousing the masses and inviting strong Roman punitive measures. That other agitator John the Baptist was dead, and at least he had operated in the territory of Antipas on the far side of the Jordan. But this Jesus who had sprung up to take his place had not kept to his own country of Galilee, and daringly and most inconveniently he had now come to the capital and was making himself heard in the Temple itself. He must be zealously watched and at all costs prevented from stirring up trouble.

The new difficulties had started when at the close of the feast of Tabernacles, on the great day of the feast, Jesus had entered the Temple and had begun to preach in the outer court. He was perfectly entitled to do this; but it was quite evident that he was not simply imparting religious instruction, he was declaiming with the voice of authority like one of the ancient prophets, crying aloud so that he could not fail to be heard. It was reported to the authorities that he was attracting excited crowds, some of the people debating dangerously whether he could be the expected Prophet or the Messiah himself. If nothing was done there might be serious developments, and the Roman commander at Fort Antonia would want to know why the Temple police were failing in their duty to keep the peace. Officers were therefore sent to bring Jesus in for interrogation. They returned empty-handed, according to the Fourth Gospel, explaining that 'never man spake like this man'. There may have been other good reasons for their failure, that Jesus was saying nothing subversive or inflammatory, that he was surrounded by tough Galileans capable of offering resistance, that intervention instead of calming the crowd might provoke an outbreak of violence. Evidently the police were satisfied that no present trouble was threatened, and that it was best to leave well alone.

So far as Jesus was concerned he was attaining two immediate objectives: he was proclaiming his message where it would have the

maximum effect, in the centre of Jewish worship, and he was bringing himself prominently to the attention both of rulers and people.
By confining his preaching to the cloisters of the Temple, where
it was customary to hold religious debate, and by refraining from
giving any support to contentions that he was the Messiah, he
avoided undue personal risk. There is no record that he ever
addressed the people in the streets of the city, and there were no
grounds on which serious proceedings could be taken against
him. Some members of his audience in the Temple might be
hostile to him, but the presence of his sturdy Galilean disciples
was an adequate deterrent to any effective attack. In the event,
no man laid hands on him. Jesus had no intention of meeting with
any other end than had been prophesied. We do not hear of him
spending a single night in Jerusalem. It was wiser that he should
not pass through the narrow streets after dark, or lodge in any
house in the city. To be spirited away to rot in a dungeon, or
die by the dagger thrust of an assassin, would completely defeat the
prophecies. As he is reported to have said: 'Are there not twelve
hours in the day? If any man walk in the day, he stumbleth not,
because he seeth the light of this world.'

Jesus did not stumble or put a foot wrong. Carefully he
matured the plans which would secure his objectives.

As the base for his operations Jesus had found a most convenient haven in the village of Bethany on the far side of the
Mount of Olives east of Jerusalem. He had been welcomed there
by a woman called Martha, who had a sister Mary and also a
brother Lazarus. A strong bond of affection was forged between
Jesus and this family.

The advantage to Jesus of having this home at Bethany was that
he had somewhere he could relax, where he could not readily
be taken by surprise, and where he was within comfortable walking distance of Jerusalem. As he constantly made his way to the
city over the Mount of Olives there was before him a panoramic
view of Jerusalem with its massive walls and noble buildings,
and particularly of the Temple crowned with the snowy marble
majesty of the Holy House, topped with its roofs of glittering

gold. As he descended into the valley of the brook Kedron, he passed close to the olive orchard, the Garden of Gethsemane, to which he sometimes resorted with his disciples, and down to the left were the ornate mausoleums of noble families, whited sepulchres. Almost every stone of the road must have become familiar.

Entering Jerusalem by the Valley Gate, in proximity to the Pool of Siloam, Jesus followed the street of the valley of cheese-makers which ran through the midst of the city and led up towards the Temple. On the left was the Akra or Lower City, the poorest quarter, and to the right the jutting spur of the Ophel which had been David's city where lived many of the priests, and where we may believe the unnamed priest, the Beloved Disciple, had his house. So he came to the Sanctuary his destination.

We take note of these topographical features, which Jesus saw almost daily at this period, because several of them helped to shape the design which was materialising in his mind. Bethany, Gethsemane, the city gate, the house on the hill, all would play their part. The whole route would be that by which Jesus would make his regal entry into Jerusalem.

It had been made clear to Jesus very quickly that there was no prospect that his message would be heeded by more than a very few in Judea and Jerusalem as had been the case in Galilee. What had been foreordained would therefore come to pass. Methodically he set about his preparations. In what he had to organise his closest Galilean associates, Peter and the two sons of Zebedee, could not assist him. They would obey his orders, but he could not confide his plans to them. Their minds rejected the thought of his suffering, and were filled with expectations that in some marvellous manner he would triumph over the Romans and their satellites and forthwith inaugurate his kingdom. But there were others who could serve his purpose, local disciples on whose fidelity he could count. We know two of them for whom he had a high regard, Lazarus and the unnamed young priest whom it will be more convenient hereafter to call John. Even to them, however, Jesus could not disclose his designs. They too might not understand, and in any case he did not wish to involve them more than was absolutely essential. The greatest secrecy and circumspection was demanded, and the less they knew the better it would be for them and the safer for himself. Each would only be informed separately of the service required of him, and what was asked would not seem too strange or unreasonable in view of the physical danger in which he would stand once he was proclaimed as the Messiah.

John would be useful in another way, for contact with secret disciples and sympathisers in the Sanhedrin. Through this channel not only could messages be conveyed; but Jesus would have knowledge of any designs of the Council against him. There was one other man among his immediate followers on whom Jesus had his eye in working out his plans, Judas Iscariot, whom the Fourth Gospel calls the son of Simon, probably Simon the Zealot, another of the twelve who immediately precedes Judas in Mark's list.

By the time Jesus left Jerusalem in January his business there was very nearly finished and the stage set for the drama to be enacted at the Passover some three months later. There was every reason why he should choose this festival in particular as the season of his revelation and of his suffering. Its symbolism and associations were altogether appropriate and in keeping with the prophecies.

The Passover was celebrated in Nisan, the first month in the Jewish calendar. It was the great festival of liberation, 'the season of our freedom'. It commemorated the wonders wrought of old in Egypt, when God delivered his people from bondage by the hand of Moses with signs and wonders, and it looked forward to the final salvation of Israel by the hand of the Messiah, the Son of David. The chief symbol of the feast was the paschal lamb offered on behalf of each household, and eaten in common by the company after being roasted whole. At the first Passover, the blood of the lamb had been sprinkled on the external doorposts and lintel of the houses of the Israelites, so that when the Angel of Death went through the land of Egypt to destroy the first-born of the oppressors he would see the sign and *pass over* the first-born of the oppressed.

Jesus saw himself not only as the predestined king and liberator of his people, but also at the present juncture as the instrument of their deliverance from the bondage of sin and death by an act of personal sacrifice, by offering himself as 'a lamb brought to slaughter'. With the unleavened bread of his body and the bitter herbs of humiliation would this Passover sacrifice be accomplished in accordance with the Scriptures, with his own blood poured out like the wine of the festival.

But afterwards he would be glorified; for the Passover spoke also of resurrection in the dedication to God of the first fruits of barley on the morrow after the Passover Sabbath, and in the prayers for dew initiated on the first day. It was written: 'The dead shall live, together with my dead body shall they arise. Awake and sing, ye that dwell in dust: for thy dew is as the dew of herbs, and the earth shall cast out the dead.'[12] 'I will heal their backsliding . . . I will be as the dew unto Israel.'[13]

Thus it was settled that at the coming Passover Jesus would reveal himself publicly to Israel as the Messiah. His hour, so long awaited, would have come.

NOTES AND REFERENCES

1. Jn. vii.
2. Jn. vii–ix.
3. Jn. i. 28. x. 40–2,
4. Jn. xi. 54.
5. Mk. x. 1; Mt. xix. 1.
6. Lk. ix. 51–3, x. 38–9.

7. Lk. xvi. 19–31. According to the parable, the fate of the rich man in hell is contrasted with that of Lazarus. The rich man begs Abraham to send Lazarus back to warn his brethren 'lest they also come to this place of torment'. Abraham replies, 'They have Moses and the prophets; let them hear them.' But the rich man insists, 'Nay, father Abraham: but if one went unto them from the dead, they will repent.' To which Abraham answers, 'If they hear not Moses and the prophets, neither will they be persuaded, though one rose from the dead.' In the

story we are not told whether Lazarus is raised from the dead as he is in John's Gospel; but the coincidence of the name associated with resurrection is unlikely to be fortuitous.

8. Mk. xiv. 49; Mt. xxvi. 55; Lk. xxii. 53.

9. See Part Two, Chapter 4, *Gospels in the Making*.

10. See Part Two, Chapter 5, *The Second Phase*.

11. See Lk. xiii. 1 and Mk. xv. 7.

12. Isa. xxvi. 19.

13. Hos. xiv. 4-5.

9

The King Comes

WHEN Jesus left Jerusalem early in January he would appear to
have made all essential dispositions for his manifestation as the
Messiah, and to have successfully contrived to alert and alarm
the Sanhedrin. They were anxious about his intentions, but could
not yet be sure what they were. Far too many people had begun
to speak of him as the Messiah, and this in itself was dangerous.
So far Jesus had not confirmed what was being said of him,
though he must have been well aware of it, but neither had he
repudiated it. This might be because he did not aspire to kingship,
or it might be that he was cunningly biding his time. They could
not tell what was in his mind. But even if he thought of himself
as no more than a teacher or a prophet, there was no denying the
strength of his personality, and he might be influenced by the
desires and folly of the people and decide to respond to their
expectations. If only they could be certain what he was up to!
One possibility was to challenge him in hope that vanity might
make him declare himself.

During the feast of Dedication in late December, commemor-
ating the Maccabean victories in the second century B.C., a number
of men had come around Jesus as he was strolling in the Temple
in the portico of Solomon. 'How long are you going to keep us
in suspense?' they asked him. 'If you are the Messiah, tell us
plainly.' These men may have been acting on instructions from
the Council.

If the incident is genuine the reply of Jesus in the characteristic
vein of the author of the Fourth Gospel to the effect that he had

already made his status clear assuredly is not.[1] At this time Jesus was still at pains to guard a secret which if revealed could abruptly terminate his activities. But it was clearly advisable to bring his work at Jerusalem to a close, and shortly after this he left with his disciples for Bethabara. There was nothing more of value he could do now for the furtherance of his plans until he joined the Galileans who would be coming to Jerusalem for the Passover, and pressures in the city were becoming uncomfortably acute. Jesus travelled east to the Jordan. Here at the spot where he had been baptised by John he would renew his strength and his vision in preparation for the ordeal that was fast approaching.

It must have been a strange experience for Jesus to stand once again by the river where the Prophet had proclaimed the near approach of the Kingdom of God, where the Voice had spoken to him, and where he had been endowed, according to the promise in Isaiah, with the gifts of the Spirit of God. Memories flooded back. John who represented Elijah was dead, and there was no vast concourse here now, only the whispering reeds and the Jordan after its long journey from Galilee hastening to its end in the bitter sea where all life became extinct. Jesus was convinced he had not been wrong. He was the foreordained Messiah, and now he must face that other baptism when he would go down into the depths of darkness and the waters of tribulation would close over his head.

We may believe that Jesus prayed earnestly for guidance and help. Luke has reproduced a story he told his disciples in this last period of his life 'to illustrate how essential it was to be constant in prayer and not to slacken'.

'There was once a judge in a certain town, who neither reverenced God nor respected man. And there was a widow in the same town who was always coming before him crying, "Protect me from my persecutor!" For some time he would not, but later he said to himself, "Though I neither reverence God nor respect man, yet because this widow keeps pestering me I will give her protection, or eventually with her coming she will completely wear me out."

' "Listen," said the Master, "to what this false judge says. And shall not God give satisfaction to his Elect, who cry to him day and night? Will he forbear in their case? I tell you, he will give them satisfaction speedily." '

It seemed like an answer to prayer that presently Jesus found himself the centre of an unexpected crowd. The people were coming to him as before they had come to hear John the Baptist. These were not critics: they wanted his instruction and advice. He taught them and was happy.

But a reminder of sterner things was not far off. Messengers arrived from Martha and Mary to say that their brother Lazarus was seriously ill. This was grave news, not only because Lazarus was dear to Jesus, but because he counted on him to carry out an important part of his prearranged plans. He must return at once to Bethany. His disciples tried to dissuade him, pointing out the risk he was running. It was useless, and they gave way.

The Fourth Gospel alone records that a tremendous miracle was performed by Jesus at Bethany in restoring Lazarus to life after he had lain dead in his place of burial, a closed cave, for four days. The truth is hidden somewhere in the legend, and the parable of the rich man and Lazarus told by Luke shows us, as we have noted, that some memory was preserved of a man Lazarus who made a surprising recovery after being apparently dead. The circumstances were such as to give rise to the report that Jesus had been responsible for his resurrection, a report that was duly conveyed to the Sanhedrin.

So far as the Council was concerned, this was the last straw. They did not credit that anything of the kind had happened; but it was enough that word was going around that it had happened. They would conclude that the supposed miracle was a deliberate fraud to gain popular support perpetrated by Jesus and Lazarus with the connivance of the latter's sisters. This could mean only one thing, that Jesus was planning to head an uprising, possibly at the coming Passover. In those days it was a common prelude to an attempted revolt for the fanatic or charlatan responsible to claim to perform or offer to perform signs and wonders to secure the adherence of the credulous masses. The steps of Jesus himself had been dogged by those who clamoured for a sign from God, and were told they would get no sign. It is unlikely that the Council knew this, and they were now positive that the intentions of Jesus were sinister. Since the raising of the dead was associated in popular belief with the inauguration of the Messianic Era, the reported 'sign of Lazarus' was proof enough that trouble was imminent and that Jesus was going to be dangerous. Already the tale was having an effect, and many more people were now persuaded that he must be the deliverer. When Moses led the people out of Egypt at the Passover it was to the accompaniment of signs and wonders. Would it not be so again when the Son of David came to save them?

The Sanhedrin hurriedly convened a special session. The subject for urgent debate was, 'What are we going to do, for this man Jesus is credited with performing many signs? If we leave him alone everyone will believe in him, and the Romans will take away our place and nation.' The presiding high priest Caiaphas brought the issue to a head by saying, 'It does not seem to have occurred to you that it is in your interest that one man should die for the people rather than the whole nation perish.' The decision was reached that there was no help for it: Jesus would have to be liquidated.

Having friends in the Council, one of whom was Nicodemus, Jesus received speedy intelligence of the result of the meeting. He promptly left Bethany and retired to the north-east to the comparative safety of the town of Ephraim on the edge of the wilderness.

The present narrative of the Fourth Gospel makes Jesus remain in the vicinity of Ephraim until just before the Passover; but the synoptic tradition is to be preferred here that after a time he made his way back to Galilee. Not only was it natural that he should wish to see his homeland again before he suffered, but also when he returned south he meant to be in the company of a substantial body of Galileans who would be going up to Jerusalem for the Passover. Among them he had numerous adherents, and it was unthinkable that the chief priests would interfere with the pilgrims fulfilling their religious obligation to attend the festival.

We thus find Jesus once more in Galilee, where at Capernaum he paid the annual Temple-tax of one half-shekel. He paid under protest since as Messiah he regarded himself as enjoying privileged immunity, but the incident, preserved in Matthew,[2] is a useful date indication, because outside Jerusalem the tax was collected one month before the Passover.

When the pilgrim band at last assembled in considerable strength for the journey to Jerusalem there was much speculation and uncertainty as to what would be the outcome. Was Jesus going to proclaim himself king, and were they going to take part in a rising to throw out the Romans and punish the sinners in high places? Did the rumour that Jesus believed he would suffer at Jerusalem portend another failure and frustration of national hopes, or would he be cut down in the hour of victory like Judas Maccabaeus, giving his life for his people? The disciples of Jesus were anxious and ill at ease. They still could not relate what he had told them of his fate with their convictions, which Jesus had confirmed, that he was the Messiah. 'They were now on the way to Jerusalem,' writes Mark, 'and Jesus was preceding them, when they took alarm, and those who followed became afraid.'[3] Jesus reiterated strongly what was in store for him; but this did not prevent representations being made to him on behalf of the sons of Zebedee, James and John, that when he became king they should occupy the seats of honour on his right and left. It was a pitiful journey marred by wrangling and gnawing doubt.

At length they reached Jericho, where their numbers were swollen by other arrivals, so that, as Jesus had counted upon, he would be going up to Jerusalem with a formidable entourage. He was going there this time as king.

When the multitude moved on from Jericho there came an interruption. A blind beggar sitting by the wayside to solicit alms, hearing that Jesus was passing, cried out, 'Pity me, Son of David!' This created a sensation. Such language was dangerous, and several people ran to the beggar to shut him up. But he refused to be silent, and went on bawling at the top of his voice, 'Pity me, Son of David!' Until now Jesus had forbidden anyone to address him in public by this messianic title. Significantly on this occasion he did not do so.

Nearing Jerusalem, the procession arrived at Bethphage close to Bethany. The time had come for Jesus to put into operation the first of the arrangements he had made privately during the winter. This task, we may believe, had been entrusted to Lazarus of Bethany, and none of the twelve knew anything about it. The foal of an ass was to be kept tethered at the entrance of the village of Bethany, and the people there were instructed that it was only to be released to messengers who would say, 'The Master needs him.' Jesus now called to him two of his disciples and sent them forward. 'Go to the village there,' he said, 'and as soon as you have entered it you will find a foal tethered, never previously ridden by anyone. Untie him and bring him here. Should any ask you, "What are you up to?" say, "The Master needs him." Then he will at once send him back here.'

Everything went according to plan. The messengers returned with the foal, wondering no doubt at the foresight of Jesus. But suddenly someone grasped the implication of what was taking place. 'The disciples had been expecting,' says Luke, 'that the Kingdom of God would be instituted forthwith.' This was what had been written by the Prophet Zechariah, 'Rejoice greatly, O daughter of Zion; shout, O daughter of Jerusalem: behold, thy king cometh unto thee, riding upon an ass, even upon a colt the foal of an ass.' Joyfully they laid their cloaks on the donkey's back, and Jesus mounted on the beast. The cry was raised, 'Hosanna [Save now], Son of David!' The word ran along the line to those in front and those who followed. 'Jesus is truly the Messiah! The prophecy is fulfilled: he has mounted on his ass.'

We may imagine the scene. For a few minutes the wildest confusion reigned. Back and forth ran the people to where Jesus sat, throwing themselves on the ground in utter abandon, acclaiming him ecstatically. Jesus sat still amidst the din created by his fervent subjects; but the light of a great gladness shone from his eyes. This experience alone was worth all the years of waiting, all the weariness and the setbacks, worth too the fate that was stretching out cold hands towards him.

At last he gave the signal to set forward. Some of his ardent followers had already claimed the privilege of grasping his bridle: others grouped themselves solidly around him. They began to move.

At this the enthusiasm doubled its intensity. The people tore off their cloaks and spread them before him, so that the feet of his ass, or at least his shadow, might fall upon them. Many hastened to cut rushes to carpet the way.

The Fourth Gospel makes Jesus halt for the night at Bethany, where Martha prepared a supper and waited upon him, while Mary received her king by producing a pound of costly spikenard and anointing his feet and then wiping them with her hair. The whole house was filled with the perfume of the ointment. Lazarus who had faithfully performed the duty Jesus had assigned to him had the honour of a seat at the table.

This account is quite probable, because Bethphage and Bethany provided one of the reception areas for pilgrims coming to the festivals. Thousands camped here because it was impossible to obtain lodgings in the overcrowded capital. The synoptic Gospels, however, make Jesus proceed directly to the city, which he reached, according to Mark, late in the afternoon, entering the Temple, and after looking around returning to Bethany. If we follow Mark, Jesus rode into Jerusalem on the Sunday, while if we accept the evidence of John's Gospel this took place on Monday.

This is by no means the only contradiction in our sources regarding the events of Passion Week. Unfortunately, as far as the Fourth Gospel is concerned, we cannot know to what extent the testimony of John the priest in his old age has been tampered with by the author of the book, what circumstances have been changed round, what have been omitted altogether. We have also to allow for uncertainty of memory on John's part. A very serious

problem arises in connection with the several evening meals
referred to in the documents in this part of their record, including
the Last Supper, but we must defer consideration of this until
later.

It is agreed by all the Evangelists that Jesus came to Jerusalem
as king in the most open manner, with crowds acclaiming him as
Son of David, and greeting him with the Hallel chant of Psalm
cxviii, 'Hosanna! Blessed is he that cometh in the name of the
Lord.' Luke tells us that some Pharisees among the onlookers
were scandalised and called out to Jesus to restrain his followers,
to which he replied, 'I tell you, if they are silent the stones will
cry out.'

The die was cast, and now there could be no turning back.
Jesus had boldly and publicly committed himself in the way
he had planned. He had accepted the plaudits of the Jewish
multitude, chiefly his own Galileans, at the capital of the nation
as their rightful ruler. By so doing he had made himself guilty
of treason against Caesar. There can be no question about this.
The action of Jesus had been intentional and deliberate, and he
was fully aware that there could be only one outcome, his arrest
and execution. He had contrived, without any show of force and
in the most peaceful manner, to make a telling demonstration that
he claimed to be the Messiah, forcing the Jewish governmental
representatives into a position where they must proceed against
him both in the interest of self-preservation and in duty to the
Roman emperor, and to do so with the knowledge that he had
identified himself to them as the heaven-sent king of Israel. In
a masterly way he was bringing it about that the requirements of
the messianic prophecies, as he interpreted them, would be fulfilled. The chief priests and elders might imagine that they were
acting on their own initiative in meeting the threat created by
Jesus, but in fact the plotting of the Galilean was progressively
reducing them to puppets responding to his control.

It had been a brilliant move on the part of Jesus to make his
triumphal entry into Jerusalem as Messiah in association with a
crowd of Galilean pilgrims coming to the city and the Temple

for the Passover celebrations. There had been no attempt to sneak into the city unobserved, as had been thought possible. He had entered openly in a manner which gave the reinforced Roman garrison no cause to take any particular notice. The Romans were familiar with the arrival of large contingents of Jews for the major festivals, who customarily approached the centre of their worship uttering glad cries and singing their sacred songs in the Hebrew tongue. After what had happened before, the troops had strict orders not to interfere with the Jews in the practice of their religion, and to avoid any contemptuous or provocative behaviour. Pontius Pilate was very wary now of getting himself into more trouble.

The stratagem of Jesus also made it quite impossible for the Council to intervene. What they had feared had now partly happened. He had finally allowed himself to be acknowledged as Messiah; but the clever way in which he had done this secured him for the present complete freedom from molestation. They had to recognise that they were up against a man of courage, cunning and ingenuity. They were puzzled and anxious, having no idea what his next step would be. So far there were no outward signs of any organised revolt, and it had proved impossible to obtain the slightest information of what the plans of Jesus were, since he had confided them to no one, not even to the closest of his followers.

The Council dare not act incautiously in case they should encourage an outbreak which at all costs they were anxious to avert at this inflammable season of the Passover. If they made representations to the governor they had as yet no proof that an armed rising was contemplated. He might well suspect them of trying to lay a trap for him. Or he might insist that if they thought their fears were well-grounded they should arrest Jesus themselves. This they could not risk at present. The business was not at all like the former affair of the aqueduct. Then it had been Pilate who had been the direct cause of disaffection, and the chief priests, who were well aware of their unpopularity with the Jewish masses, could claim national sympathy and support in their opposition to the hated governor. It would be different now: the wrath of the people would be turned against the Sanhedrin as lackeys of the Romans. Yet if they kept silence, and did nothing to bring the new pretender to the Jewish throne to justice, they could be accused of aiding and abetting treason, and would probably be sent to Caesar for trial and punishment. In Jerusalem there might be another bloody massacre. This Jesus, in his mad folly, had placed them between the devil and the deep blue sea. Somehow a way must speedily be found to seize him without incurring the odium of the people or precipitating a crisis. But how?

In the meantime the object of their concern was in full command of the situation and had carried out a measure calculated to win him the increased approbation of the people. In the Court of the Gentiles, that part of the Temple which was accessible to everyone, Jesus had launched an attack on the merchants and bankers who served the needs of those who came to make their offerings. He had laid about him with a whip of cords which had been used to tether the beasts sold as sacrificial victims, and had overturned the tables of the money-changers and the stalls of the pigeon-sellers. 'Take these things hence,' he had cried imperiously. 'It is written: My House shall be a house of prayer for all nations; but you have turned it into a den of thieves.'

With the Temple at Jerusalem, as with other great temples, it was difficult to avoid using part of the sacred precincts commercially; and additionally in the Jewish sanctuary it was needful to exchange heathen coinage stamped with idolatrous images for the Jewish currency which was free from such presentations in accordance with the second commandment of the Decalogue. But what otherwise might have been a legitimate activity was converted into an evil by profiteering and the pursuit of gain. The chief priests themselves had a vested interest in the Temple market and grew rich on their share in the transactions. Poor people were often in distress in having to meet artificially inflated prices in discharging their religious duties. Many pious Jews were scandalised by what went on, and some of the more affluent would often force costs down to aid those with limited means.

Apprised of what Jesus had done, the chief priests were greatly incensed but too fearful of the consequences to call upon the Temple police to restore order. It did not add to their composure that the urchins of Jerusalem were having a glorious time sporting among the wreckage, and shouting gleefully, 'Hosanna, Son of David!'

The following day there was a duel of wits in the Temple. The Council had decided that they must use every endeavour to alienate the people from Jesus. If they could succeed in discrediting him they would have a chance to get him into their power. But their scheme failed ignominiously. Jesus met every barbed question with an effective answer, and more than once followed up his advantage with a telling thrust of his own. Only initially did the authorities approach Jesus directly, asking him by what right he acted as he was doing. Jesus replied that he would tell them if they would first inform him whether they regarded the baptism of John as divinely inspired or not. This put them in a quandary. If they agreed that John had been sent by God, Jesus would say, 'Why then did you not believe him?' If they said the opposite, the people would be angered, because they held John to have been a prophet. They took refuge in being non-committal. 'We cannot tell.' 'In that case,' said Jesus, 'I do not have to inform you by what right I do what I am doing.'

After this, other tactics were tried. Questions would be put to Jesus on party lines by persons standing in the crowd in an attempt to create a strong difference of opinion. He could hardly avoid antagonising some part of his audience, and agents mingling with the people would be ready to exploit any unwise answer and turn it against him.

Jesus was too intelligent and experienced to be deceived by these approaches. He knew they were not genuine, and what was their purpose. The most testing and fateful question was put by a man, who prefaced it with a eulogy. 'We know how completely honest and straightforward you are, and that you are

not influenced by anyone. What is your view, then? Ought we
to pay the poll-tax to Caesar, or not?'

This tax was adjusted on the basis of a census taken in the
Roman provinces every fourteen years. When it had first been
levied in Palestine with the census of A.D. 6–7 it was bitterly resented as an infringement of Jewish law against numbering the
people and as a measure of enslavement to an alien and heathen
power. The question was loaded, and was all the more dangerous
because of its topicality. The year A.D. 34–5 was a census year,
and the Roman tax was now due for payment.[4]

The people gasped and growled at the audacity of the challenge.
Whatever one's opinions on such a subject no one in his senses
would ventilate them in public, especially here in Jerusalem.
Fearfully they waited to hear what the answer would be.

Jesus appeared unperturbed, but he spoke sternly. 'Why do
you try to trap me?' he asked. 'Show me a denarius.' The coin
was produced. He would not touch it, for that would have offended the Zealots. 'Whose is this portrait and inscription?' he
demanded.

'It is Caesar's,' he was told.

'Then,' said Jesus, 'render to Caesar what is Caesar's,' he
paused, 'and to God what is God's.'

An excited babble broke out. What a wonderful answer! No
one could say that Jesus had uttered anything subversive. His
words seemed to mean that we have distinct duties to God and to
Caesar: they do not conflict. But his listeners knew better. They
knew he meant that God is our only Lord, as Judas of Galilee
had proclaimed when the census was first taken.[5] If our hearts
are given to him all Caesar would get would be his miserable
silver with not a jot of love or loyalty. The words of Jesus expressed subtle contempt for those Jews in high places who served
the interests of Rome. Here was a denarius: it bore Caesar's
image, was inscribed TIBERIUS CAESAR DIVI, divine Caesar. Let
those who claimed to be the ministers of the God of Israel reconcile it with their consciences how far they were prepared to ack-
knowledge the theistic pretensions of the emperor.

With equal assurance Jesus dealt with other questions. At the end not only was his authority unshaken, he had scored a personal triumph. The stone which the builders had rejected had become the headstone.

NOTES AND REFERENCES

1. Jn. x. 25–30. See the argument (above pp. 80 and 82).
2. Mt. xvii. 24–7.
3. Mk. x. 32.
4. The chronology favoured by the present writer would date the Crucifixion at the Passover in the spring of A.D. 36. Reasons are given in Part Two, Chapter 6, *Some Gospel Mysteries*. The question about the tribute does not conflict with this view, and gives it some measure of support.
5. See Part One, Chapter 3, A Child is Born (above p. 53).

10

The Plot Matures

THE sequence of events in Passion Week cannot be determined with any assurance. Enormous pains have been taken by scholars, employing astronomical and other data, to ascertain the year and date of the Crucifixion and to decide whether the Last Supper was the paschal meal eaten on the 14th of the Jewish month Nisan (synoptic tradition) or another meal on the 13th (Fourth Gospel). Gallant and ingenious efforts have been made to reconcile the conflicting statements, one of the more recent suggestions being that while Jesus was crucified on the Friday, Passover eve according to the official lunar calendar, he and his disciples kept the Passover on Tuesday evening in conformity with the Qumran solar calendar. While it would be gratifying if conclusive results were obtainable, we have to accept that there is little prospect of this. We are not prevented thereby from catching on to important things which the documents communicate when read with historical insight, and venturing on a judgement which is consistent with evidences which it is essential to respect.

Looking at the Gospels as we have them, it is apparent that in setting out what took place in Passion Week the Gospel of Mark is more orderly than the others. It furnishes a number of indications of time. Jesus makes his triumphal entry into Jerusalem late in the day and in the evening retires to Bethany. The next day he enters the city again and casts out those who sold and bought in the Temple. He leaves in the evening, and comes once more to the Temple on the third day, where he answers questions and teaches. At the end of the day he leaves the Temple for the last time, and we are then told that 'after two days was the Pass-over and the feast of Unleavened Bread'. It seems that Jesus spends the fourth day at Bethany, in the evening in the house of Simon the leper. The fifth day the feast of Unleavened Bread commences when the paschal lamb is slaughtered, and Jesus sends two disciples to the city to prepare. The same evening he comes to Jerusalem with the twelve for the Last Supper, which is the Pass-over meal. That night they go out to the Garden of Gethsemane, where Jesus is arrested and brought before the Council. Early on the sixth day Jesus is brought before Pilate, and at nine o'clock that morning he is crucified. He dies about 3 p.m., and in the evening, which is the eve of the Sabbath, he is buried.[1]

This is a very convincing time-table if it stood by itself, and we should be careful how we quarrel with it. But it is open to certain objections, and in part is challenged by the Fourth Gospel.

Like other matters in Mark his version of the Passion conveys a sense of compression, as if some things have been condensed in order to fit in with the rather narrow limits of time allowed. It is difficult to imagine that Jesus was brought before Pilate much earlier than six o'clock in the morning when the Jewish day began. Yet within three hours everything is decided and Jesus is at the place of execution. In the interval Pilate has heard the charges against Jesus, has interrogated him, has listened and responded to a plea to release a prisoner according to custom and the people have chosen Barabbas: he has yielded to the demand that Jesus should be crucified, and ordered him to be flogged; the soldiers have taken him away and had their sport with him, and then have led him at a slow pace some distance outside the city to Golgotha. Pilate must surely have condemned Jesus with extraordinary haste, which is not what the other sources convey. According to Matthew, the wife of Pilate sends to tell him of a dream she has had and begs him not to proceed against Jesus, and so reluctant is the governor to act that he sends for water and publicly washes his hands to signify his guiltlessness. Luke introduces another element of delay. Pilate, learning that Jesus is a Galilean, has him sent to Herod Antipas, in residence at his palace in Jerusalem. Antipas questions Jesus at length, and finally mocks him and returns him to Pilate. The Fourth Gospel makes Pilate by various devices postpone judgement as long as he possibly can, and it is about the sixth hour when at length he gives way, midday by Jewish reckoning. Jesus would then have been crucified more than three hours later than asserted by Mark, and if he died at about the ninth hour he would not have been more than three hours on the cross. It has been proposed that the Fourth Gospel is employing Roman reckoning, and that the trial was therefore virtually over by six o'clock in the morning. But it is hard to credit that Pilate was called out of bed in the middle of the night to deal with the case.

The tendency of the Christians as the Church developed was increasingly to stress the guilt of the Jews and to whitewash Pilate, and we have to allow for this in the later Gospels. Their emphasis of Pilate's reluctance and delaying tactics may therefore partly be discounted; yet even so Mark's account does seem to be rushing things a little.

But we must return to earlier events in Passion Week. The traditions are confused, particularly in relation to certain significant meals. The Fourth Gospel brings Jesus to Bethany six days before the Passover, immediately prior to his triumphal entry into Jerusalem. There he is the guest of Martha and Mary, and Mary anoints his feet with a costly unguent. Judas protests that the ointment should have been sold and the proceeds given to the poor. Mark, however, places this supper several days later and locates it in the house of Simon the leper at Bethany. He does not name Mary or Judas as playing any part. An unknown woman comes and anoints the head of Jesus, not his feet as in John, and several disciples complain of the waste of money. After this Judas goes to the chief priests and makes a compact with them to betray Jesus. Luke does not connect the story of this supper with Passion Week at all. He brings it in much earlier in the ministry. The scene is the house of Simon a Pharisee, and the woman is a sinner of the town, who bathes his feet with her tears, dries them with her hair, and anoints them with precious ointment. The argument is not about the waste of money, but about the failure of Jesus to discern the character of the woman in allowing her to touch him.[2]

The problem of the meals is further complicated by the curious construction of the Fourth Gospel. As regards the Last Supper, we cannot tell what memories of John the priest have been altered or omitted to make room for the long discourses created for Jesus by the author and which occupy chapters xiv–xvii. There is no reference in this Gospel to the Passover ceremonial of the bread and wine, which Jesus used to speak of his sacrifice. The author does not appear to want to recognise the Last Supper as the Pass-over meal, since he makes the point that it was the eve of the Passover the following day when Jesus was crucified.[3] For him the Last Supper took place *before* the Passover.[4] To support this view he seems to have telescoped the synoptic tradition, so as to combine elements of the supper in Bethany on Wednesday evening with the Passover supper on Thursday evening in Jeru-salem. The scene of the Wednesday supper is shifted from Beth-any to Jerusalem, so that it becomes the Last Supper, while the main features of the Wednesday event are pushed back by intro-ducing an account of an earlier supper at Bethany six days before the Passover. At this supper Mary anoints the feet of Jesus with ointment and Judas protests at the waste. When the author fuses the Wednesday meal with the Last Supper he obviously cannot use this incident again, and so he substitutes for it an action of Jesus himself in washing the feet of his disciples.

After the incident of the anointing in the Markan tradition Judas leaves to bargain with the chief priests. Luke, as we have seen, backdates the incident; but he confirms that before the festi-val Judas went to the chief priests, telling us, 'Then entered Satan into Judas surnamed Iscariot.'[5] These key words relating to Wednesday evening are echoed by the Fourth Gospel in relation to Thursday evening, 'And supper being ended, the devil having now put it into the heart of Judas Iscariot, Simon's son, to betray him.'[6] So the decision of Judas to betray Jesus was taken at Jerusalem instead of Bethany. This Gospel, however, retains from the Passover meal tradition the inquiry by the disciples as to which of them would betray Jesus. We may note one other point. In Mark, followed by Matthew, the saying of Jesus, 'Rise up, let us go,' is spoken at Gethsemane after the agony in the garden and immediately before he is arrested; but in the Fourth Gospel the words are uttered before Jesus leaves the place of the Last Supper, and he only goes to the garden after further discourse.

We have an eloquent illustration here both of the uncertainties of the tradition as they reached the hands of the Evangelists and of the freedom they used in employing them to serve their aims and designs. It is quite exciting really that we do not possess a wholly reliable and unvarnished story of the life of Jesus. It means that the quest for the truth is a continuing pursuit, with every now and then opportunity arising for important fresh discoveries. The disagreements themselves bear witness that inherent in them are recollections of genuine events and experiences which we have to endeavour to reconstruct. Our business is not to seek to iron out or explain away the differences, an impossible undertaking, in order to demonstrate the validity of the curious doctrine of the plenary inspiration of the Scriptures: it is rather to sift and probe to get at the facts which have not been completely or exactly represented, but to which the documents, sometimes insensibly and unwittingly, contribute their quota of valuable evidence.

When we have grasped what considerations governed the activities of Jesus and compelled him to scheme to bring about a particular sequence of events it becomes easier to assess the relative worth of the traditions. Our line of inquiry in this work had been directed to demonstrating the effect, as regards understanding of the personality of Jesus, of the conviction which was never doubted in the early Church and has been reinforced by modern researches, that of set purpose he embarked on a programme calculated to fulfil what he believed the prophecies demanded of the Messiah. He was obsessed with this necessity. Its requirements shaped his every move and engaged his constant vigilance. As he understood it, the greatest issues for humanity depended on his success. It was a singular, fantastic and heroic enterprise, though in the strange apocalypticism of the time perfectly comprehensible. It called for intense messianic faith, acute perceptiveness, an iron will, and a very high order of intelligence.

The programme was now approaching its climax, and its stipulations were becoming more varied, more complex, more difficult to achieve, because they involved producing certain essential reactions on the part of others. Everything had to be foreseen, timed and dovetailed. The sense of the crisis is present in the Gospels in the amount of space which they devote to it. They had here their richest inheritance from the impressions left upon the minds of the immediate followers of the Messiah.

The destined road for Jesus led to torture at Jerusalem on a Roman cross, to be followed by resurrection. But these things had to come about in the manner predicted by the Scriptures and after preliminaries entailing the most careful scheming and plotting to produce them. Moves and situations had to be anticipated, rulers and associates had to perform their functions without realising that they were being used. A conspiracy had to be organised of which the victim was himself the deliberate secret instigator. It was a nightmarish conception and undertaking, the outcome of the frightening logic of a sick mind, or of a genius. And it worked out.

In the middle of Passion Week, following the Markan outline, Jesus left the Temple at Jerusalem for the last time, and appropriately at this point the Gospel introduces, in response to the questions of the two pairs of brothers, Simon and Andrew, James and John, an apocalyptic discourse in which Jesus foretells the destruction of Jerusalem and the Temple and the tribulations of the Last Times which will precede his return to earth in glory.

Jesus had finished with his public ministry and teaching. The verbal duel with the authorities was over. Both he and they retired to prepare for the final contest. The Council had to find a way to capture Jesus and have him executed which would not have dangerous popular repercussions. Jesus had to assure that he would not be taken until he was ready and further vital things

had been accomplished. The full messianic significance of his
end had to be registered to comply with the prophecies, otherwise
his sufferings would not be seen by his disciples in their true
light and communicated to Israel.

While our eyes are on the central figure of the unique drama,
we should spare a thought for all those who must have been specu-
lating at this time on what was going to happen, what Jesus
was going to do. He had come forward in the clearest manner
possible as leader of the Jewish people, whether as a prophet or as
the Messiah in person was disputed; but it was known throughout Jerusalem to multitudes that he had assumed a position of
authority and had openly joined issue with the rulers. No one
would do this without a purpose, without further intentions of a
more startling nature. What would be the next move of the Galilean? Would he attempt a coup? There was nothing yet to indicate
what his plans were. From the highest to the lowest, and according to the different opinions of Pharisees, Sadducees, Zealots and
the uncommitted masses, he had everyone guessing. Jerusalem
waited breathlessly on the eve of this portentous Passover, in
hope, in doubt, in fear.

The Council was in a state of tension. As yet they had no
answer to their problem. It was agreed that Jesus must not be
apprehended on the feast day, which argues that they were
coming very close to a decision to risk the consequences
later.

The disciples of Jesus were no less on edge. We may infer this
from Mark's account of the woman at Bethany who anointed
Jesus. They upbraided her for her prodigal wastefulness, when
the oil might have been sold for the benefit of the poor. The
Fourth Gospel may well be right that Judas Iscariot was the
most vehement of the critics, and that it was he who named the
figure of three hundred denarii which the perfume would have
fetched on the market. This Gospel offers the explanation, perhaps editorial, that Judas was a thief and angry at losing a chance
of personal gain. What the incident in any case suggests is that
the disciples were keyed up. They were not really thinking of

the poor, and took it out on the woman to relieve their nervous tension. In their minds was a nagging uneasiness because of what Jesus had said was in store for him; and he had taken them no further into his confidence. They were deeply anxious and in an explosive mood, not daring to ask him to be more explicit. It would seem that Judas, who perhaps was the most sensitive and highly strung of the twelve, was very near breaking point. The woman's gesture triggered things off. It did not help at all when Jesus calmly told the disciples that his body had been anointed for burial.

Through the confused but still eloquent remembrances of what transpired we may be afforded here, without those who handed them on realising it, an insight into another ingredient of the Passover Plot. We have previously seen how Jesus had privately arranged, no doubt with Lazarus, to have a young ass tethered at the eastern end of the village of Bethany, ready to be released to his messengers on speaking the prearranged signal words. Lazarus was the only man in Bethany with whom we are told that Jesus was on intimate terms. Jesus could trust him completely to honour his request, so that at the psychological moment the beast would be there to enable him to fulfil the prophecy of Zechariah and stage his triumphal entry into Jerusalem as king. It is noteworthy that outside the ranks of the twelve apostles it is particularly said that Jesus loved Martha and Mary and their brother Lazarus of Bethany, and the unnamed disciple, whom we have called John the priest, of Jerusalem. These Judean confidants were essential to his plans, and we can trace the parts played by Lazarus, Mary and John.

Here we are able to detect the private arrangement made by Jesus with Mary, who, according to the Fourth Gospel, was the one who brought in the flask of costly oil of nard to anoint Jesus. Jesus had asked her to perform this office, again without declaring his purpose, in order to bring to the boil his betrayal by one of his disciples, thus fulfilling the prophecy, 'Mine own familiar friend in whom I trusted, which did eat of my bread, hath lifted up his heel against me.'[7]

Let us look at the matter more closely. Ever since the revelation of the messiahship of Jesus at Caesarea-Philippi he had informed his disciples that his end would result from his rejection by the chief priests, elders and scribes. At intervals he had dinned this into them with increasing emphasis, adding that he would be betrayed to these rulers. He did not say specifically that one of the twelve would be the traitor, but it must have been in his mind both in view of the prophecy and because he had told no one else of his predestined fate. Only the Fourth Gospel credits Jesus with knowing from the beginning who would betray him.[8] This is improbable, though he may quickly have formed a strong suspicion that it might be Judas. We are informed that Judas became treasurer of the band, and he is accused of embezzling the small funds. If this is true, it was apparently unknown to the rest of the twelve, or they would have done something about it. Perhaps only Jesus was aware of the cupidity of Judas and his instability of character, and in the end revealed it to the Beloved Disciple alone. By harping on his betrayal and the circumstances of his death he was not only insisting upon what it was vital for his disciples to apprehend, he was cleverly prompting reactions which would confirm what he must know. His stratagem now was designed to pile on the pressure at the crucial moment and induce the traitor to act. To obtain a positive result he had enlightened his disciples no further about his plans at this stage, so that they were in a highly charged emotional condition, and he had arranged with Mary the incident of the precious ointment in order deliberately to let fall the words about his body being anointed for burial. He would have used these words whether or not the question of the poor had come up; but it seems likely that the value of the perfume was intended to play on the weakness of Judas. The episode had the desired effect, as Jesus could observe. The conjunction of the idea of wealth and anointing for burial registered. In Luke's words: 'Then entered Satan into Judas surnamed Iscariot, being of the number of the twelve. And he went his way, and communed with the chief priests and captains, how he might betray him unto them. And they were glad, and covenanted to give him money.' Mark's testimony is that this decision by Judas followed immediately after the incident of the precious perfume.

Judas knew that Jesus expected to be betrayed. He had been saying so again and again, and once more now he had spoken about his death. We may believe, however, that not until this moment had Judas thought of himself as the betrayer. It was the worth of the ointment and Jesus talking about his burial which put it into his head. Suddenly like an inspiration it came to him that money was to be made by doing what Jesus plainly wanted. It seemed as if in a subtle way Jesus was telling him this, inviting him to profit by doing his will. The tempter came in the guise of his Master.

What else may have been in the mind of Judas it is impossible to judge. It has been suggested that he was bitterly disillusioned about Jesus, having imagined that he would speedily establish his kingdom and that there would be great material rewards for his followers. But Jesus had said he would be killed, and the rewards would come in an uncertain future in circumstances of the performance of strange prodigies incomprehensible in practical terms. Judas therefore betrayed Jesus, on this estimation, because he felt that Jesus had betrayed him.

To the chief priests it must have seemed an act of Providence when Judas came to them with his offer. They had been at their wits' end to devise a means of removing the menace Jesus represented without inflaming popular feeling and thus stimulating the revolutionary outbreak which at all costs they had to prevent. With the leader removed, they were confident that excitement would abate and that the threatened insurrection would fizzle out. Now to their enormous relief one of his intimate associates was ready to deliver him into their hands.

In fairness to the Council it must be said that their motives were not inherently evil. They believed there was a real risk of an abortive Jewish rising prompted by the new pretended Messiah, a Galilean like the notorious Judas of Galilee. They knew how the Romans were hated, and the Sadducean hierarchy not much less. A very small spark could set the country ablaze. There would be bloodshed followed by heavier oppression.

We have evidence that the chief priests at the time were arrogant and high-handed, loving wealth and power and position. This has been true of hierarchies of different lands at many periods. But in Palestine just now they were also responsible in the difficult conditions of alien domination for the maintenance of public order, for assuring the continuity of national existence and the survival of the Temple as the world-centre of Jewish faith. Their present fears were by no means ill-founded, as Jewish history of the following decades abundantly confirmed. Better that one man should die than multitudes, including innocent women and children. The liquidation of individuals was commonplace in those days, and notorious during the closing years of the reign of Tiberius.[9] It is still tolerated two thousand years later with all our vaunted concern for human rights. We must beware of judging what happened in the light of what Christians believe about Jesus. We have to see him as he appeared to the Council in their grave predicament. From their point of view the decision they arrived at was fully justified, and Jesus, well knowing what he was doing, had quite deliberately forced them to take it by his skilfully planned and calculated activities. If he had not presented himself as a claimant of the throne of Israel and a menace to national security he would have been completely ignored by the Sanhedrin. He had himself made doubly sure that they would proceed to extremes against him by goading them with his words and behaviour, so that any possible mitigation of their severity would be offset by the personal animus he had intentionally created.

The Council might imagine they were exercising their own free will in determining to destroy Jesus, and Judas Iscariot might believe the same in betraying him; but in fact the comprehensive engineer of the Passover Plot was Jesus himself. Their responses were governed by his ability to assess their reactions when he applied appropriate stimuli. Thus it was assured that the Scriptures would be fulfilled.

The hour was now coming very close towards which all the astuteness and careful strategy of Jesus had been directed. The betrayer had been revealed and brought to the point of playing his part. We may believe that this had been the most painful task Jesus had to perform, and it must have grieved him deeply that the traitor had to be one of his chosen twelve. But so it was written. There was little time left and much still to be accomplished.

It was vital to the messianic thinking of Jesus that he should keep the Passover with his disciples in Jerusalem. This meant going there in the evening, something he had never done before, and making sure that the Council would not know where he was until the Last Supper was over and he had again left the city. The prophecies required that he alone should be the victim, and no others must be involved in his fate. He was in agreement with the Council here that there must be no violence in the Holy City. Accordingly, he had had to make secret arrangements of a dramatic kind with his trusted young disciple John the priest to celebrate the Passover at his home, and had stipulated the precautions to be taken. Not even the most intimate of the Twelve, Peter, James and John, had been informed of these arrangements.

On the Thursday morning at Bethany the disciples came to Jesus to inquire where he wished them to prepare for him to eat the passover. As in the case of the ass at Bethany he again instructed two of his disciples. Luke alone says they were Peter and John the son of Zebedee. They were to go into the city where, by the gate near the pool, they would be met by a man carrying a water-pot. Normally it was women who went to draw water, so they would easily pick him out. They were to follow this man to the house which he would enter, go in themselves and say to the owner, 'The Master says, which guest-room am I to have to eat the passover with my disciples?' They would then be shown a large upstairs room ready laid out, where they were to prepare the passover.

Again what Jesus had required of his Judean friends had been carried out to the letter. There was no hitch. The man with the water-pot was at the rendezvous. All was made ready, and in the evening Jesus came with the twelve to their destination. The circumstances had made it impossible for Judas to notify the Council in advance where Jesus was. Such incidents as this are extremely revealing, because they illustrate the generalship of Jesus and furnish concrete examples of the devices to which he was prepared to resort to accomplish his ends. When given the value they merit, they compel us to look at him with new eyes and a different kind of respect.

There were fourteen, not thirteen persons, who reclined at the table for the paschal meal. There was Jesus and the Twelve, and additionally in a place of honour was the Beloved Disciple as the master of the house.[10] Jesus leaned on the breast of Peter, and this other disciple on the breast of Jesus. With the familiar faces around him, including that of the betrayer, Jesus was deeply moved. 'I have greatly longed to eat this passover with you before I suffer,' he said to them, 'for I tell you I shall not partake of another until its fulfilment in the Kingdom of God.'

The age-old service (seder) began. Jesus recited the blessing over the first of the four obligatory cups of wine of the evening, and handed it on for them to share it, saying, 'I tell you, from this time forth I will not drink of the fruit of the vine until the Kingdom of God is inaugurated.' It seems probable that it was during the paschal meal which preceded the second part of the service that Jesus announced that one of those eating with him would betray him. Deeply distressed, one after another demanded to know if he was the one. Jesus refused to be drawn. He would not put Judas to open shame, and he could not take a chance that he might be stopped or deterred. He would only say: 'It is one of the twelve dipping in the dish with me. Though the Son of Man goes the way that is written of him, woe, nevertheless, to the one by whom the Son of Man is betrayed. Better for him had he never been born.'

Peter was not satisfied, according to the Fourth Gospel. He leaned across Jesus to John the priest, who was not one of the Twelve, and whispered, 'Ask him who he means.' The Beloved

Disciple complied, and Jesus told him, 'It is the one for whom I dip a morsel and offer it to him.' Thereupon he plunged a piece of bread in the bowl of food, lifted a portion, and presented it to Judas, saying, 'What you have to do, do quickly.' Judas accepted and hastily rose from the table. He knew that Jesus knew, and that he wanted him to proceed. He made his exit into the night. The company in general thought nothing of this. They concluded that Jesus was requiring Judas as purser to buy something for the festival which had been overlooked or to give alms to the poor.

When the betrayer had left, Jesus broke the last bread of the evening at the close of the meal and distributed pieces to his disciples, telling them that it signified his body. After grace he took the third cup of wine, known as 'the cup of blessing', recited the benediction, and passed round the cup, saying, 'This signifies the New Covenant in my blood, which is poured out for many.' The service concluded with the drinking of the fourth cup of wine and the chanting of Psalms cxv–cxviii.

Jesus embraced and parted with his Beloved Disciple, and then led the remaining eleven out into the street, out of the city, across the Kedron to the Garden of Gethsemane on the lower slopes of the Mount of Olives. As they went, he said to them, 'All of you will waver in your loyalty, for it is written, "I will strike at the shepherd, and the sheep will be scattered." '[11] Nostalgically he added, 'But after I have been raised up I will go ahead of you to Galilee.'

Peter responded stoutly, 'Even if everyone else wavers, I shall not.' Jesus looked at him. 'Simon, Simon,' he said, 'Satan has begged to have you that he may prise you loose like husks from the grain. But I have prayed that your loyalty may not fail, and on your restoration you must confirm your brothers.'

'In your cause, Master,' he replied, 'I am ready to go to prison and to death too.'

Jesus shook his head. 'I tell you for a fact, Peter, the cock will not crow today before you have denied three times that you know me.'[12] He turned to the rest, 'When I sent you out without purse, or wallet, or sandals, did you go short of anything?'

'No, nothing,' they answered.

'Yet now,' he said, 'whoever has a purse let him take it, and a wallet as well, and whoever has no dagger let him sell his cloak and buy one. For I tell you that this scripture will have its accomplishment in me, "He was classed with outlaws."[13] Yes, indeed, whatever has reference to me will have its fulfilment.'

'Here are two daggers, Master,' they said.

'That will do,' he told them.

NOTES AND REFERENCES

1. See Mk. xi. 11, 12, 15, 19, 20, 27, xiii. 1, xiv. 1, 3, 12, 17, 26, 32, 46, 53, xv. 1, 25, 34, 42.

2. Lk. vii. 36–50.

3. Jn. xviii. 28, xix. 14.

4. Jn. xiii. 1.

5. Lk. xxii. 1–6; Mk. xiv. 10–11.

6. Jn. xiii. 2.

7. Ps. xli. 9; Jn. xiii. 18.

8. Jn. vi. 64, 70–1.

9. The Roman historian Tacitus says: 'Among the calamities of that black period the most trying grievance was the degenerate spirit, with which the first men in the senate submitted to the drudgery of becoming common informers; some without a blush, in the face of day; and others by clandestine artifices. The contagion was epidemic. Near relations, aliens in blood, friends and strangers, known and unknown, were, without distinction, all involved in one common danger. The fact recently committed, and the tale revived, were equally destructive. Words alone were sufficient. . . . Informers struggled, as it were in a race, who should be first to ruin his man; some to secure themselves; the greater part infected by the general corruption of the times' (*Annals*, Book VI, vii).

10. That the Beloved Disciple had a house in Jerusalem is confirmed by the Fourth Gospel, which states that on the cross Jesus entrusted his mother to him 'and from that hour that disciple took her into his own home' (Jn. xix. 27). The disciples were in this house after the crucifixion, where Mary Magdalene came to Peter and the Beloved Disciple (Jn. xx. 2; Lk. xxiv. 33). At the beginning of the Acts we find the disciples assembled in an upper room of a house at Jerusalem, presumably the upper room of the house of the Last Supper, and it is identified with the home of John the Beloved Disciple since the mother of Jesus is there with his brothers (Acts. i. 13–14).

11. Zech. xiii. 7.

12. Mark says: 'Before the cock crow twice, thou thalt deny me thrice' (xiv. 30). We must not stress the figures, which are only a Hebrew form of emphasis found frequently in the Bible. What Jesus said to Peter simply means, 'You, the loyal one, will disown me just as much as the others.' In the Gospels the saying is literalised, not appreciating the Hebrew idiom, so that the cock has to crow, twice in Mark, and Peter has to deny Jesus on three occasions.

13. Isa. liii. 12. Again the saying of Jesus is not to be taken literally. He was not instructing his disciples to arm themselves, but telling them they would now be left to their own resources and treated as rebels.

11

It is Finished

THE little plantation of Gethsemane was a favourite spot for Jesus while he stayed at Bethany. We are told that he often went there with his disciples. It was quiet, and he had Jerusalem and the Temple in full view. He came there again now as he had done at other times. He wanted to pray, but tonight he felt in need of the solace of human companionship. He therefore took Peter, James and John with him when he went aside from the others. Mark says he was restless and depressed, and confessed to them, 'I am in very low spirits.'[1]

Until this day he had regarded the physical suffering in store for him almost impersonally. It had always been in the future, the most solemn ordeal which the Messiah was destined to undergo. There had been a certain glory and majesty about it, a sublimity of heroic behaviour as it was set down in the prophetic passages. Jesus had been so involved with his planning, with move and counter move, with the exhilarating exercise of his wits to bring events into conformity with the predictions, that he had had neither the leisure nor the inclination to dwell upon the details of what he must experience. Now it was different. The hour had come, and his flesh and his spirit quailed. To die under torture! Had he the strength and the fortitude to go through with it? What was written was going to happen to him, Jesus, not to some ideal figure of the imagination.

The Gospels have captured the agony of Jesus at this juncture, though we must appreciate that the tradition behind them is an imaginative one since no soul was present. Jesus prays that if possible he may not have to drain the bitter cup, yet only if this be God's will. Coming back to his three intimates he finds them sleeping. It is brought home to him that he is now on his own. No longer will there be any human prop to lean on, no friend on earth to whom he can turn in facing his ordeal. He addresses the drowsing Peter almost desperately: 'Are you asleep, Simon? Could you not manage to stay awake a single hour? Be vigilant and prayerful, or you may find yourself tempted. The spirit is willing enough, but the flesh is frail.' But he is speaking as much to himself as to his follower, and from Peter there comes no reply. Unnoticed, Jesus goes away again, and prays as before, so earnestly that Luke says the sweat poured from his brow like great drops of blood.

Again we have the emphatic three of Hebrew idiom. Three times Jesus prayed, according to Mark, and three times he returned to his sleeping disciples. The excitement and sadness, the meal they had eaten, the wine they had drunk, had proved too much for them. They could not keep their eyes open. Only Jesus was alert, with every nerve in his body taut, and his brain functioning with crystal clarity. 'Are you going on sleeping,' he said, 'and taking your rest? That's enough! The time has come. Look, the Son of Man is betrayed into the hands of sinners! Come, let us be going. See, my betrayer approaches!'

Hardly had Jesus finished speaking when Judas arrived and with him a force dispatched by the Council armed with swords and clubs. From the description in the Gospels they were members of the Civil Guard under the authority of the Sanhedrin together with some of the servants of the chief priests. The reference to 'sinners' in the words of Jesus indicates that the force consisted mainly of Gentiles.[2] Judas had given instructions to secure the man he would embrace.

The arrest was made with speed. Jesus said something to Judas and to the captain of the band. The texts disagree on what it was. There must have been considerable confusion with the disciples in their dazed condition. Someone, the Fourth Gospel says it was Peter, drew a sword and struck at the high priest's officer whose

name was Malchus, and therefore probably an Arab,[3] severing his
ear. But otherwise there was no resistance. With Jesus taken the
disciples scattered and fled, and it is unlikely that any attempt was
made to pursue them. It was the ringleader who was wanted,
not the small fry.

Mark alone has a postscript about a young man clad only in a
linen wrap, who followed behind when Jesus was led away.
They seized him; but he struggled free, leaving the wrap in their
hands, and escaped naked. It is tempting to think that this may
have been the Beloved Disciple, since there are so many tantalis-
ing gaps in the records. Could it be that news reached him at
Jerusalem that the Council was sending a troop with Judas to
arrest Jesus in the Garden of Gethsemane? He at least knew that
Judas had left the Last Supper to betray him, because Jesus had
pointed out the traitor to him, and it would be surprising if he
had taken no steps whatever to find out what was afoot. Definite
information may have come when John had retired, and just as
he was in his night robe he raced to Gethsemane to warn Jesus.
But he was too late. When he arrived Jesus had just been taken
prisoner. He began to follow, was seized, and only got away by
leaving his garment in the hands of the guards. He ran back to the
city, dressed hurriedly, and made at once for the house of Annas
where, according to the information he had had, Jesus was being
conducted. Where so much is a mystery, this possibility—it is
rated no higher—is by no means fanciful. The Fourth Gospel
says that John did follow Jesus to the high priest's palace, and
went in after him; but it omits any explanation of how he came
to be there. The only one of the twelve to recover himself and
follow at a discreet distance was the faithful Peter. But he had
to stay outside the palace until the other disciple, who was known
to the high priest,[4] spoke to the porteress and had him admitted
to the courtyard.

It was a chilly spring night, and a charcoal fire was burning in
a brazier. The servants and guards were standing around, and
Peter joined them to warm himself. From his speech he was
recognised as a Galilean, and strongly suspected of being a

follower of Jesus. A kinsman of Malchus was convinced he had seen Peter in the Garden of Gethsemane. Thus challenged, Peter swore he did not know Jesus, but it was risky to remain any longer, and he left. Recalling what Jesus had said he wept bitterly.[5]

Meanwhile the prisoner had been brought before Annas son of Seth, former high priest and head of the most powerful sacerdotal family of the time. He was also the father-in-law of the reigning high priest Caiaphas. Annas proceeded to question Jesus closely about his teaching and following. He was anxious to discover if he could how far things had gone, and what was the extent of the danger of a rising. What was Jesus aiming at? How many people were at present involved? Was the conspiracy still in its infancy, limited to a handful of the pretender's peasant dupes who would be helpless if deprived of their leader, or were more important individuals implicated? Jesus had fully regained his composure and flatly denied that he was engaged in any secret subversive activities. What he taught had been spoken openly and publicly in the synagogues and in the Temple. 'Why do you ask me?' he said. 'Ask those who listened what I said to them. They know what I said.'

He was cuffed by a guard for insolence to the high priest; but the shrewd Annas judged that he was sincere. He was convinced that as yet they really had only one person to deal with, and he was greatly relieved. Sending Jesus on to the Council, manacled and under escort, he no doubt communicated this opinion by a verbal message or written note to Caiaphas. It was only necessary to have Jesus executed and whatever was brewing would be nipped in the bud. The man was clearly a deluded fanatic, and for that very reason dangerous in the present state of Jewish affairs.

We have no certain information where the Sanhedrin was meeting, probably it was in the Council Hall (*Bouleuterion*) on the west of the Temple precincts and not far from the high priest's palace at the north-eastern end of Mount Zion. The Gospels tell us nothing of where Peter went, or what had become of the rest of the eleven. They appear later to have made their way to the house of John the priest on the Ophel where the Last Supper had been held and which was known to all of them. Some of the women of Jesus' company were staying there. The Beloved Disciple was perhaps the only follower of Jesus who kept on the track of where he was taken that night and the next morning.

For what transpired from the arrest of Jesus to his agony on the cross we are dependent on the varying accounts of the Gospels. These are reconstructions from traditions of what could be gleaned afterwards from various sources, interlarded with legends and deductions from Old Testament testimonies. The story has also been amplified and adapted in accordance with the development of Christian doctrine and apologetic needs. We must be content, therefore, to use this material with reservations and qualifications, following as much as can be perceived of the authentic drift of the narrative.

There has been much learned discussion of the trial of Jesus, citing the rules of the Sanhedrin as they were ideally represented long after this body had ceased to function. Nowadays reputable scholars do not set much store by this evidence. In fact we know comparatively little about the procedure, and in the case of Jesus there does not seem to have been a trial at all. The Sanhedrin met in special session that night not to try Jesus but to find grounds on which to formulate the indictment which would procure from the Roman governor the condemnation of Jesus to summary execution. This is plainly stated by Mark. It was not the theology of Jesus which was at issue or any offence against the laws of Moses: it was his political pretensions. To make a political charge stick, meriting capital punishment, it was desirable to be able to produce witnesses. Some individuals had been got hold of or bribed to act as informers, but their statements were indecisive and contradictory. Jesus had been much too circumspect in his public utterances for any words of his to be used to establish that he was engaged in treasonable activities. The nearest indication offered by any of the witnesses was a cryptic remark he had made about the Temple. He had said something like, 'Destroy this temple, and in three days I will rebuild it.' The

Fourth Gospel claims that he was speaking of his own body. The witnesses converted his words into a positive intention, 'I will destroy this Temple.' Here was some sort of threat to the existing order; but even so, the saying as a whole with its suggestion of the miraculous sounded more like the language of a madman or a charlatan than of a dangerous rebel. It would never convince Pilate.

While all this went on Jesus remained silent. He was fulfilling the prophecy of Isaiah, 'As a sheep before her shearers is dumb, so he openeth not his mouth.' The Council was getting restive and anxious. At last the high priest challenged him, 'Have you no answer to make to these charges?' Jesus made no reply. The only hope now was to force him to incriminate himself. Caiaphas bluntly put the question to him on oath, 'Are you the Messiah?'

This time Jesus answered: 'Yes I am. And hereafter you will see the Son of Man sitting on the right hand of Power, and coming with the clouds of heaven.'

It was enough for the Sadducean rulers. The high priest rent his tunic, a formal sign of sorrow. 'What further evidence do we need?' he cried. 'You have heard his traitorous confession. What is your decision?' The Council judged him to be deserving of the death-penalty. By admitting that he was the Messiah, the rightful and foreordained king of Israel, Jesus had committed a 'blasphemy', not of God in Jewish law but of Tiberius Caesar in Roman law. He was guilty, they held, of *laesa maiestas*, violation of the emperor's sovereignty, and it was therefore proper for the scandalised authorities, not as Jews but as Roman subjects, to act as *delatores* and inform against Jesus to Caesar's representative.

Because a Jewish court reached this verdict, we are not to imagine, as the Church was later concerned to establish, that Jesus had declared his deity, and consequently from the viewpoint of the Mosaic Law[6] had blasphemed the name of the Lord. In that case the penalty would have been stoning, not crucifixion. Jesus had not even uttered the sacred Name of God, and referred to himself as the Son of Man. Early Nazorean teaching knew nothing of trinitarianism. The Council had neither cause nor any interest to condemn Jesus on religious grounds, since their whole purpose was to stand well with Rome and at the same time to divert the odium of the Jewish people for what they were doing from themselves to Pontius Pilate.

The calumny that the Jewish people were responsible for the death of Jesus has all along been an antisemitic fraud perpetrated by the Church when it became paganised, and has been a direct cause of untold suffering and persecution inflicted on the Jews down the centuries. The present-day qualified second thoughts of the Roman Church on the subject of Jewish 'deicide' has come very belatedly and is a totally inadequate retraction. But the Church is obviously in a quandary, for it can only go all the way to remove the stigma it has inflicted by relinquishing the absolute veracity of its sacred doctrines and documents.

Yet the oldest tradition in the Gospels witnesses against the Church. Jesus never said he would fall into the hands of the Jewish people, but into the hands of the chief priests, elders and scribes. The Gospels testify that the commons of the Jewish nation heard him gladly, and that the Council acted secretly without the knowledge of the people, because they feared a popular demonstration by the Jews in Jesus' favour. We have the evidence that they decided on the removal of Jesus in private conclave, and, taking advantage of his betrayal by one of his own disciples, arrested and interrogated him by night so that the Jewish people assembled in their multitudes at Jerusalem for the Passover should be totally ignorant of what was taking place.

We have already considered the motives of the Council, which in the main were those of self-preservation and self-interest, though not wholly divorced from considerations of national and spiritual survival. These wealthy aristocrats knew they were out of favour with the Jewish masses while they served a foreign heathen government and that their standing with Rome was precarious. Shorn of many of their former powers they were walking a tightrope, clinging to office, inherited prestige and luxurious living, maintaining their position by high-handed action and tortuous intrigue. There were good men among them, a dissentient minority, chiefly Pharisees, who endeavoured to use their influence to curb the dominant Sadducean party as much as they could. Probably some of the Pharisee members of the Council absented themselves from the assembly which dealt with Jesus. Certain of them may not even have been called to attend the hastily convened gathering. The fact that not long after this the presiding high priest Caiaphas was deposed from office by the legate of Syria suggests that some serious representations were made against him.[7] But fully granting that the action of the lordly hierarchy and its supporters was dictated by expediency and was morally indefensible, we must remind ourselves again that Jesus had deliberately manœuvred them into the position where they were forced to proceed against him. Had he not roused their ire, and given them cause to anticipate some nationalistic demonstration, they would not have concerned themselves with him at all.

As early as possible on Friday morning Jesus was brought before the governor Pontius Pilate. The indictment formulated by the Council was in purely political terms. 'We have found this man subverting our nation, forbidding the payment of tribute to Caesar, and claiming to be the Messiah, a king.'

The scene was the Herodian Palace on the west of the city, close to the modern Jaffa Gate. It was the official residence of the Roman procurator when he came to Jerusalem from his seat at Caesarea. Pilate would not at all relish being called upon at an early hour by a deputation from the chief priests bringing with them a Jewish prisoner. The circumstances were highly suspicious, and he came out to them on the broad terrace—they would not enter the building and incur defilement—gruffly demanding to know what the charge was. He was told that the man was a criminal. 'In that case,' said Pilate, 'take him yourselves and sentence him in accordance with your own law.' They reminded him that they no longer had authority to execute anyone. They had lately been deprived of that power by the Romans. So the crime was a capital one, and not religious, and Pilate was bound to deal with it. But he had the feeling that something was wrong, and that an attempt was being made to trap him. He did not trust these priests, and well knew the hostility of the Council towards him because of his disrespect for Jewish institutions. It seemed unnatural that the chief priests should be accusing a fellow Jew of conspiracy against Rome. Likely as not the prisoner was a man of no consequence who was being used to make trouble. He had heard no reports of agitation in Jerusalem lately. The man standing passively before him did not look in the least like a militant Zealot.

Incredulously, Pilate asked Jesus, 'Are you king of the Jews?' He expected either a denial or an indication that the prisoner was a harmless lunatic. Irritatingly, Jesus replied, 'Are you asking this of your own accord, or did others suggest it to you about me?'

'Am I a Jew?' roared Pilate. 'Your own people, the chief priests, have handed you over to me. What have you done?'

Jesus explained that his kingdom did not belong to the existing world order. Had it been otherwise his followers would have fought to save him from arrest. How could the coming messianic kingdom be made intelligible to a heathen Roman official? It was quite beyond his comprehension.

To Pilate the man was talking nonsense. 'You *are* a king, then?' he persisted, trying to get him to be more explicit.

'I am a king, as you say,' Jesus answered. 'I was born and came into the world to witness to this truth. All who heed the truth listen to me.'

Now Pilate was sure he was dealing with a deluded maniac. 'What does truth mean?' he shouted. It was impossible to treat the charge seriously. He jumped up, and went out to the waiting accusers. 'I find nothing against him,' he told them shortly.

In substance we have followed the Fourth Gospel so far, but here we have to make room for a tradition preserved by Luke. According to this version the chief priests pressed their charge, insisting, 'He rouses the people, teaching all over Judea, beginning with Galilee and ending up here.'

The governor was quick to see an opportunity to end the

business. He inquired whether the man was a Galilean, and learning that he came under the jurisdiction of Herod Antipas tetrarch of Galilee he told them to take Jesus and their accusations to him. Herod was in Jerusalem for the Passover staying at the Hasmonean Palace further east along the hill. For a long time he had wished to see Jesus, and hoped to see him perform some wonder. He questioned him at length while the representatives of the Council vehemently accused him. Jesus made no response, even when Herod and his men mocked him. Tiring of the sport, the tetrarch returned the prisoner to Pilate with a message that he was quite harmless. 'That day,' says Luke, 'Herod and Pilate became friends with one another; for previously they had been at enmity.' They had quarrelled, no doubt, because Pilate's soldiers had killed many Galileans in the recent demonstration of protest over the seizure of the sacred funds for the aqueduct.

The chief priests were now in difficulties, and realised that they would have to bring strong pressure on Pilate. They therefore packed the courtyard of the praetorium with their slaves and henchmen. The governor still insisted that the charge was frivolous. He would have Jesus flogged and then release him in accordance with a Passover amnesty custom. But instigated by the chief priests the crowd shouted that they wanted Barabbas not Jesus released. Pilate must have become choleric at this demand, because Barabbas was in prison for fighting back when his troops had attacked the aqueduct demonstrators, and there was reason to believe he had caused the death of at least one Roman soldier. So this was it. The prisoner was being used by the priests as a means of taking revenge on himself for requisitioning the Temple treasure. They did not forgive, these arrogant priests.

Pilate was forced on the defensive, but he was not yet beaten. He had Jesus flogged, and his guards decked the prisoner out as a mock king with a crimson cloak round his shoulders and a wreath on his head made of thorns. Cruelly the governor presented this pitiful insult to Jewish sentiment to the crowd. 'There's your king!'

It would have been an intolerable spectacle for the Jewish

people, and probably caused a riot. But the crowd consisted of the chief priests' men, including many Gentiles, and obediently they yelled, 'Crucify him, crucify him!'[8]

Pilate cared nothing about Jesus. He did care about his own position if he should be accused to Tiberius of fomenting disaffection by executing a Jew on unsupported testimony. At Rome they did not take kindly these days to provocative action in the Provinces, and the governor was already in trouble enough because of the disturbances resulting from his flouting of Jewish customs. What decided him finally to give way was the threat of an even more sinister accusation: 'If you free the man you are no friend of Caesar's. Whoever claims to be a king is in opposition to Caesar.'

Barabbas was released, and Jesus was condemned to be crucified. But Pilate could still strike back at his tormentors by having their own charge posted upon the cross: JESUS THE NAZOREAN, KING OF THE JEWS. He refused point-blank to change the wording to, 'He said, I am king of the Jews.'

The chief priests had had their way. They had browbeaten the governor into compliance, but they could take little comfort from their victory. It had been a necessary yet nasty business, and they were by no means confident now that the death of Jesus would be the end of the matter and that they were free from blood-guilt. The Jewish people might react to their deed if it leaked out that they had taken the initiative, and hold them in greater disfavour. The future held little promise of peace. History indeed records that within thirty-five years the palaces of the nobility were sacked by mobs and the chief priests were hunted down and murdered.

Weakened by his flogging Jesus was led out of the western gate of the city by Roman guards, with two others who were being crucified with him. A Cyrenian called Simon was requisitioned to bear the cross-beam of his cross. Tardily Jerusalem began to awaken to what was going forward. There had been rumours of the arrest of Jesus; but for the most part, as had been intended, the people knew nothing of what had transpired on

Government Hill. It was the beginning of the festival, and everything had happened too quickly and secretly for any organised demonstration. There was no one to give a lead. The crosses were up on Golgotha and the victims were suspended on them before the ill news had penetrated very far. Fear and horror and respect for the sufferers decided the majority of those who heard to keep away from the scene. Perhaps some hirelings of the chief priests were there to watch and to jeer, but it is quite incredible, and probably the result of delving into the testimonies, that the chief priests, elders and scribes were present in person as the synoptic tradition states.[9] The Jerusalem tradition of the Fourth Gospel makes no such assertion. But we may believe that some angry and pious people were there to lend the solace of their presence and to pray for the dying. A retinue of mourning women had been furnished, according to Luke, to accompany Jesus to the place of execution. Of those near to him who stood by the cross, we have mention only of his mother and the Beloved Disciple. None of the apostles was there, but Mary of Magdala, Mary the mother of the younger James and of Joses, Salome the mother of Zebedee's sons James and John, and some other women of his following, were looking on at a distance.

The traditions which have come down to us of what happened on Golgotha are not in full agreement, as we would expect, since it could not have been easy afterwards to collect reliable information. Each of the Gospels has some circumstance which is not in the others. Imagination has clearly been employed to build up a picture and to lend solemnity and significance to the Crucifixion. Some of the effects are reminiscent of the revelation on Sinai and convey an anticipation of the Last Judgement.[10] We are told of darkness, an earthquake, and the rending of the veil of the Temple, even of the resurrection of the bodies of dead saints. With various incidents there is a reflection of the language of the Scriptures, especially of Psalm xxii, the psalm which begins: 'My God, my God, why hast thou forsaken me?' The soldiers cast lots for the robe of Jesus in fulfilment of Psalm xxii. 18. They pierce his hands and his feet in fulfilment of xxii. 16. The chief priests and scribes mock him and wag their heads in derision in fulfilment of xxii. 7. They cry, 'He trusted in the Lord to deliver him: let him deliver him, if he delight in him,' in fulfilment of xxii. 8. Bystanders give Jesus vinegar mingled with gall in fulfilment of Psalm lxix. 21. When he is believed to be dead they do not break his legs, as they do those of the robbers, in fulfilment of Exodus xii. 46. Instead, his side is pierced with a lance in fulfilment of Zechariah xii. 10.

There is the strongest consciousness here of the prophetic testimonies. We may grant that certain things happened, some of them usual, which seemed to answer to such Scriptures. But there has been invention as well to obtain a more exact correspondence and to supplement the paucity of facts.

The question arises, how far, anticipating as he did the detailed realisation of the predictions, was Jesus in his pain concerned with all that was taking place, of prophecies coming to pass? We would expect him to cling grimly to the last to what had been the motivation of his whole life in his role of Messiah. When Jesus cried aloud the opening words of Psalm xxii: 'My God, my God, why hast thou forsaken me?', was this only an exclamation of anguish, or did he continue the silent recitation of the psalm which was so relevant to his sufferings until he reached and voiced its closing words? It is customary among Jews at prayer to emphasise in speech the commencement and conclusion of a liturgical composition, psalm, praise or prayer, covering the intermediate matter in an undertone. Possibly the Fourth Gospel unrealising makes Jesus say, 'It is finished,' when in fact he had come to the last words of Psalm xxii: 'He has done it.' However this may be, the Gospel does at least credit him with the assurance 'that all things were now accomplished, that the Scriptures might be fulfilled'.[11]

In his sufferings Jesus could know that he had triumphantly passed the messianic test, successfully carrying out the exacting stipulations of the Oracles. The tremendous task to which he had applied his mind and heart was concluded. But in these moments he still had something to do, to provide for the mother he had

been forced to neglect to pursue his mission: he now entrusted
her to the care of his dear disciple. His last effort was to call out, 'I
thirst.' In response someone standing by raised to his lips a sponge
saturated with wine vinegar. Almost immediately he passed into
oblivion.

Never had Jesus been more the Messiah of his oppressed people
than when he hung there with bowed head at rest, on a cross of
imperial Caesar bearing a placard which announced him poignantly to all the world in Greek, in Latin, and in Hebrew, as
king of the Jews. Wretched representatives of human degrada-
tion and of pitiless society were his royal attendants. Thus lifted
up as an ensign to the nations[12] he had already begun to reign.

NOTES AND REFERENCES

1. This is the meaning of the Hebraic words, 'My soul is exceeding sorrowful,
even unto death.'

2. The Gentiles were thought of as sinners because they did not observe the
laws of God given to Moses, just as those Jews were sinners who lived like
Gentiles in violation of the Law. See Gal. ii. 14–15; Mt. ix. 10–11. The chief
priests had at their disposal a small force recruited from many nationalities, and
also non-Jewish servants and slaves.

3. From inscriptions and from Josephus the name Malchus or Malichus was
in common use among Arabs and Syrians.

4. The nature of the connection is not certain. Some scholars hold that John
the priest was a kinsman of Annas, reading *gnorimos* instead of *gnostos* as in the
Purple Codex of Patmos. It is clear at any rate that he was a person of some
standing, and not to be confused with the stormy Galilean fisherman John the
son of Zebedee.

5. See Chapter 10, Note 12.

6. See Lev. xxiv. 16.

7. The Syrian legate Vitellius was eager to conciliate the Jewish people by
making concessions to national sentiment, and one of his acts in this connection
was to depose Caiaphas (Josephus, *Antiq*. XVIII. iv. 3). Many years later when
Annas son of the Annas of the Gospels was high priest James the brother of
Jesus was arrested and executed by an illegally convened meeting of the Sanhedrin while a new governor of Judea was on the way to take up his appointment.
Some of the leading citizens of Jerusalem protested to the governor at this high-
handed action, whereupon he wrote threatening the high priest with punishment
and Agrippa II deposed Annas from the highpriesthood after he had been only
three months in office (*Antiq*. XX. ix. 1).

8. The reiteration is found only in Luke, but John has the repetition of the cry, 'Away with him, away with him!' (Jn. xix. 15). If we can rely on these reflections of the Jerusalem tradition they would point to a largely non-Jewish crowd customarily given to 'vain repetitions' (Mt. vi. 7). An example is, 'Caesar, let the prisoners be dragged! Caesar, let the prisoners be dragged!'

9. These august personages would not have demeaned themselves by attending the crucifixion in person, and in any case it is clear from the Gospels that they were most anxious not to be associated with the execution in the minds of the Jewish people. John the priest, who was at the cross, makes no mention of their presence. Jesus had said he would fall into the hands of these authorities and that they would mock him. This was enough to create the story on the basis of the testimony in Psalm xxii. 7–8.

10. See Part Two, Chapter 6, *Some Gospel Mysteries*.

11. Jn. xix. 28–30.

12. Isa. xi. 10–12.

Thou wilt show me the Path of Life

JESUS had been convinced that his crucifixion would not be the end. Provided that he faithfully discharged the duties incumbent upon him as the Messiah in his manifestation as the Servant of the Lord, he was assured that God would exalt him in readiness for his further manifestation as ruler over the Kingdom of God. The glorification would be initiated by his resurrection. According to the synoptic Gospels, as his last trials approached, he had spoken to his disciples with confidence of his rising on the third day. He even went so far as to make an appointment to meet them afterwards in his beloved Galilee.

The expectation of resurrection was a Jewish one, involving the reanimation of the body which in some way would have become immortalised. When the time came for the inauguration of the Kingdom of God the faithful dead would rise to share its bliss, and in Paul's view the surviving living saints would undergo a change.[1] It is claimed in the Gospels that persons raised from the dead were able to resume normal existence, except that in the Kingdom of God there would be no sex relationship. In the curious story in Matthew of the appearance of dead saints at the time of the crucifixion it is their bodies which arise, come out of their tombs, and go into Jerusalem. The resurrection of Jesus was understood to be of the same order: his body was believed to have left the tomb and could be handled: the revived Jesus could speak, eat and drink and walk about. There was no impairment of those faculties and capacities he had in his lifetime.

At the same time new capacities were acquired such as the ability to appear and disappear at will.

We are not dealing in the Gospels with hallucinations, with psychic phenomena or survival in the Spiritualist sense. These possibilities do not fit the circumstances as they are narrated. However the traditions of the resurrection of Jesus are to be explained it cannot legitimately be on these lines.

The Gospels in this part of their narrative exhibit the same characteristics we have encountered in earlier parts. There is some conflict between Galilean and Judean versions of what took place. There is a heightening of the miraculous in the later Gospels, and emphasis of the deity of Jesus in the Fourth Gospel. There is a paucity of material, and consequent absence of vital information. In Mark, the least legendary of the Gospels, the text breaks off abruptly and tantalisingly at a crucial point, the point at which the women of Jesus' company coming on Sunday morning to the tomb in which he had been laid on Friday evening find it empty. Inside a young man clothed in white is sitting, who gives them the message that Jesus is risen, and bids them tell his disciples that he will meet them in Galilee. In fear and trembling they depart hastily, and from this Gospel we learn no more. Some suspicion is created that the lost end of Mark was not necessarily accidental.

In the supernatural details furnished in the other Gospels we are reminded of the character of the Nativity Stories. The end of the records of Jesus as they were set down some seventy years later is of the same quality as the beginning. What was given out as fact has become blended with fairy-tale. Complete with all its legendary features, the proposition of the resurrection of Jesus is being stated, not argued. There is no inquest on the strange occurrences, no examination of witnesses, no analysis of the evidence. We have only what the Evangelists report, what little data they had at command now embellished and adorned, totally inadequate to prove anything. Much could have happened of which there was no knowledge, no recollection, to throw a different light on the circumstances. Various possibilities can be suggested;

but we cannot know the truth, one way or the other. We should frankly admit this. Yet we are fully entitled to investigate to the extent that is practicable, and it is more probable that we shall be on the right track if the clues we employ are derived from what is presented for our attention. On that basis let us quest for further enlightenment.

There cannot at this stage be absent from our thinking that Jesus would be concerned to plan for his resurrection as he was for the events which led up to his execution. This is to assume that he did speak in advance of rising on the third day and rejoining his disciples in Galilee. To be so explicit he would be unlikely to be relying solely on an act of God quite beyond his control. From this viewpoint the story of the resurrection would not begin with his burial: it would begin much earlier. We must grant that the same imperatives were present, the need to realise the messianic predictions as Jesus had interpreted them. These predictions, as in Isaiah liii, foreshadowed renewal of life after suffering and the grave, for there followed on: 'He shall prolong his days, and the pleasure of the Lord shall prosper in his hand. He shall see of the travail of his soul, and shall be satisfied.' We are therefore bound to go over again some of the ground we have covered, to detect whether anything is revealed which can assist us.

What we chiefly note is that the plans of Jesus were laid with remarkable care for timing. He had singled out a particular Passover as the season when he would suffer, and had taken every precaution to ensure that he would not be arrested beforehand. During the first half of Passion Week, keeping himself in the public eye by conducting his activities in the Temple, he had aggravated the ecclesiastical authorities to the pitch that they were determined to destroy him as soon as it should be feasible without risk of a tumult; but he was careful not to help them by staying in the city after dark. Not until Wednesday evening did Jesus apply the pressure that decided Judas to go to the Council with an offer to betray him, and by his secret arrangements he saw to it that the arrest would not take place until Thursday evening after he had partaken of the Last Supper in Jerusalem with his disciples. All this suggests that he intended that his crucifixion should be on Friday, which would be the eve of the Sabbath. Calculating that it would require some hours on Friday morning for the Council to obtain his condemnation by Pilate, which could not be withheld as the charge was treason against the emperor, and knowing that in accordance with custom he would not be left on the cross over the Sabbath, but would be taken down well before sunset when the Sabbath commenced, Jesus could roughly reckon that he would experience crucifixion for not much more than three or four hours, whereas normally the agonies of the crucified lasted for as many days.

Jesus, as we have appreciated, relied on the Old Testament Oracles, and what these intimated to him was that while there would be a conspiracy of the rulers to destroy him (as in Psalm ii), yet by the mercy of God he would be spared complete extinction of life. To illustrate this we must repeat here some of the passages which he would have regarded as prophetic.

'Though I walk in the midst of trouble, thou wilt revive me: thou shalt stretch forth thine hand against the wrath of mine enemies, and thy right hand shall save me. The Lord will perfect that which concerneth me. The bands of the grave compassed me about: the snares of death prevented me. In my distress I called upon the Lord, and cried unto my God: he heard my voice out of his temple. He sent from above, he took me, he drew me out of great waters. He delivered me from my strong enemy. God shall redeem my soul from the grasp of the grave. My flesh also shall rest in hope. For thou wilt not leave my soul in the grave; neither wilt thou suffer thy holy one to see corruption. Thou wilt show me the path of life. Come, and let us return unto the Lord: for he hath torn, and he will heal us; he hath smitten, and he will bind us up. After two days will he revive us: and on the third day he will raise us up, and we shall live in his sight. The king shall joy in thy strength, O Lord . . . He asked life of thee, and thou gavest it him, even length of days for ever and ever.'[2]

It could be interpreted, therefore, that the Messiah would survive his terrible ordeal. To this end it was essential that the duration of his sufferings should be reduced to a minimum. The planning of Jesus had contributed effectively to assuring this.

Provided that crucifixion was not too prolonged it was possible for the life of the victim to be saved. First-hand information about this is furnished by Josephus. He tells us in his autobiography that during the last stage of the siege of Jerusalem by the Romans he had been sent by Titus, the general in command, to inspect a potential camp site at Tekoa, about twelve miles south of the city. On his return he passed a number of prisoners who had been crucified, and recognised three of them as acquaintances. When he got back he went to Titus and pleaded for them. Titus ordered that they should be taken down and given the best possible treatment. Two of them died, but the third recovered. The indications are that these men had been on the cross longer than was Jesus, yet even so one of them survived.

If Jesus was convinced from the Scriptures that he was to suffer on the cross, but not to perish on it, there was no reason why he should not have been concerned to make what provision he could for his survival. We have had ample evidence that Jesus used his intelligence to assure the fulfilment of the predictions. He believed that as Messiah the spirit of wisdom and understanding had been conferred on him, and that it was God's will that he should employ these powers of the mind to accomplish what must come to pass. He did not expect, indeed it was alien to his nature, to sit with folded hands waiting for things to happen whether in a natural or supernatural manner. His whole ministry was purposeful, masterful and practical. He plotted and schemed with the utmost skill and resourcefulness, sometimes making secret arrangements, taking advantage of every circumstance conducive to the attainment of his objectives. It is difficult to credit that he had neglected to do anything about the supreme crisis of his career, when it was imperative that he should outwit the forces arrayed against him and wrest victory from the very jaws of death.

We have already made the point that Jesus had sought to

bring it about that he would be on the cross not much more than three or four hours. If we follow the Fourth Gospel the ordeal lasted barely three hours, from a little after midday to about three o'clock in the afternoon. But this obviously was not enough. If he was to cheat death it was essential that well in advance of the time, which could not be much after five o'clock, when in any case he would be taken down because of the incoming Sabbath, he would have to give every appearance of being dead. Otherwise his actual death would be expedited by the soldiers in charge of the execution. Further, help must speedily be forthcoming. Unless his body came into possession of friendly hands there would be no possibility of his recovery. The 'corpse' would be thrown into the grave of a common criminal.

If the Gospels afforded us no assistance we would have to imagine how Jesus contrived to give the impression of death, and suggest a way in which his body could have been secured by his friends. It is by no means a novel theory that Jesus was not dead when taken from the cross, and some will have it that he subsequently recovered. The idea was used in fiction by George Moore in *The Brook Kerith* and by D. H. Lawrence in *The Man who Died*. However, we have to imagine very little since Mark and John agree on what is essential to the requirements of the situation. We have only to allow that in this as in other instances Jesus made private arrangements with someone he could trust, who would be in a position to accomplish his design. This person is identified to us in the Gospels as Joseph of Arimathea. He is one of the great mysteries of the Gospels. He is represented as a wealthy man, and a member of the Sanhedrin; and since he is said to have been waiting for the Kingdom of God he would have been a messianically-minded Pharisee. He enters the story unheralded, and after his task is fulfilled he disappears completely from the New Testament records. There is no indication whatever of his association with the apostles or that he openly joined the Nazorean movement.

One of the possibilities we have to face is that the scantiness of information available to the Evangelists led them to build up their narrative not only by historicising Old Testament testimonies but also by ransacking the writings of the Jewish historian Flavius Josephus. Luke especially seems to have made use of information gleaned from Josephus.[3] We have also to allow for confused memories and anachronisms entering into the Gospel tradition. It is therefore necessary to remark here that the account of two robbers being crucified with Jesus could have arisen from the crucifixion of the two 'brigand' sons of Judas of Galilee, James and Simon, by Tiberius Alexander when he was governor of Judea in the reign of Claudius, which is reported by Josephus.[4] This incident might have become connected, as far as the part played by Joseph of Arimathea is concerned, with what we have already mentioned, that Josephus relates how three of his friends were crucified, and that he begged Titus for them. When they were taken down two died, but one recovered. This is very close to what the Gospels say. The two robbers crucified with Jesus died, but he was resurrected after Joseph of Arimathea had begged Pilate for his body. According to Mark, by the crucifixion of Jesus with two robbers the prophecy of Isaiah liii was fulfilled: 'He was numbered with the transgressors.'

The very name Joseph of Arimathea is questionable. Josephus, again in his autobiography, telling of his own eminent ancestry, states that his grandfather Joseph begot Matthias in the tenth year of the reign of Archelaus (A.D. 6). The Greek text of the words 'Joseph (begot) Matthias' is simply *Josepou Matthias*. The name Joseph of Arimathea is given in the Greek of Mark as *Joseph apo Arimathias*. The similarity is striking. It is certainly curious that we have Josephus, himself a *Josepou Matthias*, begging the Roman commander for the bodies of three crucified friends, one of whom is brought back to life.

But this is not all. In the resurrection story in the Gospels Mark refers to a young man dressed in white seen at the empty tomb. Matthew more elaborately tells a story of a guard at the tomb. An angel descends to the accompaniment of an earthquake wearing a robe white as snow, 'and for fear of him the keepers did shake, and became as dead men'. Now we find in Josephus an account of the capture of the Jewish leader Simon bar Giora after the fall of Jerusalem. He tried to effect his escape from the city by tunnelling a way out from ancient subterranean caves; but failing in this he resorted to a stratagem. 'Simon, thinking he might be able to scare and delude the Romans, put on a white robe, and buckled upon him a purple cloak, and appeared out of the ground in the place where the temple had formerly stood. Those who saw him were at first aghast and remained motionless; but afterwards they drew nearer and inquired who he was.'[5]

Such correspondences cannot easily be put down to coincidence. It has to be allowed that sources like Josephus have been employed to supplement the paucity of genuine recollections which outlasted the overwhelming catastrophe of the Jewish war with Rome.[6] We are consequently warned that we should not accept the testimony of the Gospels at face value, and must employ every external agency available to check the information where we can. Generally, we must probe to extract elements in the traditions on which we can reasonably rely. Otherwise we shall be building a house on sand, and arguing about matters and sayings which have not been established as authentic. Continually we must be aware of the circumstances which contributed to and helped to shape and develop the story of Jesus as we find it in the Gospels.

There is no cause to doubt the crucifixion of Jesus, or that he had assistants to aid him in his bid for survival. We may accept that one of them was a member of the Sanhedrin, and we may agree to speak of him as Joseph of Arimathea, even if we cannot be positive that this was his name. Jesus could have got to know him through Nicodemus, mentioned only in the Fourth Gospel, during the three months from the previous October to January when he was at Jerusalem working out details of the Passover Plot. He needed highly placed individuals on whom he could count to give him inside information of what measures were being taken against him by the Council, and also to advise him about relations between the Council and the Roman governor, procedures in political trials, and other pertinent matters with which he was unfamiliar, but which had a bearing upon his course of action and affected his plans. Evidently Joseph was deeply impressed by Jesus and was ready to co-operate in frustrating the intentions of the Sadducean chief priests. Luke says that he had not consented to their counsel and deed, and John describes him as a secret disciple.

It transpired that Joseph had property in close proximity to Golgotha, the hill of execution. Part of this was under cultivation as a kitchen garden, and also on the site was a new tomb cut into the rock. That is to say, the tomb was a cavern, containing a chamber with a ledge or ledges on which the dead would be laid, and secured by a heavy stone rolled across the mouth. We learn about garden plots in this area, again from Josephus,[7] for Titus was nearly trapped among them by a sally of the Jewish defenders of Jerusalem when with a few horsemen he rode down towards the north-west corner of the city to reconnoitre. The tomb in question could not have been more conveniently placed, and lent itself admirably to a plan to bring Jesus there in the event of his crucifixion.

Two things, however, were indispensable to the success of a rescue operation. The first was to administer a drug to Jesus on the cross to give the impression of premature death, and the second was to obtain the speedy delivery of the body to Joseph. No other manner of survival could be entertained by Jesus, since he was adamant about the fulfilment of the prophecies which demanded his suffering.

If we allow that the story of Joseph going to Pilate is trustworthy,[8] then with the help of the common factors in the traditions we can attempt to reconstruct what happened. Considerations of safety and secrecy will have dictated that as few people as possible should be in the know or involved, and these would not have included any of the apostles, to whom Jesus never seems to have confided his plans as we have already noticed on several occasions. He dealt individually and singly with Judean individuals who were in a position to carry out the various parts of his design. His was the master-mind, and those to whom he gave his instructions neither worked together nor were acquainted with more than their specific function.

The first stage of the present action was the cross. We are told that there were bystanders there, and that one of them saturated a sponge with vinegar, impaled it on a cane and put it to the mouth of Jesus. He did not perform this office for either of the two robbers crucified with Jesus, which he might well have done if his intention was purely humanitarian. The incident took place, according to Mark, after Jesus had cried, 'My God [*Eli* in Hebrew], my God, why hast thou forsaken me?' Mark gives the words in Aramaic, which Peter would have used in describing the crucifixion; but Jesus no doubt quoted from Psalm xxii in Hebrew. This prompted some onlookers to suppose that he was calling for Elijah. The man who acted, who was sent there by Joseph to administer the drug, said: 'Quiet! Let us see if Elijah will come to take him down.' The man here showed his initiative by taking advantage of an opportune moment for his intervention, which no one would suspect was favourable to Jesus. Mark gives no reason for his action, but the Fourth Gospel says that Jesus called out, 'I am thirsty,' which could have been a signal. There was nothing unusual for a vessel containing a refreshing liquid to be at the place of execution, and it presented no problem to doctor the drink that was offered to Jesus. The plan may indeed have been suggested to Jesus by the prophetic words, 'They gave me also gall for my meat; and in my thirst they gave me vinegar to drink.'[9] If what he received had been the normal wine vinegar diluted with water the effect would have been stimulating. In this case it was exactly the opposite. Jesus lapsed quickly into complete unconsciousness. His body sagged. His head lolled on his breast, and to all intents and purposes he was a dead man.

Directly it was seen that the drug had worked the man hastened to Joseph who was anxiously waiting for the news. At once he sought an audience with Pilate, to whom he would have ready access as a member of the Sanhedrin, and requested to have the body of Jesus. Pilate was greatly astonished, as well he might be, to hear that Jesus was already dead, and being on his guard in view of all that had happened he sent for the centurion in charge of the execution to obtain confirmation. When this was forthcoming, he readily gave the necessary permission. It has been noted by scholars that Joseph asked for the body (*soma*) of Jesus, which could indicate that he did not think of him as dead. It is only Pilate who refers to the corpse (*ptoma*).[10]

Joseph hurried to Golgotha with clean linen and spices. The Fourth Gospel says he was accompanied by Nicodemus. It also reports another circumstance. In view of the need to hasten death because of the Sabbath the two robbers had their legs broken with mallets, but Jesus was spared this treatment because he was believed to be dead already. To make sure, however, one of the soldiers thrust a lance into his side. The incident may have been introduced to historicise certain Old Testament testimonies. The passage[11] suggests that some doubt was thrown on this new information when it was published. If it is correct, the chances that Jesus would recover were heavily diminished. Much would depend on the nature of the wound. The reported emission of blood shows at least that life was still in him.

As arranged, Jesus was conveyed carefully to the nearby tomb. The women of his following, who had been observing everything at a distance, saw where he was taken. Sorrowfully they made their way back to the city, proposing to return on the morning after the Sabbath to pay their tribute by anointing his body. It is evident that they were not expecting any resurrection.

NOTES AND REFERENCES

1. I. Cor. xv. 51-3.

2. Ps. cxxxviii; Ps. xviii; Ps. xlix; Ps. xvi; Hos. vi; Ps. xxi. Even Ps. xxii, the 'crucifixion' psalm, speaks of help in extremity, and deliverance (vv. 20-5).

3. See Part Two, Chapter 5, *The Second Phase*.

4. Josephus, *Antiq.* XX. v. 2.

5. Josephus, *Wars*, VII. ii. 2.

6. See Part Two, Chapter 1, *Messianism and the Development of Christianity*.

7. Josephus, *Wars*, V. ii. 2.

8. The adverse evidence we have cited is from the autobiography of Josephus, published soon after A.D. 100. If Mark made use of it his Gospel must have been written later than that date, which seems unlikely, unless we hold the theory of an earlier draft of Mark (*Ur-Markus*) which did not give the particulars in question. On the whole, having noted the coincidences, it is safer to treat them in this instance as no more than that. With Matthew's additional incident, and in general with Luke, the case for dependence on Josephus is stronger since the connection is with works of this historian published between A.D. 75 and 95.

9. Ps. lxix. 21.

10. Mk. xv. 43, 45.

11. Jn. xix. 34–7.

13

He is not Here

JESUS lay in the tomb over the Sabbath. He would not regain consciousness for many hours, and in the meantime the spices and linen bandages provided the best dressing for his injuries. We may dismiss the story in Matthew alone that the chief priests requested Pilate that a guard be set over the tomb, and that they posted a watch, presumably on Saturday evening at the end of the Sabbath. The fantastic details make it appear that the story was a late reply to allegations that the body had been stolen by the disciples, which is confirmed by the words that 'this saying is commonly reported among the Jews until this day'.[1] Part of the story, as we have shewn, may have been suggested by the Simon bar Giora incident recorded by Josephus (above p. 165). The Jewish allegation, however, was a rational one and has to be entertained. As a distinguished Christian scholar has stated: 'When stripped of supernaturalism the empty tomb may point rather to a removal of the body from the place where the women had seen it laid and its burial elsewhere.' He concludes: 'Thus when Jews spread abroad the story that the disciples of Jesus had "stolen" the body, they spoke the truth.'[2] But if the body of Jesus was taken from the tomb by his friends on Saturday night, we should be ready to agree with the Gospels that the immediate disciples of Jesus knew nothing about this, and they would be quite sincere in indignantly repudiating any contention that they had been guilty of perpetrating a fraud.

Christians are surely right in protesting that the Church could not have been established on the basis of a deliberate falsehood on the part of the apostles, and therefore there must be another explanation for the removal of the body than an intention to pretend that Jesus had risen from the dead. An alternative to the accusation of theft is given by the Church Father Tertullian of Carthage at the end of the second century. Rhetorically addressing the Jews who are confounded by the Second Coming of Christ, he says, 'This is he whom his disciples have stolen away secretly, that it may be said he is risen, or the gardener abstracted that his lettuces might not be damaged by the crowd of visitors!'[3]

So another story was also current in the second century, which placed responsibility on 'the gardener', who took away the body of Jesus to save his vegetables. In the same century the *Gospel of Peter* speaks of crowds from Jerusalem and the neighbourhood who came early on the morning of the Sabbath (Saturday) to see the sepulchre of Jesus. A Coptic manuscript from Egypt now in the British Museum entitled *The Book of the Resurrection* and attributed to the Apostle Bartholomew has a variant of the story. The gardener is called Philogenes, whose son Jesus had cured. He speaks to Mary at the tomb, though the Mary here is the mother of Jesus not the Magdalene, and tells her:

'From the very moment when the Jews crucified him, they had persisted in seeking out an exceedingly safe sepulchre wherein they might lay him, so that the disciples might not come by night and carry him away secretly. Now I said to them, There is a tomb quite close to my vegetable garden; bring him, lay him in it, and I myself will keep watch over him. I thought in my heart saying: When the Jews shall have departed and entered into their houses, I will go into the tomb of my Lord, and will carry him away, and will give him spices and sweet-smelling unguents and scents.'[4]

This strange tale may have originated from what is uniquely stated in the Fourth Gospel, where Mary Magdalene sees a man at the tomb whom she supposes to be the gardener, and says to him, 'Sir, if thou have borne him hence, tell me where thou hast laid him, and I will take him away.'[5] But what is this incident doing in the Gospel? Was it due to something which came to light later? We may never know. In any case we are bound to take seriously whatever may help to solve the mystery of the empty tomb. If we discard the charge that the body of Jesus was removed in order to claim that he had risen from the dead, or that the gardener on his own initiative had done it to preserve his crops, we are left with the perfectly natural and fully justifiable reason that Jesus was taken from the tomb at the first possible opportunity for the entirely legitimate purpose of reviving him. For this action at least two persons would have been needed, one of whom could well have been the gardener.

The argument of the last chapter will then hold good, that a plan was being followed which was worked out in advance by Jesus himself and which he had not divulged to his close disciples. What seems probable is that in the darkness of Saturday night when Jesus was brought out of the tomb by those concerned in the plan he regained consciousness temporarily, but finally succumbed. If, as the Fourth Gospel says, his side was pierced by a lance before he was taken from the cross his chances of recovery were slender. It was much too risky, and perhaps too late, to take the body back to the tomb, replace the bandages left there, roll the stone across the entrance, and try to create the impression that everything was as it had been on Friday evening. It would also have been thought most unseemly. Before dawn the mortal remains of Jesus were quickly yet reverently interred, leaving the puzzle of the empty tomb.

From this point we are dealing with the accounts of the resurrection as related in the Gospels, and it has to be seen whether they are consistent with our hypothesis. We are nowhere claiming for our reconstruction that it represents what actually happened, but that on the evidence we have it may be fairly close to the truth. We have to allow that the Gospel accounts come to us from a time when the figure of Jesus had become larger than life, and his story had acquired in telling and retelling many legendary features. Yet we must not treat them as wholly fictitious and they have preserved valuable indications of what transpired.

We can almost see the process at work which transformed the deep despondency of the companions of Jesus into the joyful conviction that he had triumphed over death as he said he would. What emerges from the records is that various disciples did see somebody, *a real living person*. Their experiences were not subjective.

It is well to remind ourselves again that Jesus was positive that he was the Messiah of Israel and applied himself in a remarkable manner to carrying out the predictions as he understood them. The Church was built on his persuasion that the messianic prophecies must be fulfilled. He was truly Jewish in being both visionary and pragmatist. His attitude towards the Messianic Hope of his time was not so unlike that of Theodor Herzl in calling for the return to Zion nearly nineteen centuries later. Jesus could have used Herzl's famous words in *The Jewish State*, 'If you will it, it is no dream.' We have seen how far he was prepared to go to compel events to answer to the predictions.

Jesus may not have overlooked that he might taste of death in spite of the measures he had secretly taken for his survival. He could have interpreted Isaiah liii in this sense: 'He made his grave with the wicked, and with the rich in his deaths [plural].' Two deaths, two burials were thus foreshadowed. He would die as it were on the cross, and yet again after the cross. But whatever would happen his faith assured him that in some way God would raise him up and receive him until his coming in glory with the clouds of heaven. Jesus knew, however, that his disciples would be in anguish, not readily crediting the prophecies. There can be no clear proof, but we are entitled to imagine him as we have done regaining consciousness after he was taken from the tomb, and using these precious minutes to beg his friends to deliver a message to his disciples. He would repeat what was so much a part of him, the Scriptures relating to his suffering and revival. 'Tell them these things,' he may have urged. 'They must believe. Tell them that when I have risen I will meet them in Galilee as I said, and afterwards enter into glory.' With this possibility in mind we have to look closely at our documents for what illumination they afford.

Very early on Sunday morning the women associates of Jesus led by Mary of Magdala set out for the tomb. Suddenly it occurred to them that they might have difficulty in rolling the stone from the entrance; but they continued on their way. When they arrived they were astounded and alarmed to find that the stone had already been moved. Had grave robbers been at work? Cases were known of entry being forced to obtain corpses or parts of them for magical or medicinal purposes. It was a capital crime to tamper with tombs and interfere with the bodies of the dead. An imperial decree found at Nazareth in 1870, which may date from the reign of the Emperor Claudius (A.D. 41–54), witnesses to this. Timidly the women approached and looked into the cave. What they saw alarmed them still more. There was a strange man there.

According to Mark's Gospel the man who was seen had been a young man in a white robe who had told the women that Jesus had risen, and that they were to inform Peter and the others that he would see them in Galilee as arranged. This is how the story came to be related afterwards. But it impresses as true that the women did find someone in the tomb, who could have been the gardener or the other unknown who had participated in the earlier events and perhaps was the man who administered the drugged drink to Jesus on the cross. If he spoke to the women, which is quite likely, they were in no state to take in what he said. All that registered at the time was that the body of Jesus was gone and that a strange man was there. Trembling and unnerved they fled, and said nothing to anyone because they were afraid. Here the text of Mark breaks off.

The story progressed in the light of belief in the resurrection of Jesus. The young man became an angel, and then two angels. The words he had used could be recalled. The Fourth Gospel may be nearest the truth in making only Mary of Magdala go to Peter and the Beloved Disciple to break the dire news on behalf of the other women. There is no word here of any message from a risen Jesus to deliver. She only blurts out, 'They've taken away the Master from the tomb, and we don't know where they have laid him.' Who 'they' are is not specified.

The news was a terrible shock and completely mystifying. At once confirmation was sought. Surely there must be some mistake! The two disciples ran to the tomb, and John the priest being much younger outdistanced Peter and got there first. As a priest he would not enter the tomb until he knew there was no corpse there to make him ritually unclean. He only looked in and saw the grave clothes lying. Peter was not concerned about defilement, and went straight in. It was true. The body was gone and only the wrappings were there neatly folded. John then entered, and suddenly it came to him that Jesus had risen. Until then, says this Gospel, it had not been apprehended that the Scriptures had foretold the resurrection. Puzzled and wondering the two returned to John's house.

This was the beginning, the empty tomb and a flash of inspiration on the part of the Beloved Disciple. But there was no confirmatory evidence.

Mary, it would appear, had followed the disciples to the tomb, and when they left she remained behind weeping. Through her tears she perceived a man standing by the tomb, whom she took to be the gardener, and said to him, 'Sir, if you have moved him, tell me where you have put him and I will take him away.' The man, according to the Fourth Gospel, then reveals himself to her as Jesus, and tells her not to catch hold of him. He gives her much the same message as it came to be reported the young man in the tomb had given the women, as recorded by Mark, to which the Fourth Gospel makes no reference.

The unknown man is the key figure so far, the most important clue we have. He could, as we have conjectured, have been the man who gave the potion to Jesus at the cross, who had assisted in conveying the body to the tomb and the next night had helped to move Jesus, and when he was found to have died to have taken part in burying him. The women had seen him dimly inside the tomb when they arrived early on Sunday morning. When they fled he was still in the vicinity, and Mary of Magdala suddenly saw him when she looked up through her tears. Her question to him had hit the nail on the head, because he had in fact been concerned in removing Jesus, and he may defensively have answered, 'Keep away from me,' or, 'Leave me alone.' But why should he have lingered at the tomb to be seen on these two occasions? It may well be that he had indeed been trying to give a message which Jesus, as we have suggested, in a brief period of consciousness, had instructed him to deliver to his disciples. He may have been too frightened to reveal himself when Peter and John came to the tomb, not knowing who they were at the time, and being fully aware he had committed a crime in taking away the body of Jesus. Because of the distraught state of the women he had encountered he could not be sure even now that his message had registered.

Clearly Mary did not recognise the man she saw as Jesus. But just finding him suddenly beside her caused her in her half-crazed condition to identify him as Jesus, who had spoken to her and then disappeared. We know that she was unbalanced, since Jesus had had to cast out of her seven demons. She was deeply devoted to him, passionately perhaps, and may have nurtured the delusion that he was in love with her. In her great grief it would be consistent with that delusion that he should appear to her to console her and call her endearingly by name.

Mary rushed back to the disciples with her tale of having seen the Master. So another ingredient was added to the story. There had been the empty tomb, the man seen by the women who was converted into an angel, the conviction of the Beloved Disciple, and now the man who had spoken to Mary of Magdala had become an appearance of Jesus himself. From this moment incredulity began to struggle with dawning faith. Simon and John could confirm that they had found the body of Jesus gone, though the linen wrappings were still in the tomb. They confessed, however, that they had not themselves seen Jesus.[6]

The mood was now one of suppressed excitement. Grave doubt was there and sorrow, but also a preparedness for anything to happen however extraordinary. If Jesus was alive who could tell how or when he would appear, what he would look like? On the testimony of Jesus himself, had not Elijah been revealed in the guise of John the Baptist? They were highly superstitious countrymen, to whom the doctrine of the transmigration of souls was not alien.

We move to the story of the two disciples on the road to Emmaus narrated only by Luke. This author appears to have written his Gospel in Greece at the beginning of the second century and Robert Graves has shown that certain ingredients in the story are strongly reminiscent of the first chapter of *The Golden Ass* by Lucius Apuleius, published at this time.[7] This does not mean that the story was a complete invention, but that Luke used the work of Lucius as a literary aid as he did various passages from Josephus.

The essence of the story is that the disciples, one of whom was Cleophas, according to tradition an uncle of Jesus,[8] were approached by a stranger as they talked sadly about the events of the past days. They told him about the hopes of Jesus which had been entertained, that he would prove to be the Messiah, and the stranger encouraged them by quoting some of the messianic predictions. They responded eagerly by requesting him to sup with them and tell them more. He agreed, and afterwards took his leave. In Luke's text he vanishes. Cheered by the stranger's discourse, the disciples were soon telling each other that the man must have been Jesus all the time. 'Did not our heart burn within us, while he talked with us by the way, and while he opened to us the Scriptures?'

According to Josephus the village of Emmaus was about four miles north-west of Jerusalem. The tomb in which Jesus was laid was also north-west of the city. The disciples may have come from the tomb, which in view of the reports they had wished to see for themselves. The stranger who caught up with them could have been the man at the tomb, trying to fulfil the behest of Jesus. He could not be sure that the distracted women he had met so far had grasped and passed on the message he had been pressed by Jesus to deliver to the disciples. Now he tried again.

This of course is only a theory which would fit the recorded circumstances. We do not know just how much of the story is authentic. Again an important ingredient is the failure to identify Jesus, this time by his own relations. The man on the road to Emmaus clearly was not Jesus.

According to Luke the two told their story when they returned to Jerusalem, to be greeted by a statement of an 'appearance' to Simon Peter. In this atmosphere there is reported to have occurred the 'appearance' to the apostles in the Judean tradition followed by Luke and John. This is at variance with the Galilean tradition followed by Matthew, which is echoed in the appended final chapter of John. In the Judean tradition Jesus positively identifies himself to the apostles in Jerusalem, exhibiting his wounds and eating food. We may regard the information as in the highest degree questionable in view of the rival record in Matthew, which suggests that the apostles did not see Jesus in Jerusalem and after the Passover returned to Galilee still unconvinced trusting that Jesus if he was alive would manifest himself to them at the place he had appointed. If the Judean version was true the apostles by this time should have been absolutely certain that Jesus had risen. This version gives the impression of being a Jerusalemite response to the Galilean story. In both there is an eating by Jesus of broiled fish.

We are then left with consideration of the 'appearances' in Galilee. The fullest version is in the Fourth Gospel, but we need only concern ourselves with the basic elements. Peter decides to go fishing, and six other disciples accompany him. They have no luck all night. Looking towards the shore in the early morning they see a man standing there who hails them and inquires if they have anything to eat. They reply that they have nothing as yet; but just then they obtain a substantial catch. The success is linked with the man on the shore. The Beloved Disciple, first to believe that Jesus had risen,[9] exclaims, 'It is the Master!' This is good enough for Peter, and he jumps overboard and makes for where the man is. The man was thus assumed to be Jesus, but John says, 'The disciples did not know it was Jesus.' When they came to land after beaching the boat they found fish cooking on a fire, and the stranger invited them to eat with him. 'None of the disciples dare ask him, "Who are you?" knowing it was the Master.' But this was just what they did not know. The essence of the matter is that the apostles who knew Jesus so well entirely failed to recognise him in the man they saw. They were only persuaded by the belief of the Beloved Disciple. The stranger here was as obviously unidentifiable as Jesus as had been the man whom Mary met at the tomb, and the man on the road to Emmaus. It would seem to be the same with the man on the mountain in Galilee referred to by Matthew. When the disciples saw him they prostrated themselves before him, 'but some doubted'.[10]

A likely explanation of the circumstances is that all along, beginning with the young man first seen at the tomb by the women, one and the same man was being seen, and he was not Jesus. This man was bent on fulfilling what was perhaps a promise to Jesus when he lay dying after his removal from the tomb on Saturday night, that he would faithfully deliver to Peter and the other disciples a message that the Messiah had risen in accordance with the prophecies, and that they would see him at the place he had told them about in Galilee. The man, who had shown his quality at the cross, did his best. He gave the message to the women and to Mary of Magdala, and spoke also to the disciples who had visited the tomb and were taking the road to Emmaus. But he could not be satisfied. He had not seen Peter and the other ten and did not know where to find them. When he did get news of them, it was that they had gone back to Galilee. The man followed: he may have been told by Jesus where the rendezvous was to be. Finally he was able to discharge his obligation.

Naturally it cannot be said that this is the solution of the puzzle. The men may not have been in every case the same. There is room for other theories, such as that the man concerned, if there was but one, was a medium, and that Jesus, risen from the dead into the After Life in the Spiritualist sense, spoke through him in his own voice, which enabled his presence to be recognised. Too little is told, and that little quickly became too legendary, and too contradictory, for any assured conclusion.

The view taken here does seem to fit the requirements, and is in keeping with what has been disclosed of the Passover Plot. The planning of Jesus for his expected recovery created the mystery of the empty tomb. Without that plan it is difficult to find a valid reason why his body should have been removed from its first resting place, and without the empty tomb belief in his resurrection would probably not have registered. It was this material fact, which seemed to confirm the faith Jesus had expressed that he would rise again in accordance with the Scriptures, which prompted the beginnings of conviction. It was reinforced by the appearance on the scene of a messenger, which is what angel means, whom Jesus before he died had instructed to communicate the faith which was his to the end to his sorrowing followers. It was an old Jewish saying, 'A man's messenger is as himself.' New-born hope and wish fulfilment caused the messenger to be identified with the Master.

There was no deliberate untruth in the witness of the followers of Jesus to his resurrection. On the evidence they had the conclusion they reached seemed inescapable. There was nothing to tell them what had become of his body. They could not know that the Prophet like Moses had been finally laid to rest like Moses himself in an unknown grave.

Neither had there been any fraud on the part of Jesus himself. He had schemed in faith for his physical recovery, and what he expected had been frustrated by circumstances quite beyond his control. Yet when he sank into sleep his faith was unimpaired, and by an extraordinary series of contributory events, partly resulting from his own planning, it proved to have been justified. In a manner he had not foreseen resurrection had come to him. And surely this was for the best, since there would have been no future for a Messiah who returned temporarily to this troubled world possibly crippled in mind and body.

By his planning beyond the cross and the tomb, by his implicit confidence in the coming of the Kingdom of God over which he was deputed to reign, Jesus had won through to victory. The messianic programme was saved from the grave of all dead hopes to become a guiding light and inspiration to men. Wherever mankind strives to bring in the rule of justice, righteousness and peace, there the deathless presence of Jesus the Messiah is with them. Wherever a people of God is found labouring in the cause of human brotherhood, love and compassion, there the King of the Jews is enthroned. No other will ever come to be what he was and do what he did. The special conditions which produced him at a peculiar and pregnant moment in history are never likely to occur again. But doubtless there will be other moments having their own strange features, and other men through whom the vision will speak at an appointed time. Meanwhile we have not exhausted the potentialities of the vision of Jesus.

'When I am raised up,' Jesus is reported to have said, 'I will go before you into Galilee.' Let those who wish to partake of the faith and strength of purpose of this amazing man seek for him there in the land he loved, among its hills and beside its living waters.

NOTES AND REFERENCES

1. Mt. xxviii. 15.

2. *The Burial of Jesus* by Prof. J. Spencer Kennard, Jr. (*Journal of Biblical Literature*, vol. lxxiv, 1955).

3. Tertullian, *De Spectaculis*, xxx. An echo of this story is found in the ninth century in the *Epistola contra Judaeos* of Amulo, Archbishop of Lyons, who quotes a Jewish tradition that Jesus when taken from the cross was put into a tomb 'in a certain garden full of cabbages' (*caulibus pleno*).

4. *The Book of the Resurrection*, translated by E. A. Wallis Budge from Oriental Manuscripts No. 6804 in the British Museum.

5. Jn. xx. 15.

6. Lk. xxiv. 24; Jn. xx. 2–10.

7. In the *Golden Ass*, 'a traveller overtakes two countrymen earnestly dis-cussing a local miracle, becomes engrossed in their talk, and continues with them until they reach their goal. Later, one of the countrymen says, "You must surely

be very much of a stranger here, if you are ignorant . . ." of a further wonder'
(*The Nazarene Gospel Restored*, p. 763).

8. Cleophas was a brother of Joseph the father of Jesus. The other disciple
may have been his son Simeon, Jesus' first cousin, who was chosen to become
leader of the Nazoreans after the death of Jacob (James) the brother of Jesus.

9. Jn. xx. 8.

10. Mt. xxviii. 16–17.

14

Faith and Deeds

WHAT has emerged most strongly from the approach to Jesus
as a real person, rather than as the theological figure of Christian
faith variously represented in the Gospels, is his dynamic character. This dynamism was so much in evidence and exerted such a
powerful influence on those who came in contact with him that
no version of his career, whatever its doctrinal intentions, could
fail to exhibit it. The positiveness and purposefulness of Jesus
was such a feature of his personality that it was ineradicable in
the memory of his first followers, stamping itself indelibly on
Christian tradition. It was this spirit of his communicating itself
in retrospect to the first believers which welded them into an
active, energetic and bold-speaking community. Nothing perhaps
acquaints us more surely with the Jesus of history than the
exuberant overspill of the kind of man he was into the circumstances and experience of the early Church. Here we may see the
true significance of Pentecost.

> For he saw ere his eye was darkened
>   The sheaves of the harvest-bringing,
> And heard while his ear yet harkened
>   The voice of the reapers singing.
>
> Ah, well! the world is discreet;
>   There are plenty to pause and wait;
> But here was a man who set his feet
>   Some time in advance of fate.

In the messianic symbolism of a source common to Matthew and Luke, when Jesus died the veil of the Temple was rent from top to bottom. So we, to reach the real Jesus, have to rend in two the embroidered silken curtain of Christian theology.[1] The man we then discover, as we have tried to show, is indeed a man of faith, but not of a passive quiescent faith. He is a man who put his intense convictions to the greatest test of all, the test of actions.

When Jesus believed he was the Messiah of Israel it meant for him doing the deeds of the Messiah as the Prophets had fore-shadowed, setting the supreme example of right conduct in rela-tion to God and Man, in defiance of the shibboleths of orthodox religion and the enactments of a powerful established government. Nothing could daunt him, neither the cares of life nor the pros-pect of a traitor's death. He used the resources of his fertile mind to outgeneral and outwit his opponents, to compel their self-interested schemes to comply with his world-interested purposes. He laid his plans and he carried them out: he both guided and guarded the words of his mouth to achieve his aims. The law of lovingkindness was on his tongue; but also the biting speech that revealed and dissolved hypocrisy. He was not haughty; but neither was he humble. He came as the Servant, but with the dignity of a master, not the obsequiousness of a slave.

The ruling passion of his life was the coming of the Kingdom of God. For him it had its Hebrew meaning, the time when war and hatred would be banished, and 'the earth shall be full of the knowledge of the Lord, as the waters cover the sea'.[2] He told the Pharisees that the Kingdom of God would not come by standing idle and watching for signs. The Kingdom of God was right beside them, under their noses, ready to appear whenever they were willing to comply with the conditions which would inaugurate it. Be alive, be alert, Jesus insisted. The goal will not be reached by a sleeping partnership with God.

Despite all the legends, all the developments of the image of him, all the changes of emphasis, the vividness of Jesus comes over to us in the Gospels, the voice of his messianic authority, the ardour of his enterprise, the utter sincerity of the man in all his dealings. The traditions, hazy in many things, remain infected and impregnated with his glowing, objective and dynamic personality. The historical Jesus has always been there for the finding, not faultless, not inerrant, not divine, but magnificently human.

Of such a man surprising miracles could be told, as of other sages and heroes, and to minds steeped in this kind of adoration they would seem only natural. Such a man could even be worshipped by pagan hearts, as a god, as the son and embodiment of the Highest God. The time when such excessive devotion was an appropriate tribute has not passed yet, since it is maintained by a functioning and erudite body of religious teachers wedded to an old inheritance. The fate and eternal welfare of the individual, a matter of deep personal concern to many, has been made to depend on acceptance of a creed claimed to be the expression of an unalterable and divinely authorised truth.

But more and more people are now achieving emancipation from such ancient thralldom, and there is a trend towards the opposite extreme which seems, but is not necessarily, more rational than what is being discarded. Jesus the Jew believed that vision and action, faith and deeds, are inseparable if man is to evolve and progress. Both are equally needed, inspiration aiding aspiration, and performance taking its incentive from creative dreams. We ignore at our peril intimations that there are ways which are not our ways, and thoughts more comprehensive than our thoughts.

The Messianic Hope which Jesus espoused and in a unique manner personified has not yet exhibited its full potentialities, and so he is still the leader, worthy to be followed, not of a lost cause, but of one ever demanding fuller realisation. He himself saw to it that he would not be forgotten, that he would be continually with us pestering and challenging us. In spite of everything done to stop him in his own time and since, not only by his enemies but by his professed champions, he has continued to come through.

So let no one leave this presentation of Jesus with the notion that it is destructive of faith, or that it reveals Jesus as a deluded fanatic. If any such impression has been formed it is very wide of the mark. What this book has aimed to reveal is that he was a man of so much faith that he dared to translate an age-old and somewhat nebulous imagination into a factual down-to-earth reality. It was useless for the Jews, or any others for that matter, to cherish a noble ideal if they were going to do nothing concrete about it, if they were not going to sweat and strive to put it into effect. Jesus prayed and then he got to work. So many do the first but not the second. They believe it to be enough to give out their fine feelings and thoughts, expecting others to perform the drudgery. This attitude is what Jesus castigated so unmercifully in his own day.

The true spirit of Jesus is manifested in the Epistle of James in the New Testament.

'Of what avail is it, brothers, for someone to say he has faith, when he has no deeds to show for it? Can faith save him? If a brother and sister are destitute, lacking even daily food, and one of you says to them, "Go in peace. Mind you keep warm and take enough nourishment," but you give them no physical necessities for the purpose, what avails it? So with faith. Unless deeds spring from it it is dead in isolation. One may put it this way. You have faith, you say, while I have deeds. Show me your faith independent of deeds, and I will show you my faith by my deeds. You believe there is one God, you say. It is well that you do believe it. But so do the demons, and they shudder. Can you not realise, you dunce, that faith without deeds is unproductive? . . . For as the body without the spirit is dead, so is faith without deeds.'[3]

Much is made of the love and compassion of Jesus, and rightly, but we see these qualities everywhere united with commitment, with doing good rather than being good. He refused to allow himself to be called good. It is said of a seemingly praiseworthy young man who had never put a foot wrong that Jesus looking upon him loved him, and the measure of his love was to tell him promptly to sell all his possessions and distribute them to the poor. Again the emphasis is on deeds as the proof of faith and love.

Because Jesus is not worshipped he is not thereby inevitably played down or diminished in effectiveness. Rather should we be strengthened and encouraged because he is bone of our bone and flesh of our flesh and not God incarnate. The mind that was in the Messiah can therefore also be in us, stimulating us to accomplish what those of more careful and nicely balanced disposition declare to be impossible. Thus the victory for which Jesus relentlessly schemed and strove will be won at last. There will be peace throughout the earth.

The Iron Chancellor Bismarck, with reluctant admiration, once said of Disraeli, another famous schemer, 'The old Jew, there is the man!' Seen in the messianic light of the Passover Plot we can with more wholehearted approbation say of Jesus, 'The young Jew, there was the Man!'

NOTES AND REFERENCES

1. Professor Hugh Anderson in his book *Jesus and Christian Origins* has said of the dialectical theologians that they 'barred the door against any direct knowledge of the human Jesus, acquired by scientific historical methods, as an element in the faith'.

2. Isa. xi. 9.

3. Jas. ii. 14–26 (translated by Hugh Schonfield, *The Authentic New Testament*).

PART TWO

The Sources and Growth of the Legend

I

Messianism and the
Development of Christianity

WITH the New Testament in our hands it may be surprising to
say that we know comparatively little about the beginnings of
Christianity. It does not register with most Christians that our information is scanty, because they are primarily concerned with the
New Testament as a revelation of what is necessary for 'salvation'
and assume that it incorporates everything of consequence.

Yet it is easy enough to see how little we are told. Although
the public life of Jesus was a brief one it must have been filled
with incidents which have not been reported. The Gospel of John
says as much.[1] And if the events of a year or two are represented so
sketchily in the Gospels, how much worse is it with the early
history of the immediate followers of Jesus occupying the thirty
years from A.D. 36 to 66! If we deduct from the Acts of the Apostles the space devoted to constructed speeches, and add what can
be gleaned from the letters of Paul, we have even less material
regarding developments in Palestine during these three vital
decades than is afforded about Jesus by the shortest of the Gospels.

The single New Testament writer who concerns himself with
the experiences of the Jewish believers in Jesus, the Nazoreans
(Nazarenes), furnishes us with little more than an idealised preface
to the career of Paul and the evangelisation of the Gentiles. It is
evident that Jacob (James), the brother of Jesus, was a figure of
outstanding significance; but we learn hardly anything about

him from the New Testament, and have to turn elsewhere for
further enlightenment.

This is a very serious matter for the student of Christian
Origins, since to a large extent the truth about Jesus is not
certified to us by any documents coming directly from those
Judean and Galilean communities which flourished in the forma-
tive period of the Nazorean Church. From that period there is
not extant a single scrap of a Hebrew or Aramaic text which
speaks of Jesus or tells us about the beliefs and experiences of his
Jewish followers. We have nothing in primitive Christian material
corresponding to the Dead Sea Scrolls. Consequently to obtain
what knowledge we can we have not only to subject the New
Testament records to the most drastic analysis: we have to study
Jewish history and traditions, the writings of the Church Fathers
and early ecclesiastical historians, and various relics of lost books
which through one or another ancient authority have been
preserved.

By far the most consequential factor which has deprived us of
access to the 'inside story' of Jesus and his early Jewish adherents
is the Jewish struggle with Rome, particularly the first revolt
which came to boiling point in A.D. 66, but also the second revolt
which broke out in A.D. 132.

Jewish resistance to the domination of heathen Rome had
been in evidence long before the public ministry of Jesus, and
through the bad government and oppressive measures of the
Roman procurators after the untimely death of the Jewish king
Agrippa I in A.D. 44 it became so intensified that war was inevitable. In this time and atmosphere Christian beginnings are set,
and no account of them is of great worth which does not recognise the effect of the situation on the minds of loyal Jews who
adhered to Jesus as their Messiah.[2]

It was agreed by the pious in Israel that Rome was the arch-
enemy of God and his people.[3] It was identified with the Fourth
Kingdom, the worst of all aggressors of the prophecy of Daniel
vii. Only the advent of the Messiah could destroy its power, as
one of the later apocalyptic writers declares:

'A Fourth Kingdom will arise, whose power will be harsh and evil far beyond those which were before it . . . and it will hold fast the times, and will exalt itself more than the cedars of Lebanon . . . And it will come to pass when the times of his consummation that he should fall has approached, then the principate of my Messiah will be revealed . . . and when it is revealed it will root out the multitude of his host.'[4]

The messianic conviction behind the revolt is stressed by the Jewish historian Josephus writing under the patronage of the Roman victors:

'What more than all else incited them [the Jews] to the war was an ambiguous oracle, likewise found in their sacred scriptures, to the effect that at that time one from their country would become ruler of the world. This they understood to mean someone of their own race, and many of their wise men went astray in their interpretation of it. The oracle, however, in reality signified the sovereignty of Vespasian, who was proclaimed emperor on Jewish soil.'[5]

With messianic fervour inspiring it, the struggle with the far superior Roman forces was a terrible one, in which terrorism, fanaticism and burning patriotism all played a part. The tragic climax was reached with the destruction of Jerusalem and the Temple in A.D. 70. As the writer has stated in an earlier work:

'The loss of life in the war was appalling. Josephus estimated that one million one hundred thousand perished in the siege of Jerusalem alone. Before this many thousands had died or been killed in Jerusalem and in other parts of the country. The total of captives taken throughout the war numbered only ninety-seven thousand. Of those who survived the siege, the combatants, the aged and feeble were killed. Eleven thousand prisoners died of starvation before their fate could be determined, and the tale of death was to continue to mount with those sent to the mines, or dispatched to the various provinces to be killed in the theatres by the sword or torn limb from limb by wild beasts.'[6]

The casualties at Jerusalem were so heavy because the population of the city was swollen with refugees who had sought safety there, and with pilgrims come to worship in the Temple, who were caught by the Roman encirclement.

The followers of Jesus, the Nazoreans, had had their head-quarters at Jerusalem. There James, the brother of Jesus, had pre-sided over their affairs until his judicial murder c. A.D. 62, reported by Josephus and others.[7] When the war threatened the capital the Nazorean community in obedience to a revelation as tradition declares,[8] abandoned the city and fled across the Jordan. We do not know how far this story is correct; but it appears that some of the leaders escaped. In any case they were only a fraction of the Nazoreans of Palestine, who were numerous in other parts of the country, and we may believe that not a few took refuge in Jeru-salem and perished there. Their fate would probably have been the same if they stayed in their own homes, as we can see from what Josephus reports regarding places they inhabited such as Caesarea, Lydda and Joppa, mentioned in the Acts, and of course Galilee down to the lakeside.

At the beginning of the revolt the Gentiles of Caesarea 'massa-cred the Jews who resided in their city; within one hour more than twenty thousand were slaughtered, and Caesarea was com-pletely emptied of Jews, for the fugitives were arrested by order of Florus and conducted in chains to the dockyards'. Reaching Lydda, Gallus found the town deserted, because the inhabitants had gone to Jerusalem, but fifty persons discovered were killed and the town burnt.[9]

Galilee, where Jesus had lived and taught and which was the home of the Jewish resistance movement, suffered particularly. 'The Romans never ceased, night or day, to devastate the plains and to pillage the property of the country-folk, invariably killing all capable of bearing arms and reducing the inefficient to servi-tude. Galilee from end to end became a scene of fire and blood; from no misery, no calamity was it exempt.' Later in the war there was heavy slaughter along the shore of the Sea of Galilee. 'One could see the whole lake red with blood and covered with corpses, for not a man escaped. During the following days the district reeked with a dreadful stench and presented a spectacle equally horrible. The beaches were strewn with wrecks and swollen carcases.'[10]

In these circumstances we may fairly hold that a high percentage of the Nazoreans of Palestine perished in the war. Mortality among the elderly and infirm was specially heavy. So if Jesus was crucified under Pontius Pilate, and therefore before A.D. 37, very few who had seen and heard him can have been alive forty years later. The war created a gap only tenuously bridgeable in early Christian history. As Dr. Brandon has expressed it,[11] Christianity went into a tunnel, and when it emerged again a decade or more later much had changed.

There is something further to be said about the survivors of the war. Early rabbinical literature reveals an inevitable consequence of the conflict, and of the troubled period preceding it, which has to be taken fully into account. Many, especially of the older generation, were gravely impaired in health and memory. People whose testimony was of importance about past events and practices made contradictory statements, got dates mixed and persons and events confused. It was very natural, but most unfortunate. The manner in which the Sanhedrin had functioned and the services of the Temple had been conducted had partly to be reconstructed on idealised lines, which can be employed by the historian only with considerable caution, a caution which some scholarly writers on the life of Jesus have failed to exercise. It is probable that some of the problems in the Gospels are attributable to the same causes, which makes it most unwise to emphasise the value of oral tradition.

In the study of the Gospels—all written after the war—it is customary to allow for the attitudes and intentions of the authors and for their editorial work in the employment and arrangement of the sources available to them. But it should also be expected that there would be different versions of the same story, comparable sayings linked with different times and events, on the ground that post-war testimony could not fail to be governed by uncertainties of memory. For the same reason, quite apart from changes in the narrative or in the words of Jesus made deliberately in view of altered conditions, we should expect passages in the Gospels to be coloured by aspects of Jewish affairs later than the time of Jesus and affecting the records by unintentional anachronism.

We shall be considering the composition of the Gospels in later chapters, when it will be of consequence to ascertain as far as possible how much about Jesus, and in what form, had gone out of Palestine before the war, and what additional material from Nazorean circles became available to Christians subsequently. What we have clarified so far is that the Jewish revolt had a messianic impetus, and that the effects of the war were profound for nascent Christianity, heavily diminishing what could be known about Jesus, depriving the Church—now become predominantly Gentile—of authoritative guidance in matters of faith, and opening the door for the increasing intrusion of alien beliefs.

But the pregnant years before the war are of the greatest import, since if they were characterised by strong Jewish messianism it is certified to us that the beginnings of Christianity were part and parcel of it. The New Testament leaves us in no doubt that the early followers of Jesus were Jews, and that they adhered to him from the conviction that he was the expected Messiah. As late as John's Gospel this is clearly stated, and when those who had been nearest to Jesus established a community in Jerusalem it was as the Messiah, the Son of David, that Jesus was proclaimed.[12] This was the sensational message to be carried far and wide. In the highly explosive circumstances in Palestine at the time, with the fervency of popular longing for the coming of the Messiah, no other message could have produced such eager response, excited and bitter controversy, and governmental hostility. The opposition did not come from the Jewish masses,[13] but from those in the seat of authority responsible to Rome. In Palestine Christianity as a new religion did not exist. The Nazoreans were zealous for the Law of Moses.

Quite soon the message was carried beyond Palestine and reached Greek-speaking people on the fringe of Judaism. Those who accepted it at Antioch in Syria were dubbed Christians. The name derives from *Christos* (Christ), the Greek translation of the Hebrew title Messiah, meaning the anointed one. We may not evade, or seek to modify, this basic fact, that the terms Christ and Christian testify that the Church was founded on messianic convictions, on belief that Jesus was the Messiah.

At the time that Christianity got going in other lands and began to attract non-Jews fresh from polytheism messianic agitation was rife in the Roman Empire. Jewish Zealots from Palestine, acting as apostles (envoys), were seeking to enlist support for their anti-Roman activities among the Jews of the Diaspora. The circumstances were repeated before the second Jewish revolt in the reign of Hadrian. These emissaries did not get much response, however, from the cities of the west, because the Jews there were very sensible of the privileges they enjoyed under Roman rule, and had no desire to see them withdrawn, leaving them at the mercy of hostile Greeks, if it should be credited that they were parties to a treasonable conspiracy. The Roman authorities were well aware of what was going on, and they were particularly concerned about Zealot propaganda in key cities where there was a large Jewish population, such as Alexandria and Rome itself. The Emperor Claudius (A.D. 41–54) actually wrote to the Jews of Alexandria warning them not to entertain itinerant Jews from the province of Syria (of which Judea was a part) if they did not wish to be treated as abettors of 'a pest which threatens the whole world (i.e. the Roman Empire)'.[14] He ordered the expulsion of foreign Jews from Rome 'who were continually making disturbances at the instigation of Chrestus (i.e. engaging in messianic agitation)'.[15]

The late Acts of the Apostles, a product of the reign of the more tolerant Emperor Trajan, in its apologetic effort to placate the Romans, does not altogether conceal the truth, but does try to disguise it in claiming that the Christian message was misrepresented by its Jewish traducers. In the light of the actual conditions we can see, however, that the Jews in the Greek cities attacked Paul and his colleagues in their missionary journeys because they believed them to be Zealot agitators, since they were proclaiming the Messiah, and in self-protection took action against them. At Thessalonica the local Jews informed the magistrates that 'these subverters of the Empire have now reached here . . . and they are all actively opposed to the Imperial decrees, saying there is another Emperor, one Jesus'.[16]

Paul was eventually indicted at Caesarea before the Roman Governor Felix as 'a plague-carrier, a fomentor of revolt among all the Jews of the Empire, a ringleader of the Nazorean party'.[17] One of the planks in Paul's platform had been *anastasis Christou* (the resurrection of Christ), which could equally be understood as 'Messianic uprising'. It was known that he had been establishing messianic groups in many places which might easily become, if indeed some of them were not, cells of the conspiracy, and also that he had been collecting funds to take to Jerusalem for the Nazoreans of Judea, which could be thought to be for the purchase of weapons.[18]

The Christian message obtained the most recruits among the slaves and underprivileged. Many of them, as we find in Paul's letters, were not only of low morality, but factious, restless and disaffected. Not a few must have been antagonistic to the Roman regime and only too willing to take part in subversive activities. Otherwise it would hardly have been needed to impress upon them to behave peacefully and correctly, pay the Roman imposts and be submissive, honour and pray for the emperor and his representatives.[19] The Romans were not fools, and must have had some justification for regarding Christianity as a dangerous and hostile superstition.[20] It is significant that after the suppression of the first Jewish revolt the Romans did not outlaw Judaism, though they tried to make it certain that non-Jews professing this faith were genuine converts; but they did outlaw Christianity. They had long been familiar with the Jewish religion and knew that militant messianism was not common to all Jews. Christianity on the other hand, stemming from a Jewish sect, was wholly messianic and committed to propaganda on behalf of an asserted king and world ruler called Jesus. It could and did produce a violent anti-Roman document in the Book of Revelation. If Christians, who were not Jews, refused to burn incense before Caesar's image, it was to be put down not to religious scruples but to treasonable opinions.

Strange as it may appear to those who think of the deity of Jesus in a religious sense, it was the messianic character of Christianity which contributed directly to his deification among believers from the Gentiles. Messianism represented the conviction that the existing world order would presently be overthrown. The empire ruled by Caesar and his legions would pass away, and in its place there would be the Kingdom of God governed by the Messiah and his people. Christianity identified the Messiah with Jesus. There was 'another king', another emperor, to whom allegiance was transferred.

The message about Jesus found a lodging among peoples who believed in the commerce of gods with mortals and were accustomed to the deification of rulers and other outstanding personalities. The Acts testifies to this. When a cripple was cured at Lystra during the mission of Paul and Barnabas, the populace cried, 'The gods are come down to us in the likeness of men,' and hailed Barnabas as Zeus and Paul as Hermes. The Greeks of Caesarea, acclaiming the speech of King Agrippa when he appeared in state, shouted, 'It is the voice of a god, not of a man.'

The whole Roman Empire was at this time knit by an Imperial cult, which conjoined the worship of Rome and the emperor. The cult had developed in the reign of Augustus, who for reasons of State policy accepted deification and authorised the building of temples in which he was worshipped. He was formally decreed Son of God (*Divi Filius*) by the Senate. A typical inscription, dated 7 B.C., hails him as 'Caesar, who reigns over the seas and continents, Jupiter, who holds from Jupiter his father the title of Liberator, Master of Europe and Asia, Star of all Greece, who lifts himself up with the glory of great Jupiter, Saviour'.

Gaius Caligula (A.D. 37–41) became obsessed with the notion of his deity, and his sycophantic officials played up to him. Suetonius reports that Lucius Vitellius, legate of Syria, returning to Rome at the end of his term of office, adored the emperor by prostrating himself on the ground and would only appear before him with head veiled. The same authority tells how Gaius 'began to arrogate to himself a divine majesty. He ordered all the images of the gods, which were famous either for their beauty, or the veneration paid to them, among which was that of Zeus Olympius, to be brought from Greece, that he might take their heads off and substitute his own . . . He also instituted a temple and priests, with choice victims, in honour of his divinity. In his temple stood a statue of gold, the exact image of himself . . . The most opulent persons in the city offered themselves as candidates for the honour of being his priests, and purchased it successively at an immense price.'[21]

A later emperor, Domitian (A.D. 81–96), insisted that his governors commence their letters to him, 'Our Lord and our God commands.' It became a rule, says Suetonius, 'that no one should style him otherwise in writing or speaking'.[22]

Among Gentile believers in Jesus as the true emperor it was not possible to hold him to be inferior in dignity to Caesar. So we find in the Gospels the term Son of God (the Imperial *Divi Filius*) conjoined with the Jewish royal title of Messiah.[23] The late Gospel of John, composed not long after the reign of Domitian, even borrows the words of address which that emperor demanded, and makes Thomas address Jesus as 'My Lord and my God'.[24]

The Christians would have had some additional justification for holding Jesus to be divine if in fact they had heard him described as Son of God in a purely messianic sense by the Nazorean preachers. The term had been applied to the great king who was the immediate son of David,[25] and could therefore be appropriated for the Messiah. Not only so; for the Messiah was regarded by the Nazoreans as the representative Israelite, and Israel was called the Son of God, the Firstborn, the Only-begotten, and Dearly Beloved One.[26]

Such Jewish thinking, however, obviously did not imply the deity of the Messiah. Even the Hellenised Paul in his mystical philosophy never went as far as speaking of Christ as God, though his doctrine of the Messiah as the pre-eminent expression of God is so delicately poised in its terminology that it could be misunderstood by those unacquainted with its peculiar esoteric Jewish background of thought connected with the Archetypal Man.[27] But in the milieu of Gentile Christianity, especially in conjunction with Pauline usage of the language of Plato and the Mystery cults, not only was there no deep-seated objection to paying divine honours to Jesus, there was the strongest natural disposition to do so. In due course in some Christian circles under gnostic influences the result was a movement towards dualism, and monotheism was only saved by the complex doctrine of the Trinity.

With these matters we are not here concerned. What does concern us is that Jesus would never have been proclaimed to the Gentiles at all had it not been for the conviction that he was the Messiah through whom the Kingdom of God would be established throughout the earth. Such proclamation finds clear utterance in the words of the Book of Revelation: 'The kingdoms of this world are become the kingdom of our Lord [i.e. God], and of his Messiah; and he shall reign for ever and ever.' In view of the Imperial cult it was bound to happen that for many Christians of non-Jewish origin King Messiah would become the Lord Christ, like the Lord Serapis, Saviour and Son of God, with Caesar stigmatised as a false god, whose pretensions were blasphemous. But we should remember that the earliest Christian reference to the Antichrist makes him to be distinguished by the claim that he is God.[28]

It is not only the title Christ which confirms that the essence of the proclamation about Jesus was that he was the Messiah. There is another word associated with it, also deriving from Hebrew in its Christian usage, the word *Evangelion* (Gospel). This translates the Hebrew *Besorah* (Glad Tidings), *basar* (to give out glad tidings).

The Glad Tidings awaited by Israel was news that the messianic deliverance was imminent. This is conveyed by Luke in the angelic announcement to the shepherds of Bethlehem, 'Do not be afraid, for I bring you glad tidings of great joy for all the people, that today in the city of David a deliverer has been born to you, none other than the Lord Messiah.' The message echoes the words of Isaiah ix: 'Unto us a son is born; and the government shall be upon his shoulder.... Of the increase of his government and peace there shall be no end, upon the throne of David, and upon his kingdom, to order it and establish it.' The gospel spread by the apostles conveyed these glad tidings. With such an electrifying message they could be no other than evangelists.

Jewish expectation of the Glad Tidings rested on passages like Isaiah xl. 9 f, lii. 7 and lxi. 1 f, where with reference to the Great Consolation the Greek version, the Septuagint, uses the verb *evangelizomai*. God would intervene to save his people in their distress, and by the hand of his Messiah demonstrate his government of the world. All nations should acknowledge the One God and cease from warfare. As an ancient Jewish prayer declares, 'We therefore hope in thee, O Lord our God, that we may speedily behold the glory of thy might, when thou wilt remove the abominations from the earth, and the idols will be utterly cut off, when the world will be perfected under the Kingdom of the Almighty, and all the children of flesh will call upon thy name, when thou wilt turn unto thyself all the wicked of the earth.'[29]

The gospel of the early Christians was no other than this gospel, the proclamation of the Kingdom of God and with it the disclosure confirmed by the Scriptures of the identity of the Messiah. So the opening of Mark's Gospel sees the beginnings of the Glad Tidings of Jesus the Messiah in the prophecy of Isaiah xl and Malachi iii. 1. Thus the word gospel had a messianic significance associated with prophetic passages of the Bible relating to the Kingdom of God and held to support the claim that Jesus was the Messiah who would inaugurate it. Since books were often titled by the Jews from their initial words, it may well have been that a Nazorean collection of Old Testament Testimonies compiled at an early date bore the name Gospel because it began appropriately with a Glad Tidings quotation. If this was so, and such a collection was a vital source of the records of the life of

Jesus, it would explain how these records came to be known as Gospels.

As we have briefly indicated, the gospel message envisaged the conversion of the heathen from idolatry. Paul regarded it as his peculiar mission to go to the Gentiles with this message.[30] But he also declared that there was a difference between his gospel and that of the other apostles. What was this difference? It did not concern the objective of the message, participation in the felicities of the Kingdom of God through faith in Jesus as Messiah. This was what salvation meant, being preserved in the Day of Messianic Judgement, and entitled to reign with the Messiah in his terrestrial kingdom. Where Paul was in conflict with his fellow-apostles was in holding, alike for Jews and Gentiles, that salvation in this sense was not obtainable by repentance and keeping the commandments of God laid down in the Law (Torah), but was wholly conditional upon acceptance of the death of Jesus as an atoning sacrifice. He stressed the cardinal efficacy of the Crucifixion as the passport to future bliss, certified by the resurrection. By this means God had made all who believe the recipients of his grace, or graciousness, in offering a free pardon in the Messiah by which converted Gentiles were assured of equal privileges with Jewish believers and would inherit with them the same promises made to Israel.

In formulating this doctrine for the benefit of the Gentiles Paul could not fail to think of the pagan mysteries with their conception of individual salvation by identification with a god in his death and resurrection. In their ignorance the Gentiles in the providence of God had stumbled upon a truth which the advent of the Messiah permitted to be seen in its real significance. Released from the cruder pagan aspects the doctrine was calculated to make a strong appeal, especially to the poorer people denied the salutary benefits of the initiatory rites of the Mystery cults. The salvation in Jesus which Paul brought could be obtained without effort and without price: it was open to all as a free gift, to slave as well as freeman, female as well as male, Gentile as well as Jew. But the salvation this gospel conferred was still expressed by Paul in Jewish terms, namely, inheritance with the saints in the enduring Messianic Kingdom through the acquisition of a deathless body on the Messiah's return from heaven.

In course of time the doctrine of salvation underwent a change. Partly this was due to non-Jewish influences upon Christianity, the philosophical concept of the redemption of the soul from imprisonment in the flesh and its reascent to God, and partly to the other-worldliness resulting from the failure of the Second Advent to materialise. The expectation of a Kingdom of God on earth was largely discarded as insufficiently spiritual, though the Church retained belief in the resurrection of the body and the Last Judgement. We can see how the new ideas were gaining ground in the middle of the second century from Justin Martyr's *Dialogue with the Jew Trypho*, though they were still unorthodox. Trypho challenges Justin, 'Do you really admit that this place, Jerusalem, will be rebuilt; and do you expect your people to be gathered together, and made joyful with the Messiah and the patriarchs and prophets . . . ?' Justin replies that he does admit this, though some who are good Christians think otherwise. He goes on to say: 'But if you have come across some who are called Christians . . . who say there is no resurrection of the dead, and that their souls, when they die, are taken to heaven, do not imagine that they are Christians. . . . But I and others, who are right-minded Christians on all points, are assured that there will be a resurrection of the dead, and a thousand years in Jerusalem, which will then be built, adorned and enlarged, as the prophets Ezekiel and Isaiah and others declare.'[31]

Christians continue to be troubled today by the Church's contradictory doctrines, which arose from the unhappy endeavour to blend incompatible Pagan and Jewish ideas. We have not wished to go further into these matters than is essential. Our purpose has been to show that Christianity was in origin a messianic movement,[32] springing from the soil of Palestine at a critical moment in Jewish history, and that its development as a new religion was conditioned by its subsequent non-Jewish environment. While retaining many of the marks of its ancestry, including the retention of the Jewish Scriptures on which its initial messianic impetus depended, it became transformed by the assimilation of alien ideas and modes of thought. In the process it ceased to be a reliable guide to its own beginnings, so that now we can only reach back to them with enormous difficulty by first of all recognising that the change did take place, and that the cause of it was not fresh illumination but fresh circumstances, and then questing in the lumber room of Christian antiquity for relics of the primitive period which somehow survived.

NOTES AND REFERENCES

1. Jn. xx. 30–1, xxi. 25.

2. See Schonfield, *The Jew of Tarsus* and *Saints Against Caesar*, also below Chapter 4.

3. *Psalms of Solomon*; *Habakkuk Commentary* (Dead Sea Scrolls).

4. *Apocalypse of Baruch*, xxxix. 5–7.

5. Josephus, *Wars*, VI. v. 4. The Roman authors take a similar view, cf. Tacitus, *Hist.* v. 13, Suetonius, *Vespas.* 4. The oracle is not specified, but Josephus was probably alluding to the Star prophecy of Nu. xxiv. 17–18. The *Targum of Onkelos* here paraphrases the passage, 'When a king shall arise out of Jacob, and the Messiah shall be anointed from Israel, he will slay the princes of Moab, and reign over the children of men; and Edom [i.e. Rome] shall be an inheritance.'

6. Schonfield, *Saints Against Caesar*, p. 142.

7. Josephus, *Antiq.* XX. ix. 1 and Hegesippus, *Memoirs* (quoted by Eusebius, *Eccl. Hist.* Bk. 2, ch. xxiii).

8. Euseb. *Eccl. Hist.* Bk. 3, ch. v. (cf. Mk. xiii. 14–18). A variation of the tradition is offered by Epiphanius, *Adv. Haeres*, XXX. ii. 2 and *Mens et Pons*, xv.

9. Josephus, *Wars*, II. xviii. 11, xix. 1.

10. Josephus, *Wars*, III. iv. 1, x. 9.

11. S. G. F. Brandon, *The Fall of Jerusalem and the Christian Church*.

12. Jn. i. 41, 45; Acts ii. 30.

13. See Acts v. 26.

14. *Letter of Claudius to the Alexandrians*.

15. Suetonius, *Claud.* xxv; Dio Cassius, lx. 6; Acts xviii. 2.

16. Acts xvii. 6–7.

17. Acts xxiv. 5.

18. The circumstances were paralleled before the Second Jewish Revolt by the

missionary journeys of Rabbi Akiba, who in fact was guilty of doing what Paul was wrongly accused of. See Schonfield, *The Jew of Tarsus*, p. 181.

19. Rom. xiii; I. Tim. ii. 1–3; I. Pet. ii. 12–17.

20. Tacitus, *Annals*, xv. 44.

21. Suetonius, *Gaius*, xxii.

22. Suetonius, *Domit*. xiii.

23. Mk. xiv. 61; Mt. xvi. 16; Lk. i. 32; Jn. i. 49, vi. 69, xx. 31.

24. Jn. xx. 28.

25. II. Sam. vii. 13–14; Ps. ii. 6–8.

26. Exod. iv. 22; Hos. xi. 1; *Apoc. Ezra*, vi. 55; Jer. xii. 7.

27. See Schonfield, *The Jew of Tarsus*, ch. vii.

28. II. Thess. ii. 3–4.

29. The *Alenu* prayer (Authorised Jewish Prayer Book).

30. Acts ix. 15, xvii. 22–31, xxvi. 16–20; Gal. ii. 7.

31. Justin, *Dial*. lxxx.

32. For a fuller treatment of Jewish-Christian history and beliefs see Schonfield, *The Jew of Tarsus* and *Saints Against Caesar*, also Brandon, *The Fall of Jerusalem and the Christian Church* and Schoeps, *Theologie und Geschichte des Judenchristentums*.

2

North Palestinean Sectarians and Christian Origins

THE name borne by the earliest followers of Jesus was not Christians: they were called Nazoreans (Nazarenes), and Jesus himself was known as the Nazorean. It is now widely agreed that this is a sectarian term, of which the Hebrew is *Notsrim*, and is not connected directly with a place called Nazareth or with the messianic *Nezer* (Branch) from the roots of Jesse.[1] In the word-plays of the time these associations were made; but the name essentially relates to a community whose members regarded themselves as the 'maintainers' or 'preservers' of the true faith of Israel. This claim was shared by the Samaritans, inhabiting Samaria (Shomron), who represented themselves as the Shamerine, the 'custodians' or 'keepers' of the original Israelite religion in opposition to the Judeans (Jews). The same may be said of a pre-Christian sect of Nazareans (Aramaic *Natsaraya*) described by the Church Father Epiphanius.

Epiphanius, himself of Jewish origin, is a very important authority on the early Jewish sects, of whom he writes in his voluminous work against heresies, the *Panarion*. Some of them were still extant in northern Palestine in his own time, late fourth century. The old Nazareans, like the Samaritans, were opposed to the Judean traditions, holding that the southerners had falsified the Law of Moses. They were vegetarians and rejected animal sacrifices, but practised circumcision and observed the Jewish Sabbath and festivals.

There is good reason to believe that the heirs of these Nazareans, though time and circumstances have wrought many changes, are the present Nazoreans (also known as Mandaeans) of the Lower Euphrates. Their literature, which largely has been rescued by Lidzbarski and Lady Drower, reveals that they came formerly from northern Palestine, to which area they had migrated from Judea because of Jewish persecution. This tradition is rather like that of the 'Penitents of Israel' of the Dead Sea Scrolls, who forsook Jerusalem and sojourned in the Land of Damascus. Among these non-Christian Nazoreans the geographical names Jordan and Hauran are particularly precious,[2] pointing to recollections of residence in northern Palestine which may go back to the second century B.C. A word-play may equally have arisen with regard to their name, for the Elder Pliny speaks of a tetrarchy of Nazerines in Coele-Syria.[3]

The Mandaean-Nazoreans have always been a baptising sect holding John the Baptist in special honour, and before they moved to Mesopotamia they could well have had a relationship with Essene and other groups who practised ritual ablution. The present writer has found a direct link between the Mandaean *Sidra d'Yahja* (Book of John the Baptist) and the Aramaic *Genesis Apocryphon* discovered among the Dead Sea Scrolls. There are various points of contact between the Mandaean and Essene traditions, and it is pertinent that Ephiphanius identifies the pre-Christian Nazareans of northern Palestine with the Daily Baptists.

From the sources of information available to us it can be demonstrated that at least from the second century A.D. onwards there was a good deal of sharing of ideas and intercommunication between the sects on the fringe of Judaism which had their home in the north. Among these sects we have to include the Christian-Nazoreans, especially the more extreme Ebionites, as we can see from the Clementine Literature, the *Homilies* and *Recognitions*, and various patristic references. Inevitably these groups, still having certain individual characteristics, were very much thrown together in the severe conditions which followed the Roman defeat of the second Jewish revolt under Bar-Cochba in A.D. 135. According to the early Christian lists furnished by Hegesippus and Justin Martyr there were then surviving not only the familiar Pharisees and Sadducees, but Essenes, Galileans, Daily Baptists, Masbutheans (Aramaic for Baptists), Samaritans, and others the implications of whose names are not clear. Some of these sects had their origin around the beginning of the Christian Era, as a consequence of belief that the Last Times had come, others were older.

'The [Jewish] people,' says the author of the *Clementine Recognitions*, 'was now divided into many sects, ever since the days of John the Baptist. . . . The first schism was that of those called Sadducees, which took their rise almost in the time of John. These, as more righteous than others, began to separate themselves from the assembly of the people.'[4] By Sadducees the writer here appears to mean the Zadokites, members of the same Essene sect as those at Qumran, who called themselves the 'Sons of Zadok' and deliberately segregated themselves to follow the Law strictly and avoid pollution. These are the kind of people of whom Jesus is made to speak: 'From the days of John the Baptist until now the Kingdom of Heaven suffereth violence, and the violent take it by force.'[5] By their way of life they were attempting to storm the Kingdom of God. The Talmud also states that 'Israel did not go into captivity [in A.D. 70] until twenty-four varieties of sectarians had come into existence.'[6]

When we seek to go further back than the reign of Herod it is much more difficult to obtain from the traditions and recovered documents precise knowledge of sectarian relationships. But it is clear that so far as Judea was concerned the Jews regarded northern Palestine as the natural home of heresy.[7] And with good reason, since evidently there existed there besides the schismatic Samaritans other groups whose tenets and customs were a legacy from the time when Israel and Judah were separate kingdoms. We do not know so much about the old Israelite religion, but it would appear to have absorbed a good deal from the worship of the Syrians and Phoenicians, and this was not to nearly the same extent eradicated, as it was in the south, by the reforming zeal of

Ezra and his successors. More of the older faith was carried down
as folklore and in the ideas and usages of clans and sects which
were active in the time of Christ. Epiphanius, whose pre-Christian Nazareans in the north have an affinity with the Samaritans,
was convinced that the Essenes derived from the Samaritans,
while the Abbot Nilus claimed them as descendants of the
Rechabites.

Of the Rechabites it is said in Jeremiah that they followed the
commandments of their ancestor, never to drink wine, not to
build houses or to own and cultivate land, and always to live in
tents.[8] Like the Kenites they led a bedouin existence, earning their
living, as Eisler holds,[9] largely as craftsmen, carpenters and smiths.
Before the time of Christ they may well have become as much a
sect as a clan, having a spiritual association with other communities who had separated themselves and dwelt in camps in the
wilderness which through northern Arabia linked Syria with
Mesopotamia. Such groups were the 'holy ones of God' and the
very term Essean-Essene which was applied to them appears to
have come from the northern Aramaic word *Chasya* (Greek
Hosios) meaning Saint.

In a valuable work, *The Scrolls and Christian Origins*, Dr.
Matthew Black, approving the views of Ernst Lohmeyer, has
this to say: 'The oldest roots of the primitive Church were in
Galilee in the wide sense of "Galilee of the Gentiles", extending
beyond Galilee eastwards to include Peraea and the Decapolis
(possibly reaching as far as Damascus) and to the north as far
as Hermon. The development in Judea and Jerusalem was an inevitable expansion as a result of the events which took place
there.'[10] There is no reference to the Essenes in the Gospels or
the Acts, and such reference would be needless if the primitive
Christians as Nazoreans came within the framework of what was
commonly called Essenism, a generic term rather than the name
of one particular sect. The followers of Jesus the Nazorean of
Galilee simply established in Jerusalem a community of their
'Way', having a kinship as can be seen from the Acts with the
communal 'Way of the Wilderness' followed by the various

Essene groups bearing different names and having distinctive characteristics, but having also a family resemblance to one another. What particularly distinguished the Christian-Nazoreans was their claim that their Master was the Davidic Messiah.

It has always been difficult to explain the journey of Saul of Tarsus to Damascus to arrest Nazoreans there. The Acts gives no indication that in the earliest days of the Nazorean community in Jerusalem the message about Jesus had been carried from there as far north as Damascus. Neither is it made clear what were the religious affiliations of Ananias of Damascus who was sent to Saul to restore his sight. He is depicted as 'a devout man according to Law, having a good report of all the Jews which dwelt there'. He has the gift of healing. He tells Saul that he has been chosen to see and hear the Just One, a title having northern associations with which we shall deal later. He urges Saul to wash away his sins by baptism. In these few particulars we have the description of a typical Essene.

The problem in Acts would be solved if we suppose that some of the community of Jerusalem had taken refuge with their pre-Christian fellows in the north of whom Ananias was one. Paul (Saul) informs us that after his conversion he went into Arabia, and later returned to Damascus.[11] This too would become intelligible if we infer that he stayed with a Nazarean community in the Nabatean country close to Damascus. We could then more readily account for several features of the Pauline doctrine (the Heavenly Messiah and Second Adam) which are still reflected in the literature of the Mandaean-Nazoreans,[12] and for passages in the Pauline Epistles reminiscent of the Dead Sea Scrolls.[13]

The Just One of whom Ananias speaks recalls the revered Teacher of Righteousness of the Qumran Essenes, who had been the leader of the Penitents of Israel, 'the student of the Law who came to Damascus'. It was in the Land of Damascus that the Penitents affirmed the New Covenant as prophesied by Jeremiah. The Talmud, representing hostile rabbinical views, has a passage about the Prophet Elisha going to Damascus to turn his servant

Gehazi to repentance, Gehazi here typifying a Jewish sectarian.[14]
The doctrine regarding the Teacher of Righteousness is not yet
sufficiently clear, but someone of this character was expected by
Essene sects to arise in the End of the Days, who would have a
priestly and prophetic mission, and who perhaps was identified
with the Priestly Messiah.

We are meant to assume that Ananias of Damascus understood
Jesus to be the expected Just One, and it is plain that the followers
of Jesus did so. Obviously they regarded the Messiah and the
Just One as identical. 'Ye denied the Holy One and the Just . . .
and killed the author of life [in the world to come] . . . But those
things, which God before had shewed by the mouth of all his
prophets, that the Messiah should suffer, he hath so fulfilled.'[15]
Similarly the deacon Stephen declares to the Sanhedrin: 'Which
of the prophets have not your fathers persecuted? And they have
slain them which shewed before the coming of the Just One;
of whom ye have been now the betrayers and murderers.'[16] In
Mark's Gospel an unclean spirit recognises Jesus as 'the Holy
One of God'. The terms 'holy one' and 'just one' belong to the
language of the Essene sects, some of whom followed a nazirite
way of life, refraining from meat and intoxicants. The Prophet
Samuel at Shiloh, whom Luke uses as an antetype of Jesus, was
a lifelong nazirite. So was John the Baptist, whose parents are
represented as blameless observers of the Law. The rules laid
down for the Community in the Qumran texts continually emphasise that the indispensable condition of membership was
absolute faithfulness to the Laws of God delivered to Moses.

It brings this kind of thinking right into the home circle of
Jesus when we find that his brother Jacob, who became head of
the Nazoreans at Jerusalem, was a typical Essene sectarian. The
New Testament epistle standing in the name of another brother
Judas (Jude) quotes from sectarian literature (the *Book of Enoch*
and the *Testament of Moses*). In the *Memoirs* of Hegesippus
(second century A.D.) it was stated that James was a lifelong
nazirite, abstaining from animal food and strong drink. He
neither shaved nor cut his hair, never anointed his body with oil

or used the public bath. He never wore woollen, only linen, garments, performed priestly offices and prayed constantly in the Temple for the forgiveness of the people. When he was executed by stoning at Jerusalem the words of Isaiah iii were fulfilled: 'Let us take away the Just, because he is offensive to us; wherefore they shall eat the fruit of their doings.' As he was being stoned he knelt down and cried, 'I beseech thee, O Lord God and Father, forgive them, for they know not what they do' (words attributed to Jesus in Luke). One of those present, who was a Rechabite priest, called out to the executioners: 'Cease! What are you doing? The Just One is praying for you.'[17]

The cumulative evidence, of which more will be said in the next chapter, points to the conclusion reached by Matthew Black, that 'the oldest root of the Christian movement in "Galilee" is to be sought in a group of dedicated Nazirites, sectarians who continued the ancient Israelite institution of the lifelong Nazirate'.[18]

We have every reason to hold that the family to which Jesus belonged was nurtured in this tradition, and much of his teaching confirms this. But his reading of his messianic mission led him in many matters to turn his back on it, which may well have been a cause of friction with his family.[19] He associated freely with the people, even with the worst of them, and would have nothing to do with a nazirite or segregated way of life. 'The Son of Man came eating and drinking, and they say, Behold a man gluttonous and a winebibber, a friend of publicans and sinners.' He relaxed the rigid Sabbath observance, and held that nothing which enters a man's mouth defiles him. He taught that all secrets (so dear to 'the Saints') were to be revealed, and that what was whispered in the ear should be proclaimed from the housetops. To many of the old Nazareans he would be an apostate. No wonder, therefore, that in the Mandaean literature he is stigmatised as a false Messiah. But, as Jesus said, 'Wisdom is justified of her children.'

Yet in his conception of his messianic office Jesus was largely indebted to northern ideas. To illustrate this we must specially consider the tradition of a Suffering Just One and deal also with the figure of the Son of Man.

NOTES AND REFERENCES

1. Isa. xi. 1.

2. *Mandaean Polemic*, E. S. Drower, *Bulletin of the School of Oriental and African Studies*, Vol. XXV, Part 3.

3. Pliny, *Natural History*, v. 81.

4. *Recog.* Bk. I. liii–liv.

5. Mt. xi. 12.

6. T.J. *Sanhedrin*, 29c. See Schonfield, *Secrets of the Dead Sea Scrolls*.

7. Jesus was suspect as a Galilean and vilified as 'a demon-possessed Samaritan'.

8. Jer. xxxv. 5–10.

9. Eisler, *The Messiah Jesus and John the Baptist*, p. 234 f. and elsewhere.

10. Matthew Black, *The Scrolls and Christian Origins*, p. 81.

11. Gal. i. 17.

12. See E. S. Drower, *The Secret Adam* and Schonfield, *The Jew of Tarsus*, ch. vii.

13. 'He left a remnant of Israel' (*Damascus Document*, Rom. xi. 5). 'God loveth wisdom, and counsel hath he set before him. Prudence and knowledge minister unto him. Longsuffering is with him and plenteousness of forgiveness' (*Damascus Document*, Rom. xi. 32–4). 'And power and might and great fury of fire (all the angels of destruction), for them who turned aside out of the way, and abhorred the Statute, so that there should be no remnant, nor any to escape of them' (*Damascus Document*, II. Thess. i. 7–9). Like the Scrolls Paul also refers to the Children of Light and of Darkness, Eph. v. 8.

14. T.B. *Sotah*, 47a. See R. Travers Herford, *Christianity in Talmud and Midrash*, p. 97 f. Among the Dead Sea Scrolls, the *Damascus Document* speaks of what Elisha said to Gehazi, vii.

15. Acts iii. 14–18.

16. Acts vii. 52.

17. Hegesippus, quoted by Eusebius, *Eccl. Hist.* Bk. II. xxiii.

18. Black, *The Scrolls and Christian Origins*, p. 83.

19. Mk. iii. 21; Jn. vii. 3–5.

3

The Suffering Just One and the Son of Man

THE current teaching about the Messiah the Son of David at the time of Christ, as we have seen in Part One, Chapter 2, was that he would be a righteous and holy king as predicted in the prophecies of Isaiah ix and xi. But we do not know whether the Davidic Messiah as distinct from the Priestly Messiah of the sectarian documents had at all been associated with the Suffering Servant of Isaiah xlii–liii. There was a belief that the Saints, the Elect of Israel, the Son of Man collective of the Book of Daniel, would perform an atoning work for sin by their faithfulness to the Law and by their sufferings at the hands of the wicked, and it would appear that at least in sectarian circles the same function was applied to a messianic personality, the Elect One and Just One, the Son of Man singular.

It is not easy to throw light on these pre-Christian ideas of tht Jewish eclectic groups because much of their teaching was noe made public and the literature to which we have access is somewhat mysterious in its expressions. We have to explore as best we can and reach certain tentative conclusions.

It was wholly in keeping with the testimony of the Scriptures that persecution and even death was the likely lot of those who followed the way of the Lord faithfully. Perhaps nowhere is this better expressed than in a famous passage of the Wisdom of Solomon.

> Let us lie in wait for the righteous man,
> because he is inconvenient to us and opposes our actions;

he reproaches us for our sins against the Law,
and accuses us of sins against our training.
He professes to have knowledge of God,
and calls himself a child of the Lord . . .
Let us see if his words are true,
and let us test what will happen at the end of his life;
for if the righteous man is God's son, he will help him,
and deliver him from the hand of his adversaries.
Let us test him with insult and torture,
that we may find out how gentle he is,
and make trial of his forbearance.
Let us condemn him to a shameful death,
for, according to what he says, he will be protected.[1]

This passage is very close to what we read in Psalm xxxvii.
30–3, on which fortunately we have a commentary from Qumran. It is in fragmentary condition, but in an important section
the sense of what is missing can be sufficiently restored.

'*The wicked watches out for the righteous and seeks to slay him.
The Lord will not abandon him into his hand or let him be condemned
when he is tried.* Interpreted, this concerns the Wicked Priest who
rose up against the Teacher of Righteousness that he might put
him to death because he served the truth and the Law, for which
reason he laid hands upon him. But God will not "abandon him
into his hand and will not let him be condemned when he is
tried".'

For the Qumran Essenes their founder had been a Suffering
Just One, though he had escaped death at the hands of his
enemies by going into exile. His sufferings are described in the
Thanksgiving Hymns, which many scholars hold to be autobio-
graphical.

By way of illustration we give an excerpt here from Hymn ii,
2, but the interested reader is recommended to study these poig-
nant compositions some of which reflect the atmosphere of the
Davidic Psalms which were interpreted in a messianic sense in the
Christian tradition.

> Violent men have sought after my life
>   because I have clung to Thy Covenant.
> For they, an assembly of deceit,
>   and a horde of Satan,
> know not that my stand
>   is maintained by Thee,
> and that in Thy mercy Thou wilt save my soul
>   since my steps proceed from Thee.
> From Thee it is
>   that they assail my life,
> that Thou mayest be glorified
>   by the judgement of the wicked,
> and manifest Thy might through me
>   in the presence of the sons of men;
> for it is by Thy mercy that I stand.[2]

We are rather in the dark, however, about what the Essenes held would be the fate of that other Teacher of Righteousness whom they expected to arise at the End of the Days. Would he too be a Suffering Just One? It appears likely, as suggested by G. Vermes, that the Teacher of Righteousness was thought of as the messianic Prophet like Moses, and identified with 'the Man' who in the Last Times would 'instruct the upright in the knowledge of the Most High'.[3] In this case there would be a direct link between the Just One and the Son of Man figure. Moses Gaster proposed long ago that the Son of Man of Daniel's vision who came with the clouds of heaven was inspired by Moses, who received the Law amidst the clouds on Mount Sinai. But we must leave this issue for the present to pursue another line of tradition concerning the Just One.

A messianic interest had attached itself to the person of the patriarch Joseph among certain sections of the Saints. Due to this, perhaps, there emerged the concept in later Judaism of a Messiah ben Joseph, who would be killed.

In Jewish teaching Joseph was the perfect righteous man, whose brethren persecuted him and attempted to get rid of him. But in

the providence of God he who was humiliated was afterwards
exalted and became the saviour of the sons of Jacob from whom
he had been separated. It was prophesied of him, 'From thence is
the Shepherd, the Stone of Israel.'[4] This curious passage had the
consequence of enlisting in the messianic cause various Scriptures
relating to the Shepherd and to the Stone, both of them having
connections with suffering or rejection. As we shall have to deal
particularly with the Shepherd aspect, we may briefly note here
about the Stone, that messianic interpretation brought together
the stone which Jacob used as a pillow when it was confirmed
to him in a dream that in his seed all the families of the earth
would be blessed, which stone he set up and *anointed* at the spot
which became the northern cult centre of Bethel,[5] the stone laid
in Zion for a foundation, 'a tried stone, a precious corner stone',[6]
the stone which the builders rejected and which would become the
chief corner stone'[7] and the stone of Nebuchadnezzar's dream,
which smote a great image representing the successive heathen
empires and became a great mountain and filled the whole earth.[8]

But to return to Joseph. In the sectarian *Testaments of the XII
Patriarchs* he is revealed as the antetype of the Suffering Just One.

'Do ye also, therefore, my children, love the Lord God of
heaven and earth, and keep his commandments, following the
example of the holy and just man Joseph. For until his death he
was not willing to tell regarding himself; but Jacob, having learnt
it from the Lord, told it to him. Nevertheless he kept denying it.
And then with difficulty he was persuaded by the adjurations of
Israel. For Joseph also besought our father that he would pray
for his brethren, that the Lord would not impute to them as sin
whatever evil they had done to him. And thus Jacob cried out:
"My good child, thou hast prevailed over the bowels of thy
father Jacob." And he embraced him, and kissed him for two
hours, saying, "In thee shall be fulfilled the prophecy of heaven,
which says that the blameless one shall be defiled for lawless men,
and the sinless one shall die for godless men." '[9]

There once existed a *Book of Joseph the Just*, mentioned in the
Ascension of Isaiah, of which we do not know the contents. But

in another sectarian work the *Book of Jubilees* it is said that the annual Day of Atonement was instituted because of Joseph. 'And the sons of Jacob slaughtered a kid, and dipped the coat of Joseph in the blood, and sent it to Jacob their father on the tenth of the seventh month . . . For this reason it is ordained for the children of Israel that they should afflict themselves on the tenth of the seventh month—on the day that the news which made him weep for Joseph came to Jacob his father.'[10]

It is by no means easy to get to the heart of this Joseph mystery; but we may venture to suggest that it has a northern background, for Joseph is synonymous with the northern Kingdom of Israel in several places in the Old Testament.[11] There is room for suspicion that as a result of strict monotheism there was transferred to the Joseph figure of a Suffering Just One some of the characteristics of the old Syrian cult of Adonis-Tammuz or Adad, Tammuz:

> Whose annual wound in Lebanon allur'd
> The Syrian damsels to lament his fate.

The death and resurrection of Adonis-Tammuz had to do with the Fertility cult, and in the ancient liturgies he is called Shepherd and Wild Ox, names used in the Joseph predictions.[12] As is well known, pagan customs and beliefs are not extinguished by a change of faith, and the Church has had to absorb and Christianise many of them. T. J. Meek has pertinently illustrated this kind of survival in writing on the theme of Canticles and the Tammuz cult. A traveller in Euboea, according to Lawson (*Modern Greek Folklore*), had observed the gloom of the people in Holy Week. Asking an old woman for an explanation, he was told, 'Of course I am anxious: for if Christ does not rise tomorrow we shall have no corn this year.' Meek regards the shepherd lover in Canticles as an original reference to the god Dad, who in Palestine was Adad, the counterpart of Tammuz. There is a connection between the god-name and that of David the shepherd king of Israel, and there is a strong probability that in Palestine the messianic expectation embodied elements of the local Fertility cult. Tammuz

in the liturgies was 'shepherd, pure food, sweet milk', and of the
Messiah it is said, 'And I will set up one shepherd over them,
even my servant David; he shall feed them, and he shall be their
shepherd.'[13] There was a shrine of Adonis-Tammuz in David's
city of Bethlehem (the place of Bread).

The view is speculative, but deserving of consideration, that
in the north in the time of Jesus a Joseph messianic concept of a
Suffering Just One existed which could readily be combined with
that of the Davidic Messiah. In the Mandaean literature John
the Baptist says of himself, 'A shepherd am I who loves his sheep;
sheep and lambs I watch over.'[14] and the words were applied to the
Messiah, 'Awake, O sword, against my shepherd, and against the
man that is my fellow, saith the Lord of hosts: smite the shepherd,
and the sheep shall be scattered.'[15] The persecuted David, destined
to be king and shepherd of Israel, is not far from the Suffering
Servant of Isaiah.

The Messianic Hope was sufficiently fluid to permit the inter-
changeability of the messianic personalities, and there is considerable evidence of such fusions. When Jesus is made to declare in
the Fourth Gospel, 'I am the Good Shepherd: the good shepherd
giveth his life for the sheep,' he is speaking with the voice of
Adonis-Tammuz-Adad, as well as in accordance with messianic
prophecies, and most appositely in his case, since he came from
Galilee and by parentage was Son of Joseph and by descent Son
of David.

The more we look into the origins of Christianity the more
we are confronted with venerable beliefs and ideas woven into
the messianic pattern by the Jewish sectarian groups, beliefs and
ideas to which Jesus to some extent had access, and to which he
was responsive, and which helped to shape his own messianic
convictions.

One of the most curious of these ideas is that which concerns
the Son of Man, or—avoiding the orientalism—the Man. It
belongs to the sphere of Jewish mystical teaching regarding the
Archetypal or Primordial Man,[16] and its messianic significance
was developed among the Essenes.

The Biblical source of the concept is Daniel, that remarkable book of the Saints. 'I saw in the night visions, and, behold, one like the son of man [i.e. a human being] came with the clouds of heaven, and came to the Ancient of Days, and they brought him near before him. And there was given him dominion, and glory and a kingdom, that all people, nations, and languages, should serve him: his dominion is an everlasting dominion, which shall not pass away, and his kingdom that which shall not be destroyed.'[17]

From the context we can see that this human figure is contrasted with the successive worldly imperialisms, described under the figures of beasts, the last to appear being the worst of all. The Son of Man stands for the Elect Ones of Israel, the people of the Saints of the Most High, who ultimately will possess the kingdom and institute the rule of righteousness.

It was natural, however, that what was believed of the Elect Ones of Israel should be applied to the ideal Israelite. Just as the suffering Holy Community was personified by the suffering Holy and Just One, so the corporate Son of Man found its epitome in the messianic Elect One, the Prophet like Moses who was brought near to God in the clouds of heaven. Jesus is described as the True Prophet in the Clementine literature of the Ebionite Nazoreans. Whether Moses was at all in the mind of the author of Daniel, we can more definitely find the image of the cloud-borne Man in the religious symbolism of Assyria and Babylonia, from whence it came to Palestine, and lent itself admirably to the mystical doctrines of the Jewish sectaries. We have a reflection of this image in the John the Baptist stories of the Mandaeans, where John is conveyed on a cloud to Jerusalem and set down there.[18]

There is some warrant for the opinion that the Qumran documents linked the expected Prophet with the Son of Man figure (the Man, *geber*) and with the Teacher of Righteousness. 'It is not so simple', writes G. Vermes, introducing *The Dead Sea Scrolls in English*, 'to define the role of the mysterious Prophet since he is named only once and his duties are not given. But if

I have understood it correctly, the functions ascribed to the persons alluded to in the Community Rule (IV) as *geber*, "Man", correspond to those of the expected Prophet: *geber* was to "instruct the upright in the knowledge of the Most High" at the end of time, and "to teach the wisdom of the Sons of Heaven to the perfect of way". *Geber*, however, seems to have been identified with the Teacher of Righteousness. In the Commentary on Psalm 37, the verse, "The steps of *geber* are confirmed by the Lord" is interpreted: "This concerns the Priest, the Teacher of Righteousness."[19] The role of *Geber* (the Man) is messianic. Through his teaching the Elect Community regains the innocence of the First Man, 'for God has chosen them for an everlasting Covenant and all the glory of Adam shall be theirs'.[20]

We are on the fringe here of Pauline Christology of the Second Adam from heaven and the doctrine of the predestination of the Elect.

But on the theme of the messianic Man there is another link between the Qumran and Christian records. In the Revelation we read:

'And there appeared a great sign in heaven; a woman clothed with the sun, and the moon under her feet, and upon her head a crown of twelve stars: and she being with child cried, travailing in birth, and pained to be delivered ... And she brought forth a man child (the *Geber*), who was to rule all nations with a rod of iron: and her child was caught up unto God, and to his throne.'[21]

This recalls an apocalyptic passage in the Qumran hymns, where it is stated:

For the children have come to the throes of Death,
  and she labours in her pains who bears the Man.
For amid the throes of Death
  she shall bring forth a man-child,
and amid the pains of Hell
  there shall spring from her child-bearing crucible
  a Marvellous Mighty Counsellor;
and the Man shall be delivered from out of the throes.[22]

Probably in both cases we are meant to understand that it is the Elect Community, the True Israel, which brings forth the Man, who here seems to be identified with the Messiah ben David, since the words of the hymn make obvious reference to Isaiah ix. 6–7: 'Unto us a child is born, unto us a son is given: and the government shall be upon his shoulder: and his name shall be called Wonderful Counsellor . . . Of the increase of his government and peace there shall be no end, upon the throne of David, and upon his kingdom, to order it, and to establish it with judgement and justice from henceforth even for ever.'

Can it be that among the Saints before the time of Jesus the Son of Man was already another term for the Messiah, whether he was the Prophet, the Priest or the King?

This would help to explain the Son of Man messianism of the *Similitudes of Enoch*, a section of the Enoch collection of documents which circulated among the Saints, which is still our principal source of information on the subject. Enoch the antediluvian patriarch who had walked with God and who was translated to heaven was one of their great heroes, as also was Noah. Both the date and place of origin of the *Similitudes* are in doubt. Fragments of other parts of the collection have been found at Qumran; but so far this section is missing. One explanation which has been proposed is that the *Similitudes* is not pre-Christian but Jewish-Christian. On the other hand it could well be that it was a product of northern Nazarean-Essenism and was not used in the south. It is consistent with this view that Jesus the Nazorean should have applied the term Son of Man to himself in a messianic sense, and when replying to the challenge of the high priest as to whether he was the Messiah, declared, 'I am: and ye shall see the Son of Man sitting on the right hand of Power, and coming in the clouds of heaven.' In his answer Jesus employs a substitute for the divine name, 'Power', which as Matthew Black, following Lohmeyer, has pointed out, 'was a northern form of speech, certainly Samaritan, and possibly no less Galilean.' As he says, 'The same substitute for the divine name (and the same type of "Son of Man" Christology) is to be encountered in the famous reply of

James (brother of Jesus), reported by Hegesippus . . . "Why do ye ask me concerning the Son of Man. He sits at the right hand *of the great Power,* and will come in the clouds of heaven". . . . We have to do with a North Palestinian idiom, attested especially in accounts of sectarian circles in this area. Here we have a very striking link between the "Galilean" Gospel tradition and North Palestinian forms of religion.'[23]

Since the Son of Man doctrine of the *Similitudes* is of major importance and will be unfamiliar to many readers we shall supply now some representative extracts. In the document Enoch relates his heavenly visions, when he is permitted to see to the very Last Times. In the divine courts he beholds the Son of Man.

'And there I saw One who had a Head of Days [i.e. the Ancient of Days], and his head was white like wool, and with him was another being whose countenance had the appearance of a man whose face was full of graciousness, like one of the holy angels. And I asked the angel who went with me and showed me all the hidden things, concerning that Son of Man, who he was, and whence he was, and why he went with the Head of Days. And he answered and said unto me, "This is the Son of Man who hath righteousness, with whom dwelleth righteousness, and who reveals all the treasures of that which is hidden, because the Lord of Spirits hath chosen him, and his lot before the Lord of Spirits hath surpassed everything in uprightness for ever. And this Son of Man whom thou hast seen . . . will put down the kings from their thrones and kingdoms because they do not extol and praise him [the Lord of Spirits] nor thankfully acknowledge whence the kingdom was bestowed upon them . . .

'And at that hour that Son of Man was named in the presence of the Lord of Spirits and his name before the Head of Days. And before the sun and the signs were created, before the stars of heaven were made, his name was named before the Lord of Spirits. He will be a staff to the righteous on which they will support themselves and not fall, and he will be the light of the Gentiles and the hope of those who are troubled in heart. All who dwell on earth will fall down and bow the knee before him, and bless and laud and celebrate with song the Lord of Spirits. And for this cause has he been chosen and hidden before him before the creation of the world and for evermore. And the wisdom of the Lord of Spirits hath revealed him to the holy and righteous, because they have hated and despised this world of unrighteousness . . . And in those days the kings of the earth, and the strong who possess the earth will be of downcast countenance . . . And I will give them over into the hands of mine Elect Ones . . . before them they will fall and not rise again . . . for they have denied the Lord of Spirits and his anointed.

'And the Lord of Spirits seated him [the Son of Man] on the throne of his glory, and the spirit of righteousness was poured out upon him, and the word of his mouth slew all the sinners . . . And all the Elect will stand before him in that day . . . And the righteous and elect will be saved on that day and will never again from thenceforth see the faces of the sinners and unrighteous. And the Lord of Spirits will abide with them for ever, and with that Son of Man will they eat and lie down and rise up for ever.'[24]

The atmosphere of the *Similitudes of Enoch* is apocalyptic and predestinarian, and is reflected in the Revelation and the Pauline Epistles. The Son of Man concept unites here with the Just One and the Messiah of Righteousness, the Branch of David. He is present in the mind of God and chosen before the creation, and from time to time revealed to the righteous for their consolation; but he is neither divine nor actually pre-existent. He is named and hidden from the beginning in the secret thoughts of God, finally to be revealed in the Last Times as the ideal Man who will justify God's creation of the world. In this sense he is the Second Adam, answering to the Light Adam of the Nazorean-Mandaeans, and the Nazorean-Ebionite 'manlike figure invisible to men in general'. From such teaching, probably while he was in the borders of Arabia, Paul acquired the inspiration from which he developed his concept of the Heavenly Messiah who had incarnated in the earthly Jesus.

At the end of the *Similitudes* Enoch is told that in the Son of Man he has seen an image of his own righteous self; so that we are not required to go beyond the idea that when the Messiah would be manifested he would embody that perfect righteousness which God from the beginning designed for humanity, and which was present in the chief Saints of all the ages. By virtue of that perfection of holiness Man in the Messiah is exalted to the right hand of God, and is fitted to be God's representative in the reborn and redeemed world from which all sin has been banished. The Son of Man is so to speak the essential Messiah embodied in all the Messiahs, the eternal principle of Righteousness exemplified in all the Just Ones.

The extent to which Jesus drew upon this heritage is evident. His language again and again echoes that of the *Similitudes*, as we can see by bringing together some of the Gospel references.

'Whosoever therefore shall be ashamed of me . . . of him also will the Son of Man be ashamed, when he cometh in the glory of his Father with the holy angels. And then shall they see the Son of Man coming in the clouds with great power and glory. Ye shall see the Son of Man sitting on the right hand of Power, and coming in the clouds of heaven. The Son of Man shall send forth his angels, and they shall gather out of his kingdom all things that offend, and them which do iniquity; and shall cast them into a furnace of fire. For the Son of Man shall come in the glory of his Father with his angels; and then shall he reward every man according to his works. Ye which have followed me, in the Regeneration when the Son of Man shall sit on the throne of his glory, ye also shall sit upon twelve thrones, judging the twelve tribes of Israel. When the Son of Man shall come in his glory . . . then shall he sit upon the throne of his glory: and before him shall be gathered all the nations: and he shall separate them one from another, as a shepherd divideth his sheep from the goats. The Father hath given him authority to execute judgement also, because he is the Son of Man.'[25]

Thus we can appreciate how among the Saints belief in the Messiah could envisage both a Suffering Just One and a Glorious King. The two apparently distinct concepts could be united, the one preceding the other, as evidently they were in the mind of

Jesus. It took a Nazorean of Galilee to apprehend from the Scriptures that death and resurrection was the bridge between the two phases. The very tradition of the land where Adonis yearly died and rose again seemed to call for it.

NOTES AND REFERENCES

1. *Wisdom*, ii. 12–20, RSV.

2. Vermes, *The Dead Sea Scrolls in English*, p. 155.

3. Vermes, op. cit., p. 50.

4. Gen. xlix. 24.

5. Gen. xxviii. 10–22.

6. Isa. xxviii. 16.

7. Ps. cxviii. 22.

8. Dan. ii. 29–45.

9. *Testament of Benjamin*, iii. 1–7. Tr. Charles.

10. *Jubilees*, xxxiv. 12–18.

11. See Ps. lxxviii. 67, lxxx. 1; Ezek. xxxvii. 16, 19; Amos. v. 6, 15.

12. See Gen. xlix. 24; Deut. xxxiii. 17; also Langdon, *Babylonian Liturgies*.

13. Ezek. xxxiv. 23–4, xxxvii. 24–5.

14. *Sidra d'Yahya*, xi. See G. R. S. Mead, *The Gnostic John the Baptizer*, p. 81.

15. Zech. xiii. 7.

16. See Schonfield, *The Jew of Tarsus*, ch. vii, where the subject is dealt with in some detail.

17. Dan. vii. 13–14.

18. *Sidra d'Yahya*, xxxii. Mead, op.cit., p. 56 ff.

19. *The Dead Sea Scrolls in English*, p. 50.

20. *The Community Rule*, iv.

21. See Rev. xii. 1–6.

22. *Hymns*, III. 4. Tr. Vermes, op. cit., p. 157.

23. Matthew Black, *The Scrolls and Christian Origins*, p. 81.

24. Enoch, *Similitudes*, xlvi. 1–5, xlviii. 1–10, lxii, 2–16. Tr. Charles. See also lxix. 26–9.

25. The passages quoted are in order, Mk. viii. 38, xiii. 26, xiv. 62; Mt. xiii. 41–2, xvi. 27, xix. 28, xxv. 31–2; Jn. v. 27.

4

Gospels in the Making

THE Four Gospels on which we must largely depend for information about Jesus were the products of historical circumstances which to an appreciable extent are ascertainable. On the showing of many Christian scholars who have devoted themselves to the study of these documents there was no special inspiration either in their origin or composition. They are dramatisations with policy features; and what inspired them was the needs and conditions of particular communities of Christians in different lands.

The Gospels belong to the period following the Jewish war with Rome, and can approximately be dated between A.D. 75 and 115. Each Gospel bears the stamp of an individual author, who treats the material at his command in his own way; but all the authors are writing outside Palestine in a substantially Gentile-Christian environment.

None of the Gospels is original in the sense that it is a first-hand authority; though we have to take account of the use of first-hand recollections and of primary documents no longer extant. The measure of faithfulness to such sources is important, and what we can glean of their character and worth. But also we cannot ignore that in the interests of theological doctrine, contemporary circumstances, and effective story-telling, nothing wrong was seen in creating views for Jesus to express, altering the sense of traditional sayings of his, supplying and colouring episodes with the help of non-Christian literature.

The character of the Gospels is biographical, making allowance for the fact that they are controlled by an established design to represent the experience of Jesus in terms of a faith, originally a purely messianic faith. The authors are endeavouring to tell a connected story of Jesus. They are not very successful, because their resources were slender and offered few indications of time and sequence. They were not in the position of a Plutarch, whose *Lives of Great Men* was composed early in the second century, or of a Suetonius, whose *Lives of the Caesars* was written a few years later. But in making the attempt at all, they have conveyed to us that they were catering for circles influenced by Greek and Roman literary art rather than Jewish, and also that confidence in the imminent return of Jesus was beginning to wane. As regards the latter, the sense of postponement is least present in Mark, one of the pointers to its relatively early date.

While all the Evangelists are aware how the public activities of Jesus began, and how they ended, they are not at all sure how long they continued, what teaching of Jesus was related to what events, and what was the order of these events. In the synoptic Gospels most of the teaching of Jesus is found in Matthew and Luke. A good deal of it comes from some written source used by them both, and that source must have concerned itself little with time and place, since Matthew and Luke felt free to make their own decisions as to where to fit the material into the structure of Mark. But building on Mark they were trying to achieve a biographical result, finding themselves in the dilemma that while the career of Jesus had a definite beginning and end it had no organised middle.

We shall have more to say later about the lost Teaching Document. The determination of its existence has been one of the most important results of the literary examination of the Gospels. We may observe, however, that this document appears to have been unknown to the author of Mark, and equally the source material for the nativity stories. This suggests that exciting fresh information became available after Mark was written, or was in circulation in other areas than where this Gospel was composed.

When Mark was published, perhaps between A.D. 75 and 80, it was unique in Christian literature; for Matthew and Luke had no alternative but to use Mark as a guide. It is evident that they could not turn for assistance to any similar composition. When Luke speaks of 'many' in his foreword it has been held to mean that a number of others had written gospels before he decided to undertake his. But in that case it is likely that there would be evidence in his work that he was familiar with some of them and borrowed from them, and there is no indication of this. Luke's reference has a certain rhetorical quality, but he could be alluding to various collections of gospel stuff applying Old Testament prophecies to circumstances in the life of Jesus, conforming to the more or less stereotyped pattern or outline of early Nazorean testimony. Long before the canonical Gospels Paul shows his acquaintance with such testimony, especially in connection with the final events in the life of Jesus.[1] Though he was concerned with the Messiah in heaven rather than with his earthly career, except as its climax reinforced his message, he did know something about it, including that Jesus was of the line of David.[2] He also felt it needful to check with the Nazorean leaders, 'lest by any means I should run, or had run, in vain'.[3]

We have pointed out above (p. 201 f.) that the very word 'gospel' in Christian usage had a messianic significance, and prophetic testimonies applied to Jesus, when written down, would be just as much the Gospel as the oral message, combining the Old Testament texts with their fulfilment. Multiplying such collections, with certain differences of detail from oral tradition, would create what could be called 'gospels'. We know what store was set by the prophetic gnosis in the early Church, and how much it was relied upon as the certification of 'our common salvation . . . the faith once and for all delivered to the Saints'.[4]

While Mark broke fresh ground in giving the proclamation of Jesus a more biographical treatment, he framed it on the Testimony tradition. In his record of events he does not bring out the fulfilments of the Old Testament as Matthew and John do; but the language he employs shows that he is well aware of them.[5] He does not hesitate to begin his book with such prophetic testimony, and to say that Jesus regarded the experiences of John the Baptist and himself as being demanded by the Scriptures.[6] That Mark's Gospel owes much to the Nazorean prophetic gnosis is further indicated by the amount of space devoted to the narrative of Passion Week, rather more than a third of the whole book. It was the fate of Jesus, if he was the Messiah, which chiefly called for evidence that it had been foretold. The circumstances had therefore to be set out in much greater detail backed by an impressive array of testimonies.

Once Mark became well known, and after a decent interval as the unchallenged authority, it was to be expected that other Gospels of this type would come into existence, at first based on Mark but subsequently becoming more venturesome. Such a medium lent itself admirably to investing various doctrines with the highest endorsement, and from about the middle of the second century onward a number of these uncanonical Gospels appeared under the names of different apostles. In the earlier essays the meat of the Testimony Gospel was in them; but the more vivid narrative presentation of these Memoir Gospels made them much more acceptable to the Gentile Church. It is interesting to note that when Justin Martyr in the middle of the second century speaks of the records of the life of Jesus read in the churches he refers to them as Memoirs, or Recollections, of the Apostles and those who followed them.[7] The essentially Testimony documents ceased to appeal for internal use by churches for whom the messiahship of Jesus was no longer paramount, and they would tend very quickly to disappear. Yet what they had represented could still be employed externally for controversial and missionary purposes in the form of *Testimonies Against the Jews*.[8]

To learn more of how the message about Jesus as Messiah came to be put into writing we have to turn to early Nazorean history in Palestine.

The period from A.D. 40 to 50 was one of dramatic events and intense religious and political excitement for the Jewish people. First there was the attempt of the Emperor Gaius Caligula to have his statue set up in the Temple as an object of worship. Such a

blasphemous design had had no equal since the Seleucid king
Antiochus Epiphanes in the second century B.C. had converted the
Temple into a shrine of Zeus Olympius, which united the nation
in arms under the leadership of the Maccabees. The intention of
Gaius similarly roused the Jews to resistance, and some took up
arms. Most, however, awaited the outcome of massive protests
to Petronius the Roman legate of Syria. A full-scale revolt was
averted only by the concern and delaying tactics of this official,
who at personal risk made clear to the emperor what the consequences would be. Gaius grudgingly gave way, yielding to the
persuasions of his friend the Jewish prince Agrippa. But he
ordered Petronius to commit suicide for disobedience, a fate
which the legate escaped only because news reached him first
that Gaius had been assassinated.

Jewish nationalists and fanatics seized upon the situation and
exploited it. All who were messianically minded saw in what had
happened a great Sign of the Times, including the Nazoreans, to
whom it must have seemed to portend the near return of Jesus.
Partial calm was restored when the new emperor Claudius made
Agrippa king of Judea; but it was necessary for the king to try
to curb the hotheads. He executed one of the 'tempestuous'
brothers, James son of Zebedee. Peter was arrested and placed
under close guard; but his escape was contrived, and he went into
hiding, the wretched guards being put to death on the king's
orders. The state of affairs was evidently more explosive than is
represented in the Acts.

Agrippa's sudden death in A.D. 44 brought Judea again under
direct Roman rule and stimulated the spirit of revolt. Cuspius
Fadus, sent as governor, had to take military action against the
disaffected and the religious enthusiasts, lumped together as
rebels. On the orders of the emperor he commanded that the
robes in which the high priest officiated in the Temple should be
returned to the custody of the Roman garrison in Fort Antonia,
and handed out on each festal occasion. This measure, as Josephus
reports, was thought so likely to provoke a hostile outbreak that
Cassius Longinus, then legate of Syria, arrived at Jerusalem, 'and

had brought a great army with him, out of fear that the injunctions of Fadus would force the Jews to rebel'.

Later, Claudius dispatched a pro-Roman Jew, Tiberius Alexander, to assist in the pacification of the country. Among those killed at this time was the prophet Theudas, and James and Simon, sons of the former resistance leader Judas of Galilee, were crucified.

In the story of this period the Old Russian text of Josephus adds a passage, which if it is not genuine is not far off the mark.

'And since in the time of those [governors] many followers of the wonder-worker [i.e. Jesus] aforementioned had appeared and spoken to the people of their master, that he was alive, although he had been dead, and "he will free you from your bondage", many of the multitude hearkened to their preaching and took heed to their injunctions. . . . But when these noble governors saw the falling away of the people, they determined, together with the Scribes, to seize them . . . for fear lest the little might not be little, if it ended in the great. . . . They sent them away, some to Caesar, others to Antioch to be tried, others they banished to distant lands.'[9]

With this we may compare the words of Tacitus, that by the execution of Christ 'the sect of which he was the founder received a blow, which for a time checked the growth of a dangerous superstition; but *it broke out again*, and spread with increased vigour, not only in Judea, the soil that gave it birth, but even in the city of Rome, the common sewer into which everything infamous and abominable flows like a torrent from all quarters of the world'.[10]

Historically, we are required to look at Christian beginnings without the rose-tinted spectacles of piety. The movement was largely composed of Zealots for the Law, and was involved in the Jewish struggle for freedom. We have previously taken some note of this, and of measures of the Emperor Claudius to counter messianic propaganda in Rome and Alexandria (above p. 197 f.). The 'pacification' of Judea at this time must be seen as a prime cause of spreading this propaganda in the Provinces and in Rome itself, partly by prominent individuals being forced to leave the country, and partly by the deliberate sending out of agents and apostles.

There is an early Christian tradition referred to by Apollonius and in the *Preaching of Peter* that Jesus told his disciples not to leave Jerusalem for twelve years, and then to go out into the world.[11] Twelve years after the latest possible date for the Crucifixion would coincide with the repressive measures of Fadus and Alexander. It is pertinent that the Acts assigns to this period, after the death of King Agrippa, the first missionary journey of Paul and Barnabas, and laconically states that 'the word of God grew and multiplied'.[12] But Eusebius, following ancient tradition, says that 'the rest of the apostles, who were harassed in innumerable ways with a view to destroy them, and driven from the land of Judea, had gone forth to proclaim the gospel to all nations'.[13]

We are now better able to comprehend the circumstances which brought about the putting into operation of what has been called the Great Commission. It was this step which required the setting down of the prophetic testimonies to Jesus as the Messiah for the service of the evangelists. Since only the Hebrew text of the Bible was regarded as authoritative by the Zealots, we must hold that the document in the first instance was written in the sacred tongue, not in Aramaic, the spoken language, or in Greek, and we cannot be far wrong in assigning the date of the Testimony Book to about A.D. 50. It would have been a short scroll inexpensive to copy and easy to carry.

There is strong evidence that the compiler of this little work was the apostle Matthew. The Church Fathers all agree that he published his Gospel in Hebrew. But canonical Matthew was certainly composed in Greek, and the mistake could have arisen from not understanding that Matthew's 'Gospel' was in fact the Testimony Book, which in the original sense was the Gospel. The earliest reference which offers some confirmation, and may have misled later writers, is that of Papias (*c*. A.D. 144), who stated in a work of his now lost that 'Matthew compiled the Oracles in the Hebrew language, and each interpreted them as he was able'.[14] The 'Oracles' (*logia*) means passages of the Old

Testament employed prophetically as in the Dead Sea Scrolls, in this case in relation to Jesus as Messiah (*logia kyriaka*). Just as in the synagogues texts from the readings of the Law and the Prophets were translated by preachers and their application expounded, so was it the function of the evangelists to interpret and explain the Oracles fulfilled in Jesus. Later, in all probability, Testimony Gospels would come into existence in Aramaic and Greek, the 'many' of Luke's foreword, in which the texts and the applications were set down together, with variations according to the information available to each evangelist. We may take an illustration from Justin, who brings forward Genesis xlix. 11, 'binding his foal to the vine, and his ass's colt to the choice vine'. He then tells us that this signified what was to happen to Christ, 'for the foal of an ass stood tethered to a vine at the entrance of a village, and he ordered his acquaintances to bring it to him . . . and he mounted and sat on it, and entered Jerusalem'.[15] Our present Gospels say nothing about a vine at Bethany.

Further evidence that the apostles who went forth from Judea in the reign of Claudius were equipped with a Testimony Book prepared by Matthew comes to us from other sources. The *Acts of Barnabas*, though late and rather legendary, tells how Barnabas, when going to Cyprus,[16] took with him documents he had received from Matthew, 'a book of the Word of God, and a narrative of miracles and doctrines'. In the synagogue at Salamis, 'Barnabas, having unrolled the Gospel which he had received from Matthew, his fellow-labourer, began to teach the Jews.' The sequel tells how, on the martyrdom of Barnabas, the manuscripts were put away secretly in a cave with his remains. The reference to the second document, 'a narrative of miracles and doctrines', may relate to the Teaching Document, the second source used by Matthew and Luke, known to modern scholars as Q, of which Kirsopp Lake has written, 'It is probably not too much to say that every year after A.D. 50 is increasingly improbable for the production of Q.'[17]

We also have the report of Eusebius that Pantaenus, an eminent Christian of Egypt in the late second century, visiting the East, 'found the Gospel of Matthew, which had been delivered before his coming to some who had knowledge of Christ, to whom Bartholomew, one of the apostles, as it is said, had preached and left them that writing of Matthew in Hebrew characters'.[18] This copy, according to Jerome, Pantaenus took back with him to Alexandria.

There is reason to believe, then, that the situation in Palestine between A.D. 45 and 50 was a major cause of the widespread missionary journeys of the Nazorean apostles and created the need for setting down the prophecies believed to have been fulfilled by Jesus with some account of his teaching and activities. These records were in Hebrew, and had been compiled by Matthew. Paul probably had a copy of the Testimony Book, to which he is referring when he writes to the Corinthians that he had delivered to them what he had himself received, 'that Christ died for our sins according to the Scriptures'.[19]

On the showing of such evidence as we possess there were written accounts of Jesus within about fifteen years of his death. Except as they are reflected in the Gospels, however, these Hebrew sources are lost and the early translations made of them. It is possible, nevertheless, to learn something of the contents and structure of the Testimony Gospel.

Evidently in presenting the material a sentence from one prophet was sometimes tacked on to or combined with the words of another prophet. Classic examples are Mal. iii. 1 running on into Isa. xl. 3, ascribed to Isaiah in Mk. i. 2–3, and a passage from Zech. xi. 12–13 mixed with some allusion to Jer. xxxii. 6, 9, ascribed to Jeremiah in Mt. xxvii. 9. It is not only that the secondary authority is substituted for the primary, but that excerpts from different works are combined to make a continuous quotation. We find the same thing in Justin's use of the testimonies, for instance, 'A Star shall arise from Jacob, and a Flower shall come up from the root of Jesse.'[20] The first part is from Nu. xxiv. 17 and the second from Isa. xi. 1; but the sentence reads as a single quotation and is attributed to Isaiah. We may assume, therefore, that this kind of combination appeared in the Testimony Book.

We know now from the recovered Dead Sea Scrolls that the composition of such a book was no Nazorean novelty: it was quite typical of what was being done by the Jewish eclectic groups, who prepared a number of Biblical anthologies, some of them messianic, with and without interpretation, as well as providing more extended explanatory commentaries on books of the Bible. Their oracular employment of the Scriptures was of the same order as that of the Nazoreans.

At an early date the Christian testimony material seems to have been arranged under headings in accordance with an outline of developments. We have a hint of this in Paul's speech before Agrippa in the Acts. 'I continue unto this day . . . saying none other things than those which the Prophets and Moses did say should come; that the Messiah should suffer, that he should be the first that should rise from the dead, and shew light unto the [Jewish] people, and to the Gentiles.' Justin, some fifty years later than the authorship of the Acts, is even more explicit: 'In these books, then, of the Prophets we found Jesus our Messiah foretold as coming, born of a virgin, growing up to man's estate, and healing every disease and every sickness, and raising the dead, and being hated, and unrecognised, and crucified, and dying, and rising again, and ascending into heaven, and being, and being called the Son of God. We find it also predicted that certain persons should be sent by him into every nation to publish these things, and that among the Gentiles (rather than among the Jews) men should believe in him.'[21] Justin was obviously familiar with an expanded Greek version of the testimonies, taking in much more of what became the Christian story of Jesus.

Elsewhere, Justin urges that Christians have not accepted Jesus without being able to produce proof, and asks: 'With what reason should we believe of a crucified man that he is the firstborn of the Unbegotten God, and himself shall pass judgement on the whole human race, unless we had found testimonies conconcerning him published before he came?' He claims that the predictions were made at five intervals of time, and this raises the question whether the Testimony Book had originally or assumed a five-book structure, which in fact is the literary structure of canonical Matthew.

A Jewish tradition has it that Jesus had five disciples, whose names are given as Matthai, Naki, Netser, Buni and Todah.[22] The first name evidently has Matthew in mind; but the discussion of the passage shows that otherwise individuals are not the subject but proof-texts from the Bible in favour of Jesus, which are met by counter-texts. The tradition thus witnesses to a five-divisioned collection of testimonies associated with Matthew, which Rendel Harris argued convincingly was the form of the Testimony Book.

In further support it is on record that the work of Papias, who stated that Matthew had compiled the Oracles in Hebrew, was also in five books and entitled, *Exposition of the Oracles relating to the Lord*. It may well be the case that the author of canonical Matthew is being more faithful to the spirit and design of the Testimony Book than any of the other Evangelists, and he may be believed to have been greatly influenced by a Greek version of it. This would account for the Gospel being attributed to Matthew.

While we are on the earliest sources of information about Jesus we must revert to the Gospel of Mark. Concerning its origin Papias had obtained secondhand some particulars on the authority of John the Elder of Ephesus which are of considerable interest. We quote his statement in full.

'Mark, having become the interpreter of Peter, set down accurately as much as he remembered, though not in order, of the things said and done by Christ. For neither did he hear the Lord, nor did he follow him; but afterwards, as I said, followed Peter, who adapted his instructions to the needs (of his hearers), but had no design to provide a connected account of the things relating to the Lord. So then Mark made no mistake in setting down some things as he remembered them; for he took care not to omit anything he heard or to include anything false.'

What Papias is telling us may be slightly elaborated to make it clear. Mark had followed Peter, and acted as his interpreter for the reason no doubt that Peter could only express himself in

Aramaic. Subsequently—and this could be much later—Mark wrote down what he could recall of what Peter had related in his addresses about various things which Jesus had said and done. Such recollections of sayings and incidents could not be arranged in consecutive order, since Peter had introduced them to suit the occasion, and had not specified the sequence in which they occurred.

How apt is this tradition as applying to canonical Mark? It cannot be denied that to a considerable extent it fits. This Gospel is episodal, with little real connection between many of the episodes. It reproduces certain words of Jesus in Aramaic, as Peter may well have quoted them. The style is not literary, and conveys the sense of a spoken rather than a written story told unaffectedly with great economy of words, yet with a rugged charm and convincing Palestinean colouring. In creating this biographical presentation the author must have depended on some personal source, and the evidence points to this source being Peter.

Canonical Mark does not allow us to agree entirely with Papias, because this Gospel betrays purposes and tendencies which reflect a situation which arose some years after Peter's death, and attitudes for which Peter could not have been responsible. We shall have more to say about this in the next chapter. But we may point out here that Brandon and others have seen in Mark the re-emergence of Pauline Christianity, which for a decade or more before the fall of Jerusalem had lost ground heavily to the Nazoreans. After Paul's arrest about A.D. 58 church after church of his founding had defected to the doctrine of the supreme Jerusalem authority,[23] and in Italy, where it is most probable that Mark was written, and where there were many Jewish-Christians, Paul's teaching was strongly opposed.[24] It would seem, however, that Mark was with Paul at the end,[25] and could have been influenced by him. The fall of Jerusalem wrought a great change, and under the new conditions much of what Paul had stood for could be reasserted and help to formulate a revised Christianity in much the same way as the rabbis after the war formulated a revised Judaism.

It could have happened that Mark's Gospel, written between A.D. 75 and 80, was an instrument in bringing about a combination of the Palestinean Petrine doctrine with the more Hellenistic Pauline teaching and Christology. At any rate the New Testament associates Mark with Peter as well as Paul, and suggests a reconciliation between the Petrine and Pauline positions.[26]

We must not, then, be carried away by favourable first impressions of Mark's Gospel, since it was performing a function which became essential if Christianity was to survive the defeat of the Jews and the cutting off of communication with the remnant of Nazorean orthodoxy in the East. But it adds greatly to its standing as an authority if it does to an appreciable extent embody remembrances of what had been told by one who had been so close to Jesus as Peter.[27] It is not surprising in these circumstances that the Gospel of Mark should have been hailed by the Gentile Church as a singularly precious possession. Incidentally, there is a link between Peter and the publication of the Testimony Book, for tradition has it that it was in the reign of Claudius that Peter came to Rome.

When we come to assess the character and worth of the Gospels it is important to know that behind them is a considerable amount of material about Jesus, which fortunately, because of Roman oppression in Palestine between A.D. 45 and 55, had been conveyed to other lands before the outbreak of the fatal Jewish revolt against Rome. This material so far as it was in documentary form is not available, though there is always the chance that some of it may be recovered. Consequently, while we can be convinced that Jesus really lived and that a good deal reported about him is worthy of credence, we must accept that we are without direct access to the oldest and most reliable sources of information.

NOTES AND REFERENCES

1. I. Cor. xi. 23–5, xv. 1–7.
2. Rom. i. 3.
3. Gal. ii. 2.

4. Jude 3.

5. Cf. Mk. xv. 24 with Ps. xxii. 18, and Mk. xv. 29 with Ps. xxii. 7. See especially Hoskyns and Davey, *The Riddle of the New Testament*, ch. iv.

6. Mk. ix. 12 and cf. Mk. xiv. 49.

7. Justin Martyr, *I. Apol.* lxvi and lxvii; *Dial.* lxxxviii, etc.

8. J. Rendel Harris, *Testimonies*, Vols. I and II; A. Lukyn Williams, *Adversos Judaeos*.

9. The passage is introduced at *Wars* II. xi. 6. All the Slavonic additions are given in the Appendix to Vol. III of Josephus in the Loeb Classical Library.

10. Tacitus, *Annals*, XV. 44.

11. Euseb. *Eccl. Hist.* Bk. V. xviii. Cf. Mk. xvi. 15; Mt. xxviii. 19.

12. Acts xii. 24–xiii. 3.

13. Euseb. *Eccl. Hist.* Bk. III. v.

14. Euseb. *Eccl. Hist.* Bk. III. xxxix.

15. Justin, *I. Apol.* xxxii.

16. See Acts xv. 39.

17. *Expositor*, VII, vii, p. 507.

18. Euseb. *Eccl. Hist.* Bk. V. x.

19. I. Cor. xv. 3–4, cf. Isa. liii. 8.

20. Justin, *I. Apol.* xxxii.

21. Justin, *I. Apol.* xxxi.

22. Sanhed. xliiia. See Schonfield, *According to the Hebrews*, p. 52 ff.

23. II. Tim. i. 15, and see S. G. F. Brandon, *The Fall of Jerusalem and the Christian Church*, ch. x.

24. Phil. i. 14–17, iii. 1–8. The Gospel had been carried by the Nazoreans to Rome long before Paul was brought as a prisoner to the city as his Epistle to the Romans shows.

25. Philemon 24; II. Tim. iv. 11.

26. I. Pet. v. 13; II. Pet. iii. 15–16.

27. Justin Martyr furnishes from 'the memoirs' information given in Mk. iii. 16–17, and the passage can be read to imply he knew Mark as the Memoirs of Peter (*Dial.* cvi). There is some doubt, however, whether the 'him' in the text refers back to Peter or Jesus, and Justin may only be speaking of the memoirs concerning Jesus and not those of Peter.

5

The Second Phase

THE Christian communities had to face a major crisis with the destruction of Jerusalem as the spritual home of their faith. They were widely scattered, with pockets of believers in many parts of the Roman Empire, with larger organised bodies in the big cities like Rome, Alexandria, Antioch, Ephesus and Corinth, diverse in background and composition. There was a certain amount of communication between the centres, but nothing approaching an integrated universal Church.

Emotional reactions to the outcome of the Jewish war with Rome must have been very mixed. It would be held that spiritually Jerusalem had deserved the fate of Sodom and the plagues of Egypt; but its overthrow had stimulated the Beast to make war with the saints, to overcome them and kill them.[1] Antagonism to Rome would be fostered, and for some time conviction would be intensified that Jesus would speedily return and triumph over the adversary. Many would be bitter against the Jews as the authors of their troubles. Greeks were prone to anti-semitism, and now it would find a lodging in the Church. It would be urged that the Jews had suffered because of their guilt in crucifying Christ, and that they were now clearly rejected by God in favour of the believing Gentiles. Ears would be ready to listen to teachers who opposed all Jewish practices and called for complete freedom from the Law, and even to some who would distinguish between the God of the Jews, the Demiurge, and the True God revealed by and incarnate in Jesus the Saviour.

The kind of reactions we have indicated here are substantiated

by Christian literature of the Sub-Apostolic Age. The position
of the Christians for some decades was a grave one. They were a
persecuted minority without legal status, in many places only
able to meet in private. Mingled with hopes that the calamities
portended the Second Advent there were nagging doubts. The
doctrine of Christ had come from the Jews. Had it been a lying
fable? The victory of Rome seemed complete. 'Who is like unto
the Beast? Who is able to make war with him?'[2] Unless these days
should be shortened there would be no flesh saved. Many found
themselves unable to heed the call to endure to the end: they fell
away and made their peace with the ruler of this world.

The situation in Asia at the beginning of the second century
was reported on to the Emperor Trajan by Pliny the Younger,
when Governor of Bithynia. Some who had been denounced as
Christians 'at first confessed themselves Christians, and then denied it. True, they had been of that persuasion formerly, but had
now quitted it (some three years, others many years, and a few as
much as twenty-five years ago). They all worshipped your statue,
and the images of the gods, and cursed the name of Christ.' On
the other hand there was an abundance of new converts as is
usually the consequence of an ideology being outlawed and pro-
scribed, and Pliny goes on to say that, 'this contagious superstition is not confined to the cities, but has spread through the
villages and the countryside. Nevertheless it seems still possible
to check and cure it.'

Ultimately persecution established and unified the Church, but
for a considerable time after the catastrophe of A.D. 70 there was
darkness and chaos, division and controversy. We obtain an
impression of conditions from the later New Testament documents, and from the Epistle of Clement of Rome to the Corinthians. They have to do with grave internal problems, false
teachers, antinomianism, faction and rivalry, loss of confidence in
the Second Advent, persecution and apostasy. The long discourse
to the disciples put into the mouth of Jesus in the Fourth Gospel[3]
has to be read as a message of exhortation from the author to
the Christian communities with which he was concerned. The

followers of Jesus are told to be at peace with one another and to love one another. Jesus promises not to leave them orphans. He will send them the Spirit of Truth to instruct them. They must remain firmly attached to Jesus or they will perish. They must expect persecution in the world, but he has overcome the world. He prays that they may be united and kept from evil.

We have previously pointed out that nothing wrong was seen in inventing sayings and speeches for individuals in the interests of doctrine or propaganda. This is why we have to be so careful with the Gospels, products of the period between A.D. 75 and 115, to note their tendencies and interests, and reflections of contemporary circumstances.

The Gospels, nevertheless, for all their mythologising and special pleading, must be regarded as among the more potent instruments for saving Christianity from disintegration. They were a tower of strength to their own and following generations of believers, wresting victory from what might well have been utter defeat. They were sorely needed at the time they appeared. They salvaged and co-ordinated enough from the past to inspire the present and assure the future. They held on to the historic Jesus as the rock on which Christian faith was founded, even if they fitted him into the framework of Gentile concepts, even if they used his name as the vehicle through which they could express what was vital for their contemporaries to be told on such high authority. And they kept alive as relevant and indispensable to the Christian hope of salvation that Jesus had appeared among the Jews as the Messiah.

There can be no doubt that the authors of the Gospels did as much as they could to utilise and hand on what they could discover about the life and teaching of Jesus from the limited written sources, and conservatively they preferred these to oral traditions as most likely to be authentic. Mark in employing the discourses of Peter is exceptional; but after him Matthew and Luke make very little use of *agrapha* (unwritten sayings) of Jesus which were current, and which men like Papias were avid to collect, and of which we have one compendium in the recently recovered Gospel of Thomas. The Fourth Gospel has an additional unique source in the memoirs of the Beloved Disciple, but even here the evidence is that these had been recorded before they came into the hands of the author of this Gospel. It is the literary sources of the Gospels with which therefore we must be chiefly concerned. We have already dealt with the Testimony Book, and must now seek more light on the Teaching Document to which we have referred, and on other material such as the nativity stories, and then deal briefly with the environment and aims of the Gospels.

The character of the second major source employed by Matthew and Luke creates the presumption that like the Testimony Book it emanated from Nazorean circles. If this work, as it would appear, was unknown to the author of Mark, a Greek version of it must have come into circulation some time after the war made from a Hebrew or Aramaic original possibly preserved by the survivors of the Palestinean community, which would argue that the Nazoreans managed to reorganise themselves. That they did so is confirmed by the information available to us.

Eusebius relates,[4] on the authority of Hegesippus in the second century, that those apostles and disciples that remained alive after the war, together with members of the family of Jesus, met and took counsel concerning who should be titular head of the Nazoreans in succession to his brother James. They chose a first cousin of his, Simeon son of Cleophas. Cleophas had been a brother of Joseph the father of Jesus. This Simeon lived to a great age, and was finally crucified by the Romans in the reign of Trajan. Also associated with the leadership were James and Sokker, grandsons of Jesus' brother Jude.

Thus there was set up in the East a government vested for the time being in the relations of the Messiah, a kind of caliphate, and rather like the position of the Booth family in the Salvation Army after the death of its founder. These relations became known as the Heirs (*Desposyni*), and we must regard it as due to them that the Nazoreans witnessed to the descent of Jesus from David, to his being the first-born of Joseph and Mary, and to his having been designated as the Messiah at his baptism in the Jordan.

It is quite untrue, as Church historians sometimes still assert, that the Nazoreans passed speedily into oblivion. Eusebius records that great numbers of Jews joined them at this time, and this is intrinsically probable because they could offer a sure Hope to those overwhelmed with despair. Rabbinical sources also testify to the influence of Nazorean propaganda on the Jewish people.[5] On Simeon's death, the succession passed to a Jew called Justus, not one of the Heirs, and he was followed in turn by twelve other Jews whose names have been preserved, down to A.D. 132. All of these, says Eusebius, 'were Hebrews from the first, and received the knowledge of Christ pure and unadulterated'.[6] The Nazoreans were in possession of a Gospel written in Aramaic, of which fragments have been preserved, and produced much other literature partly known to us. Their communities were still active as late as the fifth century in the north and east of Palestine.

To what extent the reorganised Nazoreans were able to communicate with Christians elsewhere we cannot tell. Mystery surrounds the epistles of James, Peter and Jude in the New Testament. Some of the Nazorean writings certainly became known to the Christian churches, and one of the earliest could have been the Teaching Document available to Matthew and Luke. Both these Gospels introduce genealogies of Jesus, and that these came from the Nazoreans is stated by Julius Africanus in his *Letter to Aristides*. He declares that they were produced and circulated by the Heirs 'coming from Nazara and Cochaba, Jewish villages, to other parts of the country'. These same survivors of the family of Jesus also related how King Herod, to conceal his own ignoble ancestry, had caused the public registers at Jerusalem to be burnt.

It would be quite in character for a Jewish-Christian Community to be responsible for issuing a book like Q, a *Maaseh Jeshua* (Works of Jesus), and in fact long afterwards a Jewish parody of the Gospel story bore this very title. Sayings of the early rabbis were collected and published, as in the *Pirke Aboth*, and many of their parables were also preserved. So what was done by post-war Judaism could equally be done by the Nazoreans. Indeed, the Talmud alludes to sayings of Jesus in connection with incidents relating to the late first and early second century.

The tone of Q is Judaic, and some of its characteristics may well be due to controversy between the Nazorean position and that of the rabbis. This became intensified in the third and fourth century, as may be seen from the Talmud[7] and from the Nazorean Commentary on Isaiah quoted by Jerome; but it had already started between A.D. 80 and 90. The Nazoreans were particularly opposed to the Oral Torah, which the rabbis claimed went back to Moses on Sinai. With the Nazoreans too, as with the Gentile-Christians, the name of Jesus was being employed in the interests of policy before the close of the first century. In all four Gospels, products of the second phase of Christian experience, we can see Jesus being magnified and becoming more symbolic, more representative of ecclesiastical concerns, whether Christian or Nazorean, in the several areas where they were produced. The miracle is that the real Jesus has managed to survive the treatment of him and persists in the Gospels despite all efforts to take advantage of his incapacity to correct the misrepresentation of his followers. The miracle has happened because so much of what is reported in the Gospels depends on sources which antedate the development of Christian doctrine in the second century.

Near the end of the second century Irenaeus, bishop of Lyons, delivered himself of cogent reasons why it was right and proper for the universal Church to have four Gospels. Among them he mentions the four winds and the four quarters of the earth. He was not entirely without justification, for the probabilities favour the view that the Gospels were produced in areas north, south, east and west of the eastern Mediterranean. We cannot say definitely that this was so, and scholars are not fully agreed, but with the evidence available the hypothesis seems to work out quite well that Mark saw the light in Italy, Matthew in Egypt, Luke in Greece and John in Asia Minor.

There is no need to repeat here what has already been said about Mark. But we do require to mention briefly the tendencies of this Gospel. When it was composed it was unique in Christian literature, a presentation of Jesus for the first time through the medium of biography. This already assured it, while it held the field, of an enthusiastic welcome. When it was written there was a risk that before long Jesus would come to be regarded as a myth, whereas it was basic to Christianity that he was no heavenly being who only appeared to be a man. Mark's Gospel was calculated to obviate this risk, by setting down what tradition had preserved and memory could recall. His work saved the historicity of Jesus. It provided a coherent account of the experiences of Jesus, related to but freed from the intricacies of the prophetic gnosis.

But Mark's Gospel also takes account of the Roman attitude towards the Christians: its tendencies are apologetic. Brandon has shown convincingly[8] that Mark does all he can to dissociate Jesus from Jewish nationalism. He initiates the white-washing of Pontius Pilate. He refrains from mentioning that the apostle Simon was one of the militant Zealots, deliberately leaving the Aramaic word *Qana* untranslated. Conceivably for a similar reason he makes Jesus emphasise his superiority to David rather than his descent from David. According to a tradition, the reigning emperor Vespasian had sought to exterminate the descendants of David to prevent another Jewish messianic uprising.

Obviously we have to note the way in which Mark's Gospel is slanted when we make use of its information.

We turn now to the Gospel in Egypt. We learn nothing from the New Testament about the Church at Alexandria. We are only told that the distinguished preacher Apollos came from that city, and in the Epistle to the Hebrews there is evidence that the author knew the writings of the Jewish philosopher Philo of Alexandria. The city had a very large Jewish population, and with its proximity to Judea must have been one of the first objectives of the Nazorean evangelists. We have already seen in the letter of the Emperor Claudius to the Alexandrians an indication that messianist agents were busy in the city, and it was in the same reign, according to Eusebius, that Mark proclaimed the gospel there. When leaving Alexandria in the eighth year of Nero (A.D. 61–2), Mark appointed a certain Annianus as first bishop, who held office until his death in the fourth year of Domitian (A.D. 84–5). This Annianus was evidently a Jew, for his name represents the Hebrew Hannaniah. He was succeeded by Avilius (i.e. Abel), another Jew.

From ancient times Egypt had been a place of refuge for Jews escaping from political troubles in Palestine. Here many had fled from the overthrow of Jerusalem by the Babylonians in the sixth century B.C., an event which Jews in A.D. 70 recalled only too poignantly. We know from Josephus that refugees again poured into Egypt as a result of the parallel disaster, including some 600 of the Zealots, and we would expect that a number of Nazoreans reached Alexandria to swell the community there.

The circumstances, as Brandon has pointed out, were conducive to the production in Alexandria rather than in Antioch in Syria, as many scholars hold, of a Gospel like that of Matthew, and would explain the characteristics of this Gospel, at once Judaic and universalistic. No other Gospel conveys so much that the great national calamity had been a punishment for the guilt of what had been done to the Messiah. No other so combines the limitation of the mission of Jesus to his own people with the recognition that Gentiles have by faith been admitted to the heritage of Israel to replace the children of the Kingdom who have been cast out.

Elements in the nativity story peculiar to the Gospel of Matthew may be thought to be another pointer to its Alexandrian origin. The account of the birth of Jesus is of course built on the legends of the birth and infancy of the great figures of Israel, Abraham and Moses, current among the Jews. But in the Gospel they are brought into relation with the virgin birth legend typical of Greek heroes like Perseus and Alexander himself, most apt for the land of Isis and the infant Horus, and having some support in the allegorical Biblical interpretations of the first-century Hellenised-Jewish author Philo of Alexandria. A feature of Matthew's story is that the infant Messiah escapes death by the flight of his parents to Egypt; so it is possible that we have here a reflection of the flight of Nazoreans to Egypt at the time of the war with Rome. This flight also was in obedience to a vision: one tradition speaks of the warning being conveyed by an angel as in the Gospel story. It seems improbable in the face of what Josephus tells us[9] that the Nazoreans fled to Pella beyond Jordan as report has it, though they were in this area much later. Pella may have replaced the original Pelusium, the Egyptian border town on the way from Palestine. In the Gospel, Herod, to destroy the Messiah, killed the babes of Bethlehem, David's city. So Vespasian, as we have mentioned, 'after the capture of Jerusalem, commanded all of the family of David to be sought, that no one might be left of the royal stock'.[10]

Since the find of a substantial collection of gnostic manuscripts in Egypt, notably the Gospel of Thomas with its Sayings of Jesus, some of which were previously known from the fragmentary Oxyrhynchus Papyri, the view has been strongly favoured that part of this material derived from Jewish-Christian sources and reached Egypt from Palestine. There are links with the Nazorean Gospel of the Hebrews, which came to be regarded by some as the Hebrew original of Matthew.

It is worthy of consideration, therefore, that Matthew originated in Egypt. If Mark did evangelise this country his Gospel, brought to Alexandria on one of the ships which sailed regularly from Rome, would be assured of a special welcome and greatly assist the Christians in Egypt to sort out their problems.

The author of Matthew united the five-book structure of the Testimony Gospel with the groundwork of Mark, and greatly impressed with the Teaching Document brilliantly assembled sayings of Jesus in the long discourse of the Sermon on the Mount. The result of his achievements was an amalgam of Eastern and Western elements, an association of Jewish and Gentile interests, a formulation of something like a Christian orthodoxy. These features, and the concern of the author with the status of the Church and its internal discipline, suggest that the Gospel was composed near the close of the first century, possibly in its last decade. The author sometimes combines his sources, so that we have two Gadarene demoniacs and two blind men cured at

Jericho, and he introduces legendary elements not only in the nativity story but in his account of the crucifixion. The community for which he wrote was still partly Jewish; but he himself was not a Jew and his written sources were Greek. No Jew would have understood the Hebrew parallelism in Zech. ix. 9, so as to suppose that both an ass *and* a foal were brought to Jesus for his entry into Jerusalem. Neither would a Jew have made the welcoming crowd cry, 'Hosanna *to the* Son of David.'

The Gospel of Matthew is most important to us for bringing us nearest to the Testimony Book, and for preserving sayings of Jesus which ring true, and which were either unknown to or omitted by Luke because of their particularist Jewish complexion.

As regards Luke, tradition has it that he gave expression to the gospel which Paul preached. This was a reasonable inference from the evidence that Luke the physician had been a companion of Paul, that the Gospel has a universalistic outlook and some points in common with Pauline teaching, and that Paul is the hero of the author's second treatise, the Acts of the Apostles. It is unlikely, however, that Luke was the author, since the Gospel must be dated around A.D. 105, and the Acts at least a year or two later. But there is no reason why he should not have had access to Lukan material, such as the diary sections used in the Acts, preserved at Philippi or elsewhere in Greece.

The character of the Third Gospel is quite different to that of Mark and Matthew. It has even stronger apologetic interests in relation to the Roman authorities, and the preface suggests that the author designed his book for, or at least had in mind, the interested non-Christian reader. He is writing at a time rather more favourable for the Christians, such as was experienced in the reign of Trajan, and he avoids reference to internal Church problems. He is a good evangelist, but not a keen controversialist: he is urbane, prone to idealise and to tone down harshness. The Jesus he portrays is a more gentle sympathetic figure, healing and teaching out of innate virtuousness and love of humanity, correcting the widespread view that the Christians were subversive and haters of mankind. The author's devotion to the Christ is rather like that of Damis, who early in the second century composed a life of his teacher, the famous sage Apollonius of Tyana.

With Luke the Hebraic and the Hellenic are happily integrated, and he is much influenced by the Greek Old Testament. In the sermon of Jesus at Nazareth there is introduced the incident of the widow of Sarepta in the time of Elijah, and the cure of Naaman the Syrian in the time of Elisha. In the nativity stories of John the Baptist and Jesus the Evangelist borrows from the story of the birth and infancy of Samuel, even to applying to Jesus the language of I. Sam. ii. 26.[11] The aged Simeon may have come from the Nazorean leader Simeon son of Cleophas, who was alive in the reign of Trajan and a reputed centenarian, but he also bears a likeness to the old priest Eli of the Samuel story, and the name of Anna the prophetess is that of Samuel's mother. Like the Old Testament Hannah, Elizabeth mother of the Baptist longs for a son, and when her petition to God is heard she dedicates the child to the Lord as a perpetual nazarite, and sings a song of thanksgiving. The Magnificat, as Rendel Harris established, is the song of Elizabeth not of Mary and to be compared with I. Sam. ii. 1–10. The correspondences are too considerable for mere coincidence. Luke is the only Evangelist to give the age of Jesus at the beginning of his ministry, namely about thirty years old. This may be quite unhistorical and based on the age at which David began to reign,[12] and perhaps also on the age that Joseph was made viceroy of Egypt.[13] We have illustrated in Part Two, Chapter 3, the combining of David and Joseph messianic material.

Luke's Gospel is more purposefully biographical than Mark. Like Matthew the author uses Mark as a groundwork and has had access to a version of the Teaching Document, and he probably follows the order of this second source more faithfully. But he brings in additional matter obtained from other sources, and evidently has been at pains to seek out supplementary information, some of which may have come from Nazorean circles. We have remarked on his probable knowledge of Simeon son of Cleophas, and he does introduce Cleophas himself in the story of the two disciples on the way to Emmaus. Conceivably the other was Simeon.

Luke makes rather a parade of his qualifications; but proves himself a better storyteller than he is a historian, and allows himself a good deal of imaginative licence. Where he has insufficient data at his disposal he does not hesitate to borrow language and incidents from non-Christian authorities to amplify his narrative and heighten effects. His requisitioning of the Book of Samuel has already come out; but his favourite authority was the Jewish historian Josephus, who was an older contemporary. From Josephus he learnt of the census carried out when Quirinius was legate of Syria (A.D. 6–7), and saw in the census decree the cause why Joseph and Mary went to Bethlehem where Jesus was born. In the autobiography of Josephus he discovered that the historian had been a precocious child, and had written: 'While still a mere boy, about fourteen years old, I won universal applause for my love of letters; insomuch that the chief priests and learned men of the city [Jerusalem] used constantly to come to me for precise information on some particular of our ordinances.' This was just the thing to help bridge the huge gap in the life of Jesus with an account of how he went to Jerusalem at the age of twelve and amazed the learned men in the Temple with his knowledge and understanding.

There is much more of this sort of embellishment. The parable of the pounds is developed from the history of Archelaus, Herod's successor, as related by Josephus,[14] who went from Judea to a far country (Rome) to obtain a kingdom, and whose citizens hated him, and sent an embassage after him to say, 'We will not have this man to reign over us.' The reference to the Galileans, whose blood Pilate had mingled with their sacrifices, echoes the riot caused by Pilate's use of the Temple treasure to bring water to Jerusalem.[15] Similarly the story of the Samaritans who stopped Jesus and his followers from Galilee entering their village, because Jesus was going up to Jerusalem, utilises the incident in Josephus of a refusal by the Samaritans to permit Galileans to enter one of their villages on the way to Jerusalem.[16] Then there is Luke's version of the healing of the centurion's servant, where he has added that the Roman official 'loveth our nation, and hath built us a synagogue'. He bears a likeness to the Roman legate of Syria who befriended the Jews when the Emperor Gaius insisted on placing his statue in the Temple, and had told them, 'For I am under authority as well as you,'[17] which is nearest to what the centurion says in Luke, 'For I also am a man set under authority.'

Apart from Josephus, Robert Graves has detected Luke's employment of elements of the first chapter of *The Golden Ass* by Lucius Apuleius (above pp. 177, 181 f.) in his account of the two disciples on the road to Emmaus. From the various indications of Luke's reading, and other considerations, his Gospel is probably to be dated as we have suggested around A.D. 105.

Another characteristic of this Evangelist is to adapt the wording of his Christian sources to suit the environment with which his Greek readers were familiar. In the Sermon, Matthew speaks of one man who built his house on rock, and another who built his on sand. Luke changes this to a man who *dug deep* and laid the foundations on a rock, while the other built his on the surface without a foundation.[18] In the case of the cured paralytic, Mark says that those who brought him uncovered the roof by breaking it up, appropriate to an Eastern mud roof, but Luke makes them remove tiles.[19]

The Jesus of Luke is still very much the Messiah, the Son of David, but he is also to be known as Son of God, revealing his quality as the seeker and saver of all lost souls, whatever their nationality. Thus Luke skilfully manages to have the best of both worlds.

The Gospel in Asia is represented by John, which while it shows some familiarity with the synoptic tradition stands largely on its own, and creates a problem which would not have been nearly so difficult to solve had not the book been quite impossibly attributed to the Apostle John the son of Zebedee, a Galilean fisherman. The error partly arose from concluding that the anonymous Beloved Disciple, who had leaned on the breast of

Jesus at the Last Supper, must be one of the Twelve. But on this occasion someone whom Jesus greatly trusted could have been present in addition to the Twelve, namely the man in whose house the celebration was held, and who would be entitled to a place of honour next to Jesus. The Twelve, minus Judas, but including John the son of Zebedee, were in hiding at the time of the Crucifixion: but the Beloved Disciple was at the cross, and was told by Jesus to take his mother Mary into his own house. It is in the highest degree improbable that the humble Galilean fisherman owned a house in Jerusalem and had ready access to the palace of the high priest.[20] Peter, also a Galilean fisherman, could not get in without the mysterious disciple's help. The house could well be the same where the disciples met later to choose a successor to Judas, and where the mother of Jesus was present.[21]

The matter of the house is simply contributory evidence. It has to be taken in conjunction with the testimony of Polycrates, bishop of Ephesus at the end of the second century, that John the Beloved Disciple, buried at Ephesus, had once served as Jewish high priest. This is an exaggeration, but it is not to be doubted that he had been a Jewish priest. As the writer has pointed out in the preface to his translation of John's Gospel: 'He betrays his priestly office not only by his accurate references to Jewish ritual and Temple worship, but when he speaks of the priests not going into the praetorium to avoid defilement, and when he will not himself enter the tomb in which Jesus had been laid until he knows there is no corpse there.'[22] This man, whoever he was, was personally known to the high priest, and it is not far-fetched to identify him with the owner of the house in Jerusalem in which the Last Supper was held. Jesus must have been very sure of the devotion of the unnamed householder to trust himself completely to him. Certainly we can say that the Galilean John was no priest, and in Luke's account of the arrangements for the Last Supper this apostle was sent with Peter to follow a man who would lead them to the secret rendezvous.

Tradition makes John the Beloved Disciple and seer of the Revelation die at an advanced age at Ephesus in the reign of

Trajan, after being persuaded against his inclination to dictate his reminiscences of Jesus. Yet the study of the Fourth Gospel shows that it is not his work as it stands. Another major hand can be detected, which from the style can be identified with the author of the Epistles of John, who is called the Elder. Eusebius speaks of the graves of two Johns being shown at Ephesus. This John the Elder was still living in the time of Papias (c. A.D. 140), and is cited as an authority by Irenaeus. As we can discern, he was able to employ the memoirs of the aged priest in a Gospel, which otherwise is entirely his own, but distinguishes himself from the Beloved Disciple in two footnotes.[23]

What the relationship was between the Greek Elder and the aged Jewish priest it is impossible to know; but in some way the Elder became the inheritor of his material and could claim to be the repository of his testimony. This put him in a very strong and authoritative position, and helped to create a confusion of identity. Through the Fourth Gospel we can still to some extent have access to the recollections of the last-surviving direct disciple of Jesus, because the book exhibits the existence of an underlying design to present Jesus as Messiah in a series of signs, introduced by the words 'after this' or 'after these events'.

When the old priest dictated his material this was some sixty-five years after the events described, and we have to allow for errors of recollection and uncertainties about time and place. Nevertheless we do get a glimpse of important circumstances not represented in the synoptic tradition. Familiarity is shown with the topography of Palestine, especially that of Jerusalem. On several occasions this authority was an eyewitness of what he related. He introduces persons of consequence not mentioned in the other Gospels, like Nicodemus and Lazarus the brother of Martha and Mary. To the Elder, a Greek whose background and Christian philosophy was very different from that of the old priest, the material was a godsend, since it invested his own peculiar teaching with an atmosphere of authenticity it would not otherwise have possessed, and enabled him to express his ideas through the mouth of Jesus. The fusion created the puzzle which the Fourth Gospel has always presented of early and late elements, Jewish and anti-Jewish, which can only be satisfactorily explained by recognition of the distinct contributions.

The second John (the Elder) is almost Marcionite in his way of thinking; so that it is not surprising that a tradition survived in the *Antimarcionite Prologues* that the Beloved Disciple had dictated his recollections to Marcion of Pontus who later turned heretic. For the Elder, if the writer may quote himself again: 'Jesus is the Divine son of the Father, whose earthly birth is not mentioned. He has come direct from God and entered the world, and returns to God. His human qualities largely disappear. He addresses the Jews as though not himself a Jew, and in disparaging terms. The Law of Moses is "your Law" . . . The peculiarity of the Dialogue (Greek-type material supplied by the Elder), in keep-with its nature, is that both the Jews and the Apostles appear in it virtually as lay figures, enabling Jesus to make his points by their interjection of unreal comments and questions. The discourses of Jesus himself are full of repetitions. He speaks indeed exactly as the author of I. John writes.'[24]

The Gospel is prefaced by a Prologue, which is of some service in locating and dating the book in its present form. The Prologue takes the form of a hymn in twelve stanzas, each declaimed line being followed by a response. The hymn is to Christ as the Divine Logos and Light of the World, and could well be the same as that mentioned by Pliny the Younger in his letter about the Christians to the Emperor Trajan, written when he was Governor of Bithynia in Asia Minor (*c.* A.D. 112). He says that the Christians 'met on a certain day, *before it was light,* and sang an antiphonal chant to Christ, as to a god'. This dawn hymn must therefore have been a popular one among Christians in Asia Minor in Trajan's reign at the time the Fourth Gospel was composed. There are other links with Asia Minor, besides this and the Ephesian testimony of the two Johns buried at Ephesus. The Apostle Philip is given greater prominence in this Gospel, and tradition has it that he and his daughters were buried at Hierapolis, where Papias became bishop. Andrew and Thomas also receive special mention, and they are quoted among the sources of information used by Papias, together with John the Elder, who was still living.

The Fourth Gospel may thus be dated about A.D. 110–15. It is the latest of the canonical Gospels, and yet preserves certain first-hand memories of Jesus in what is left of the record of the Beloved Disciple. This man lived to such an advanced age that in his lifetime he became a legend, so that it was believed he would not die before Jesus should come again.[25]

NOTES AND REFERENCES

1. Rev. xi. 7–8.
2. Rev. xiii. 4.
3. Jn. xiv–xvii.
4. Euseb. *Eccl. Hist.* Bk. III. xi.
5. See R. Travers Herford, *Christianity in Talmud and Midrash.*
6. Euseb. *Eccl. Hist.* Bk. IV. v.
7. R. Travers Herford, op. cit.
8. S. G. F. Brandon, *The Fall of Jerusalem and the Christian Church*, ch. x.
9. See Brandon, op. cit. ch. ix, p. 169 f.
10. Euseb. *Eccl. Hist.* Bk. III. xii.
11. Lk. ii. 52.
12. II. Sam. v. 4.
13. Gen. xli. 46.
14. Joseph. *Antiq.* XVIII. xi; see Lk. xix. 12–27 and cp. Mt. xxv. 14–30.
15. *Antiq.* XVIII. iii. 2; Lk. xiii. 1.
16. *Antiq.* XX. vi. 1; Lk. ix. 52–3.
17. Joseph. *Wars*, II. x. 4; Lk. vii. 1–10.
18. Mt. vii. 24–7; Lk. vi. 47–9.
19. Mk. ii. 4; Lk. v. 19.
20. Jn. xviii. 15–16.
21. Acts i. 13–14.
22. Schonfield, *The Authentic New Testament*, preface to John's Gospel.
23. Jn. xix. 35 and xxi. 24; cp. I. Jn. i. 2.
24. *The Authentic New Testament*, preface to John's Gospel.
25. Jn. xxi. 21–3.

6

Some Gospel Mysteries

IT IS outside the scope of this work to go into the more abstruse aspects of the study of the Gospels, textual criticism and the like, which are in the domain of the specialist and much too technical. Our aim has been to afford some insight into the character of the Gospels and the circumstances in which they originated, restricting our survey to what would sufficiently illustrate and inform.

There was need to be aware that a variety of influences helped to shape the Gospels. There was need to be aware that they were designed to meet situations alien to and later than those prevailing in Palestine in the lifetime of Jesus, and to an extent reflect those situations. There was need to be aware that the Gospels were not only bent on preserving genuine information about Jesus, but were also seeking to guide contemporary Christian affairs. There was need to be aware that the state of the Christians after the Jewish war with Rome affected their attitude both towards the Jews and the Roman authorities. There was need to be aware of the sources of knowledge of Jesus available to the authors of the Gospels, and the ways in which they employed them.

Now we have to move nearer to a position where we can use the Gospels rightly to obtain a dependable picture of Jesus and his activities. Bultmann has pointed out, though he was by no means the first to do so, that 'the proclamation of Jesus must be considered within the framework of Judaism. Jesus was not a "Christian", but a Jew, and his preaching is couched in the thought forms and imagery of Judaism'.[1] We have to qualify this a little, because the Judaism of Jesus was Galilean and partly

sectarian; but the statement is broadly correct. It applies equally
to those who initially transmitted information about him. There
is involved, therefore, for the Gentile, be he believer or sceptic,
an adjustment of his thinking if he is to be sufficiently at home
in a quite unfamiliar environment. The effort, hard for both, must
be harder for the convinced Christian, because so much of what
is dear to him from the Gospels has to be relinquished as un-
authentic or occasionally interpreted differently. With all that
the Church has taught and insisted upon down the centuries,
the Jesus whom informed Christian scholars are in process of
discovering is something of a stranger, and at first contact less
pleasing and acceptable than the idealised quasi-mythical divine
being of Christian faith. Are Christians to be encouraged to get
to know the real Jesus and learn to appreciate him, or is the
Church to seek escape from its dilemma by formulating what
amounts to new myths about him?

At present there is a strenuous effort to salvage that part of
the traditional image which is associated with the Great Teacher
and Revealer of God. Yet having determined that a number of
cherished elements in the teaching of Jesus were not his, this
enterprise is not very successful. The real Jesus did teach, of
course, but essentially about the messianic Kingdom of God,
and how to be worthy of participating in it. He had no cause to
reveal or explain God to his Jewish audiences. What is attributed
to him in this respect, chiefly in the Fourth Gospel, was put into
his mouth for the benefit of non-Jews.

The Jesus of history can be more correctly known only by
those who are willing to see him as a Jewish Messiah. The Gospel
writers tried to tone down the national and political implications
of this cardinal doctrine. For this they had no small excuse in the
circumstances of their time. But they still affirmed it: it simply
could not be eradicated. But every step they took to depict Jesus
in another guise took them further from him. We cannot now
find him again by falling into the same error.

Allowing for the aims and tendencies of the authors of the
Gospels, there probably was not much in their sources which all

of them left out so that no trace of it remains. One of the important values they have is that they retained a good deal which they could not always understand. These things are of special interest. We have also to appreciate, as we have noted in discussion, that before the Gospels were composed the traditions about Jesus had been changing and expanding, and that right from the beginning much information was excluded from record because it served no useful purpose in proclaiming Jesus as the Messiah whose return to inaugurate his kingdom was imminent. Consequently we have to search most thoroughly both in the Gospels and outside them for whatever may assist us in filling in some of the blanks.

The Gospels could not be other than quite short books if they were not to be substantially works of fiction, and we have no right to criticise them for not being full-length studies of the Life and Times of Jesus. Their authors had no such object, neither had they the equipment to achieve it. They were as biographical as their limited information allowed; but, except to a slight extent Luke, they felt no call to engage in historical research, and it would have been almost impossible to undertake it in view of the conditions in Palestine after the war. While speaking about what had happened there at a particular period they furnish no more than a rough and none too reliable an indication of time and place, and references to contemporary life and conditions are mainly incidental. Some officials and certain other persons are named, but there is no attempt to tell us more about them than their connection with events in the life of Jesus. For background information about what was going on we have to turn to other sources. Where should we be without the help, for instance, of the histories of Josephus?

By delving into a variety of records we are able to reconstruct the circumstances, religious, social, political and economic, with tolerable accuracy; and when we have done this, and set what we have learnt beside the Gospel story, we realise that much of what we have discovered is reflected in it and confirmed by it, which testifies to the general reliability of the traditions. But we would not know this without independent investigation. From the Gospels alone we would be unable to see the relevance of what we read to the situation at the time: we could not consider the experiences of Jesus in relation to the external circumstances, or apprehend from his words and activities his reactions to them.

A great deal obviously depends on the chronology of the life of Jesus, because this may be expected to provide important clues to his conduct and to his fate. It is necessary here, therefore, to bring together and somewhat expand points made in the course of the narrative in Part One.

The Gospels tell us that the public ministry of Jesus began shortly before John the Baptist was imprisoned by the tetrarch Herod Antipas, and that Jesus was crucified not very long after the Baptist's execution and when Pontius Pilate was governor of Judea and Caiaphas was high priest. This gives us something tangible to go on, but not nearly enough to suggest that the information was of any great consequence. Yet it could matter very much in which year of Pilate's administration (A.D. 27–36) Jesus was crucified. We are driven to seek further enlightenment from the pages of Josephus.

The governorship of Pontius Pilate was brought to an abrupt end towards the close of A.D. 36 or very early in 37, when his superior the legate of Syria Vitellius ordered him to go to Rome to answer charges brought against him by the Jews and Samaritans. Vitellius came in person to Jerusalem because the Jews were in a dangerous anti-Roman mood due to Pilate's high-handed actions. There at the Passover of A.D. 37 he deprived Caiaphas of his highpriesthood. The latest date for the crucifixion of Jesus is therefore the Passover of A.D. 36, and we cannot rule out that there may be some connection between this event and the fact that within a year both the officials concerned in the death of Jesus had been removed from office. It is pertinent that in A.D. 62 another high priest was deposed for illegally convening a Sanhedrin and passing a death sentence on James the brother of Jesus while a new governor was on the way to Judea and had given no sanction.[2]

According to the Gospels the period of the public activities of Jesus extended from not long before to not long after the imprisonment and execution of John the Baptist. Therefore it must assist us if we can date these events. The ostensible cause of the Baptist's imprisonment by Antipas was that John had denounced as unlawful the tetrarch's marriage to Herodias, widow of his brother Philip.[3] On the evidence of Josephus, Philip died at the end of A.D. 33 or early in 34, and the marriage must be presumed to have taken place in 34. The former wife of Antipas would not tolerate the new union and fled to her father Aretas, king of Arabia Petraea. Aretas did not take the insult to his daughter lying down and prepared for war. Herod had to defend himself. He sent John as a prisoner to the fortress of Machaerus near the Arabian border and made his own headquarters there. Here, before hostilities commenced, John was beheaded. In the battle with the forces of Aretas the army of Herod was heavily defeated, and this, says Josephus, many Jews regarded as a divine judgement on him for killing John.[4] Herod appealed for help to the Emperor Tiberius, who thereupon ordered Vitellius legate of Syria to make war on Aretas and capture or destroy him. Vitellius assembled his forces and was about to launch his attack when news reached him that Tiberius had died (March A.D. 37) and he did not proceed. Following Josephus, we are accordingly able to assign the imprisonment and execution of John the Baptist to the year A.D. 35 shortly before the battle between the forces of Antipas and Aretas in the winter of 35–6. It is to be noted that when Antipas gave the order to behead John this was at a royal banquet, at which Mark mentions that the tetrarch's military commanders were among those present.[5] The baptism of Jesus must then be placed late in 34 or more probably in the spring of 35, and his crucifixion at the Passover of 36 in the last year of Pilate's administration.

The chronology of Luke supports this. He dates the birth of Jesus at the time of the census carried out when Quirinius was legate of Syria, which was in A.D. 6–7, and the commencement of the preaching of John the Baptist in the fifteenth year of the reign of Tiberius (A.D. 28–9). When Jesus was baptised by John he 'began to be about thirty years of age'. So that in A.D. 35 he would have been twenty-nine. Luke's system thus fits in with the evidence of Josephus, on whom, as we have seen, he relies a good deal. Matthew's chronology does not affect the date of the ministry and crucifixion of Jesus: it only makes him a considerably older man, born in 6–5 B.C. in the reign of Herod the Great, who died in 4 B.C. Therefore at the date of his crucifixion in A.D. 36 Jesus would have been about forty-one, which would more nearly agree with John's Gospel, where the Jews of Jerusalem say to Jesus, 'Thou art not yet fifty years old.'[6]

We cannot by any means get away from the fact that it is the imprisonment and execution of John the Baptist which governs the date of the ministry and crucifixion of Jesus, and since we know the time of the former we know that of the latter also. We can say that Jesus was crucified at the Passover of A.D. 36 and this information obviously makes all the difference to the understanding of the Gospel story.

Let us take first the controversy in the Temple in Passion Week. When Jesus was challenged to state his authority for disrupting the Temple market he replied by asking the priests whether the baptism of John was divinely inspired or not. This put his opponents in a quandary because the people regarded John as a prophet. The question of Jesus is seen to have much more force and relevance when we appreciate that the death of John was fresh in the public mind, and that they regarded the recent destruction of the army of Antipas as a punishment from God because the tetrarch had executed the Baptist.

Light is also thrown on the question put later to Jesus as to whether the Roman poll tax should be paid to Caesar. The census for the purpose of this tax was made every fourteen years, and the year 34–5 was a census year. So the detested tax, which the Jews regarded as tantamount to enslavement, was currently due for payment when the barbed question was posed. Only a few days earlier there had been growls of protest when Jesus had elected to spend a night under the roof of Zacchaeus the tax-collector at

Jericho. We may have an echo of public feeling at this period in the statement of Josephus that Vitellius when he came to Jerusalem the following year relieved the citizens of the tax on fruit and vegetables. He could of course do nothing about the poll tax which was the emperor's perquisite, but his action was obviously intended to placate the people to the extent that lay in his power. We should further note that the Roman proclamation of the year 35 as census year, which signified the mastery of Caesar, was countered by Jesus as Messiah in proclaiming in the synagogue the very same year as 'the acceptable year of the Lord'. This was as good a riposte as his answer to the question about the tax in the Temple.

The ministry of Jesus is thus seen to have coincided with a period of public unrest and of political disturbances. In A.D. 35 Herod Antipas was in trouble with his subjects on account of John the Baptist, and had a war on his hands with Arabia, which compelled him to deplete Galilee of armed forces in order to send them to Perea across the Jordan. He had every reason to be concerned that the Galileans, hostile to the Herodians, would seek to profit by the circumstances and stage a rising, and he would know that the Baptist had told the people to expect the coming of one mightier than himself. Jesus could hardly have chosen a more opportune or a more dangerous moment to conduct a campaign in Herod's territory announcing the near advent of the Kingdom of God. We have the report in Luke that some of the Pharisees warned Jesus that Herod was out to kill him, and urged him to make good his escape.

Antipas was not the only one in trouble. So was Pontius Pilate, governor of Judea. He had earned the detestation of the Jews, both the hierarchy and the people, by employing the sacred funds of the Temple to bring water to Jerusalem. They had staged a massive protest. Pilate had the crowds surrounded by his soldiers garbed as civilians, but with daggers concealed under their cloaks, who at a prearranged signal fell on the people when they refused to disperse and killed many of them. It is at this point in his history[7] that Josephus introduced his reference to

Jesus, not the bogus passage we read now, but one which will have been less complimentary and which Christian hands amended. We can be confident that Galilean Zealots will have been among the angry crowd, and so it would have been proper at this juncture, and chronologically right, for Josephus to refer to the Galilean prophet Jesus. Luke's copy of Josephus would no doubt have had the genuine passage; for he seems to depend on the incident as he read it when he tells us of those who reported to Jesus about those Galileans whose blood Pilate had mingled with their sacrifices.[8] Did Luke also obtain his story of the fall of the tower at Siloam from the same source? It would appear to be in relation to the rioting that broke out over Pilate's requisitioning of the sacred funds that Mark speaks of Barabbas being in prison in chains 'with them that had made insurrection with him, who had committed murder in the insurrection'.[9]

Pilate was also in bad odour with the Samaritans. They too at this time were expecting a messianic personality, the Taheb, who would bring to light the sacred vessels of the Tabernacle hidden in ancient times on Mount Gerizim. A man now appeared claiming to be the Taheb, and multitudes of Samaritans assembled to follow him up the mountain. Pilate, treating this activity as the beginning of a revolt, sent his forces against them, killing many and capturing and executing the leaders. The Council of the Samaritans at once wrote to Vitellius, accusing Pilate of murdering innocent people.[10] This incident underlines the peril in which Jesus stood in proclaiming the Kingdom of God to the multitudes in Galilee, even though Pilate had no jurisdiction in this area, and explains what the Gospels do not clearly reveal—the reasons why he had to be so guarded and circumspect in his speech, and why until nearly the end he had to keep secret that he was the Messiah and refuse to allow himself to be addressed as the Son of David.

We can also now see the difficult position of Pontius Pilate when Jesus was brought before him by the priests as an instigator of revolt. The governor was fully aware that both the Jews and Samaritans were his bitter enemies and that the gravest charges of cruelty and tyranny were hanging over his head. He would have every justification at this time to be extremely wary, and that the Jewish authorities were inviting him to try a fellow-Jew on such a charge would put him at once on the defensive. The way in which he acted only makes sense if it is brought out that Pilate, who had earned a reputation for arrogance and harshness, was just now in a particularly vulnerable position. No doubt he had already been admonished by Vitellius, and, as we have seen, at the end of 36 he was ordered back to Rome. Pilate's dilemma is not made sufficiently clear in the Gospels, though we get some impression of it from Luke and John.[11] If Jesus was innocent and Pilate condemned him this would be another count against him at Rome. If Jesus was guilty and he released him he would be condoning treason against Caesar.

Interpretation of the Gospels can so easily go astray because of their reticence and their apologetic tendencies, and we have to compensate for their deficiencies from external sources. If we wish to know the real Jesus we have to be acutely conscious of all that was going on at the time, the highly charged atmosphere and political tension. We have to think of him not as a divine being or teacher of ethics, but as a son of his country, a man with the blood of kings in his veins, exercising authority, because he believed it to be his messianic destiny, in circumstances of great danger and difficulty, addressing himself to a populace longing for inspired leadership and national liberation.

The Gospels speak of the eager crowds, but only occasionally, as when they would have taken him by force and made him king, do they grant us a glimpse of what was in the mind of many who flocked to him. They tell of those who regarded Jesus as a menace; but they would have us understand that the opposition was largely religious. They fail to make adequately plain that Jesus spoke in parables, when he proclaimed the Kingdom of God, because of the presence of spies and informers, a security system introduced by Herod the Great. There would be an end to argument about the implication of some of the sayings of Jesus if these had been set squarely in the context of the contemporary conditions. Nothing makes Jesus so incredible historically as treating him as a kind of palimpsest superimposed on the records of his period, a being who was in his desperate world but not of it, making pronouncements in hot-blooded Galilee, of all places, with an air of Olympian detachment.

The paucity of information in the Gospels and the special pleading is at times quite aggravating. A number of sayings of Jesus are extremely doubtful and it is uncertain with others what is their correct context. Some of them were coined in answer to later adverse criticisms like, 'Think not that I am come to destroy the Law' and 'Think not that I am come to send peace on earth.'[12] When we seek to go further back the problem is harder because we do not know what was going on inside the Nazorean community in those days, what internal controversies there were, what disagreements between individuals, what things about Jesus and those associated with him were altered or suppressed.

The authors of the Gospels must bear the responsibility for changes they made themselves, but they cannot be blamed for obscurities inherent in their sources. Indeed we must be grateful to them that frequently they simply reproduced what they found 'warts and all'. But we are still surprised at certain of the things they did not appear to know about, and some which they left without any explanation.

It is curious that the synoptic tradition has a little information about Joseph of Arimathea, but none at all about Nicodemus. And why do we not hear more about Joseph of Arimathea, who comes into the Passion Story abruptly, and almost immediately disappears without trace? It is also curious that the synoptic tradition knows about Martha and her sister Mary, but not about their brother Lazarus. What relationship to them, if any, was Simon the Leper at Bethany?

We may wonder too why there was nothing in any of the sources about the life of Jesus before his baptism. Admittedly, the Testimony Book would have begun with the Baptism, because this was regarded as his inauguration as Messiah. But something might have been told us elsewhere. The Nazorean community at Jerusalem included the mother of Jesus and his brothers, from whom information was obtainable. We learn in the Bible of incidents in the boyhood of David. Why not about the Messiah his descendant? Was there a deliberate silence for reasons of policy? Later generations of Christians did not see why there should be this hiatus, and they partly filled it in after their own fashion with extravagant tales. All we have in the Gospels is the one doubtful story contributed by Luke.

There is another matter which strikes us as strange. When we read the Fourth Gospel we are impressed by the recollections of the unnamed disciple of events at some of which he was present, notably towards the end of this Gospel, his being at the Last Supper, his securing Peter's entry into the palace of the high priest, his presence at the cross, and his later accompaniment of Peter to the tomb. Why is there no mention of any of these things in the synoptic Gospels? If Mark reflects the reminiscences of Peter it would be natural that he should refer to them. It is difficult to avoid concluding that the omission in the synoptic tradition of all knowledge of the mysterious disciple was intentional.

Events of a highly dramatic character, most important for the understanding of the life of Jesus, receive no explanation, though the circumstances clearly call for one. Two instances will suffice, both relating to Passion Week. The first concerns the triumphal entry of Jesus into Jerusalem when he sent two disciples forward to Bethany to obtain an ass which they would find tethered at the entrance to the village. The second event took place later the same week when Jesus and his disciples were at Bethany. In this case Jesus again sent two of his disciples (Luke says they were Peter and John son of Zebedee) to follow a man with a water-pot whom they would encounter at the gate of Jerusalem, who would lead them to the house where he would keep the Passover.

These stories show Jesus making secret arrangements in advance with people whom obviously he trusted implicitly, plans which were so vital that he had not disclosed them even to his closest disciples. They involved signs of recognition. The two who were dispatched by Jesus were furnished with agreed pass-words, in respect of the ass, 'The Master needs him,' and in the case of the owner of the house, 'Which guestroom am I to have to eat the passover with my disciples?' In the first incident the emissaries were to expect to be challenged with the words, 'What are you up to, untying the ass?' In the second they were to look out for a man with a water-pot. The signals were clear on both sides, and everything went according to plan.

The stories, intriguing as they are with their cloak and dagger atmosphere, are straightforward and serve no theological pur-pose. We have no reason to doubt their truth. They throw im-portant light on the behaviour of Jesus. But it would seem as if the sources did not wish to disclose why Jesus had turned to others than the Twelve, to others than Peter, James and John. Why could it not be told afterwards who was the owner of the ass at Bethany and the owner of the house at Jerusalem?

The Gospel mysteries are not confined to those which arise from very early ignorance, neglect and possible concealment of material facts: they extend to the legendary features. For the most part the Evangelists did not create the legends: they inherited them. When we speak of legends we are thinking of occurrences of a miraculous or superhuman character, such as the birth stories in Matthew and Luke with which we have dealt already. We exclude the cures reputed to have been performed by Jesus, which, however exaggerated and multiplied, especially in the interest of the fulfilment of prophecy, do not call for any assumption that Jesus possessed supernatural powers. We may accept that he was a healer and could effect cures of certain complaints where there was co-operative faith. It was the normal thing in those days both among Jews and Gentiles to expect of sages and saints that they should exercise powers of healing, blessing and cursing in a magical fashion. We are more concerned here with other classes of happening, like Jesus stilling the storm and walking on the water, the miraculous feeding of the multitude, and the abnormal circumstances connected with the Crucifixion.

It may be said, of course, that such stories were simply the products of popular superstition; but some of them can be traced to the use of the primitive Testimony Book.

The Nazorean prophetic gnosis inevitably had the potential of inspiring the creation of events. Passages were found in the Scriptures which seemed to demand that some experience of Jesus should realise them. The oracular interpretation of the Scriptures in vogue among the Nazoreans evidently delighted the early Christians, who proceeded to ransack the Greek Old Testament for texts to apply to Christ and Christianity. It became a kind of spiritual game. Gentile believers could go much further than Jews because they accepted the deity of Jesus. References to the Lord (*Kyrios*) in the Greek Bible, and even to God (*Theos*), could be enlisted in the service of the Lord Christ (*Kyrios Christos*). We have an early example in the first chapter of the Epistle to the Hebrews.

For the most part, however, these exercises in oracle hunting would not get into the Gospels. Those would have the best chance which were related to an authentic incident. Three stages would be involved. First there would be the incident itself, reported by tradition. Then the expositors would bring Old Testament oracles to bear on it to exhibit the messianic significance. Finally, the imagery of the oracles would be added to the tradition so as to invest the incident with miraculous features. Let us then look at the stories we have taken as examples.

The basis of the story of Jesus stilling the storm is quite clear. He had been teaching all day from a boat moored at the edge of the Sea of Galilee and was very weary. He gave orders to cross to the other side of the lake, and as soon as it left the shore he fell fast asleep. A tempest arose, but he was so exhausted that it failed to waken him. The boat began to ship water rapidly, and the anxious disciples roused him. Jesus rose, and as he did so the ftorm subsided. The phenomenon is not uncommon on the Sea of Galilee, where the wind will suddenly come rushing through the adjacent gorges lashing the calm waters of the lake to fury, and just as suddenly the tempest will die away.

Since everything which happened to the Messiah must be

meaningful, the expositors were reminded of many passages in
the Psalms which spoke of the Lord in relation to storm and
tempest. 'Which stilleth the noise of the seas, the noise of their
waves'; 'The waters saw thee, O God, the waters saw thee;
they were afraid'; 'Thou rulest the raging of the seas; when the
waves thereof arise, thou stillest them.'[13]

Finally the incident was embellished from the oracular texts.
When Jesus is roused from sleep he rebukes the wind and bids
the sea be still. The fearful disciples ask themselves, 'What manner
of man is this, that even the wind and the sea obey him?'

A similar process has been at work with the story in Mark of
Jesus walking on the water, which is elaborated in Matthew to
include Peter also walking on the water, but sinking. Again the
basis is a storm on the lake. On this occasion Jesus had told his
disciples to cross over by boat, while he went up into a mountain
to pray. But the boat did not get far because a storm came up and
they were forced inshore. As they were struggling with the oars,
Jesus suddenly loomed up before them on the bank in the failing
light of evening, and the superstitious fishermen momentarily
took him for a malignant spirit supposed to haunt these parts.
They were greatly relieved when he called to them, and wading
into the shallows he was taken aboard. As he clambered into the
boat the wind subsided.

When it was said that Jesus walked *by* the sea this was easily
converted to *on* the sea, since the Hebrew word *al* has both
meanings. The oracles said of God, 'Thy way is in the sea, and thy
path in the great waters, and thy footsteps are not known,'[14]
and again, 'Which treadeth upon the waves of the sea.'[15] The
addition about Peter probably derived from teaching about the
Lord's care of believers in peril. 'Save me, O God; for the waters
are come in unto my soul. I sink in deep mire, where there is no
standing: I am come into deep waters, where the floods overflow
me'; 'He sent from above, he took me, he drew me out of great
waters.'[16] The incident emerged fortified by the oracles. Jesus
walks on the water, and Peter cries to him, 'Lord, if it be thou,
bid me come to thee on the water.' And he said, 'Come.' And

when Peter was come down out of the ship, he walked on the water to go to Jesus. But when he saw the wind boisterous, he was afraid, and beginning to sink, he cried, saying, 'Lord, save me.' And immediately Jesus stretched forth his hand and caught him, and said unto him, 'O thou of little faith, wherefore didst thou doubt?'

A not dissimilar type of story development is represented by the feeding of the five thousand of which there is another version in the feeding of the four thousand. Behind the story as we now read it there was no doubt an account of Jesus giving food to the hungry, and search was made to build up its significance. Oracles would be quoted like: 'Can he give bread also? Can he provide flesh for his people?'[17] 'The people asked, and he brought quails, and satisfied them with the bread of heaven.'[18] The Prophet like Moses would perform miracles like Moses. There was another association also, with the antetype Joseph, who had given corn to his brethren in time of famine.

It is observable that the oracles were brought into relation with incidents in the life of Jesus not only to illustrate the fulfilment of prophecy, but to provide sermon lessons. In our previous example there is the teaching that the Lord will be with his people in time of tribulation, and that salvation depends on holding on to faith in him. Such sermonising exposition may be detected in the feeding of the multitude, and the figures quoted will be allegorical. The five loaves may represent the fivefold Testimony Book, the two fish Baptism and the Eucharist, all signifying the Gospel of which those who partook would be abundantly satisfied.[19] The twelve baskets of surplus fragments will perhaps represent the further distribution of the Gospel to all nations, the mandate given to the twelve apostles. The alternative version with seven loaves and seven baskets could bring in the seven deacons (Acts vii) and their subsequent evangelical activities.

With the last story we wish to consider, the strange circumstances connected with the Crucifixion, we are more definitely in the area of Nazorean exposition. The fullest form of the story is found in Matthew xxvii: 'Now from the sixth hour there was darkness over all the land unto the ninth hour . . . Jesus, when he had cried again with a loud voice, yielded up the ghost. And, behold, the veil of the temple was rent in twain from the top to the bottom; and the earth did quake, and the rocks rent; and the graves were opened; and many bodies of the saints which slept arose.' For the rending of the veil of the Temple, the Gospel of the Hebrews stated that the lintel stone of immense size fell. We have also to note that ancient versions at Lk. xxiii. 48 make the people who were present at the Crucifixion cry, 'Woe unto our sins; for the Judgement and the end of Jerusalem is drawn nigh.'[20]

What is being offered to us here is a solemn comparison between the giving of the Old Covenant at Sinai and the sealing of the New Covenant in the blood of the Messiah. There is an associated comparison between the happenings at Sinai and those at Golgotha in relation to the Day of Judgement.

The oracles enlisted to build up the account of the death of Jesus and reveal its messianic significance were inevitably more abundant than for any story connected with his life. Some of the testimonies are still preserved in the Gospels; but we are concerned with those which are not quoted and yet exercise a powerful influence. The following are a few specimens. 'And Mount Sinai was altogether on a smoke . . . and the whole mountain quaked greatly . . . Moses spoke, and God answered him by a voice.'[21] 'And the posts of the door [of the temple] moved at the voice of him who spoke, and the house was filled with smoke. Then said I, Woe is me, for I am undone.'[22] 'Yet once, it is a little while, and I will shake the heavens, and the earth . . . and I will fill this house with glory.'[23] 'Sound an alarm in my holy mountain: let all the inhabitants of the land tremble; for the Day of the Lord cometh, for it is nigh at hand; a day of darkness and of gloominess, a day of clouds and of thick darkness.'[24]

In the ancient Samaritan eschatology we have a direct comparison of the events at Sinai with the Day of Judgement. 'All the signs and wonders which happened at Mount Sinai will be repeated on the Day of Requital, namely, a day of turmoil and lightnings and heavy cloud . . . and a great fear and a mighty sound of a trumpet . . . And so will it be on the day of Requital, the Lord will cover his faithful servants with the cloud of the Garden of Eden, while the wicked will be . . . in deep darkness and anguish of soul . . . Then the bodies will revive, and will come out of the earth.'[25]

From this kind of thinking came the miraculous accompaniments of the Crucifixion, seen by the early expositors as a repetition of the experiences at Sinai appropriate to the New Covenant and as the presage of the coming Day of Judgement. There was the darkness, the quaking of the earth, the voice that cried, the fear of the people, and the rising of the saints.

In such cases as those we have looked at, and there are others, we find incidents made more meaningful and imaginative by teaching arising from Old Testament oracles, so that the events were invested with a legendary character when they were set down in the Gospels. Unless we are familiar with the early Christian methods of exposition and instruction we might suppose that certain miraculous stories in the Gospels were pure invention. We have to understand that between the Evangelists and the originally natural events we have the intervening Christian prophets and teachers, who in Paul's list come next after apostles.[26] What began as edification ended as accepted fact.

NOTES AND REFERENCES

1. Rudolf Bultmann, *Primitive Christianity in its Contemporary Setting*, p. 84 (Fontana Library).

2. Josephus, *Antiq*. XX. ix. 1.

3. The Philip known to the Evangelists (Mk. vi. 17; Mt. xiv. 3; Lk. iii. l) was Philip, the tetrarch half-brother of Herod Antipas, and it is understood that this Philip was the former husband of Herodias. The same assumption is made in a passage introduced into the Slavonic version of Josephus' *Jewish War* (see Appendix to the Works of Josephus, Vol. III, pp. 646-7, Loeb Classical Library). However, according to *Antiq*. XVIII. v. 4, the previous husband of Herodias was another half-brother called Herod, son of Herod the Great by Mariamne, daughter of Simon the high priest. There is no evidence that he also bore the name of Philip.

4. Josephus, *Antiq*. XVIII. v. 1-2.

5. Mk. vi. 21.

6. Jn. viii. 57.

7. Josephus, *Antiq.* XVIII. 3.

8. Lk. xiii. 1.

9. Mk. xv. 7.

10. Josephus, *Antiq.* XVIII. iv. 1–2.

11. In Luke the governor tries to shelve responsibility by passing Jesus on to Herod Antipas, and when the tetrarch exonerates Jesus we are told that 'the same day Pilate and Herod were made friends together; for before they were at enmity between themselves' (Lk. xxiii. 12–16). In John when Pilate tries to release Jesus he is threatened, 'If thou let this man go, thou art not Caesar's friend: whosoever maketh himself a king speaketh against Caesar' (Jn. xix. 12).

12. Mt. v. 17, x. 34.

13. Ps. lxv. 7; lxxvii. 16; lxxxix. 9.

14. Ps. lxxvii. 19.

15. Job. ix. 8.

16. Ps. lxix. 1–2; xviii. 16.

17. Ps. lxxviii. 20.

18. Ps. cv. 40 and lxxviii. 24; cp. Jn. vi. 30–1.

19. Deut. xiv. 29; Ps. xxii. 25–7; Jer. l. 19–20; Joel ii. 26.

20. In the Old Latin and partly in the Curetonian Syriac, also in the *Gospel of Peter*.

21. Ex. xix. 18–19.

22. Isa. vi. 5–6.

23. Hag. ii. 6–7, and cp. Heb. xii. 26.

24. Joel ii. 1–2 and 31.

25. *Yom al-Din* (Day of Judgement). See Gaster, *Samaritan Eschatology*, pp. 153–7.

26. I. Cor. xii. 28–9.

Bibliography

The authorities listed, ancient and modern, are those to which direct reference has been made. A very large number of others have been profitably studied or consulted in preparation for this work, and absence of mention must not be taken to imply any lack of familiarity with or appreciation of their varied contributions. Where translations have been employed consideration has sometimes been given to readiness of accessibility.

Acts of Barnabas, translated by Alexander Walker (Ante-Nicene Christian Library, Vol. xvi), T. & T. Clark (Edinburgh, 1870).

Amulo, Archbishop of Lyons A.D. 841–52, *Epistola, seu Liber contra Judaeos, ad Carolum Regem,* quoted by A. Lukyn Williams in *Adversos Judaeos,* Cambridge University Press (1935).

Anderson, Hugh, *Jesus and Christian Origins,* Oxford University Press (New York, 1964).

Apocalypse of Baruch, translated by R. H. Charles, Adam & Charles Black (London, 1896).

Apocalypse of Ezra, translated by G. H. Box, S.P.C.K. (London, 1917).

Apollonius, Christian martyr late second century, quoted by Eusebius, *Ecclesiastical History,* Bk. V. ch. xviii, translated by C. F. Crusé, Geo. Bell & Sons (London, 1874).

Apuleius, Lucius, *The Golden Ass,* translated by Robert Graves, Penguin Books (1950).

Aron, Robert, *Jesus of Nazareth: The Hidden Years,* translated from the French by Frances Frenaye, Hamish Hamilton (London, 1962).

Assumption of Moses, translated by R. H. Charles, Adam & Charles Black (London, 1897).

Black, Matthew, *The Scrolls and Christian Origins,* Thomas Nelson & Sons Ltd. (1961).

Brandon, S. G. F., *The Fall of Jerusalem and the Christian Church*, S.P.C.K. (London, 1951).

Bultmann, Rudolf, *Primitive Christianity in its Contemporary Setting*, translated by R. H. Fuller, Collins, The Fontana Library (1960).

Burkitt, F. Crawford, *The Gospel History and its Transmission*, T. & T. Clark (Edinburgh, 1925).

Cassius, Dio, *Roman History*, Tauchnitz Edition (Leipzig, 1890).

Clement of Rome, *Epistle to the Corinthians*, translated by J. B. Lightfoot in *The Apostolic Fathers*, Macmillan & Co. (London and New York, 1891).

Clementine Homilies (Ante-Nicene Christian Library, Vol. xvii), T. & T. Clark (Edinburgh, 1870).

Clementine Recognitions (Ante-Nicene Christian Library, Vol. iii), T. & T. Clark (Edinburgh, 1871).

Dead Sea Scrolls, translations by Millar Burrows in *The Dead Sea Scrolls*, Secker & Warburg (London, 1956), and G. Vermes, Penguin Books (1962). Scrolls quoted or referred to: *Community Rule (Manual of Discipline)*; *Damascus Document*; *Genesis Apocryphon*; *Habakkuk Commentary*; *Hymns (Thanksgiving Psalms)*; *Psalms Commentary*.

Drower, E. S., *Mandaean Polemic*, Reprinted from the Bulletin of the School of Oriental and African Studies, Vol. xxv, University of London (1962); *The Secret Adam*, Clarendon Press (Oxford 1960).

Eisler, Robert, *The Messiah Jesus and John the Baptist*, Methuen & Co. Ltd. (London, 1931).

Enoch, Similitudes of, translated by R. H. Charles, *The Book of Enoch*, Clarendon Press (Oxford, 1893).

Epiphanius, *Against Heresies (Panarion)*, edited by Francis Oehler (1859).

Eusebius, *Ecclesiastical History*, translated by C. F. Crusé, George Bell & Sons (London, 1874).

Gaster, Moses, *Samaritan Eschatology*; *Samaritan Oral Law and Ancient Traditions*, Search Publishing Co. (London, 1932).

Gospel of Peter, from *The Apocryphal New Testament*, translated by M. R. James, Clarendon Press (Oxford, 1926).

Graves, Robert, *The Nazarene Gospel Restored*, by Robert Graves and Joshua Podro, Cassell & Co. Ltd. (London, 1953).

Harris, J. Rendel, *Testimonies*, Vols. I–II, Cambridge University Press (1916 and 1920).

Herford, R. Travers, *Christianity in Talmud and Midrash*, Williams & Norgate (London, 1903).

Hoskyns, Sir Edward and Noel Davey, *The Riddle of the New Testament*, Faber & Faber Ltd. (London, 1931).

Hunt, B. W. P. Stather, *Primitive Gospel Sources*, James Clarke & Co. Ltd. (London, 1951).

Irenaeus, *Against Heresies* (Ante-Nicene Christian Library, Vols. v and ix), T. & T. Clark (Edinburgh, 1868–9).

Isaiah, Ascension of, translated by R. H. Charles, S.P.C.K. (London, 1917).

James, M. R., *Apocryphal New Testament*, Clarendon Press (Oxford, 1926).

Jashar, Book of, Sepher Hajashar (Prague, 1840).

Josephus, Flavius, Works of, translations by William Whiston and in the Loeb Classical Library by H. St. J. Thackeray and Ralph Marcus, William Heinemann Ltd. (London) and Harvard University Press (Cambridge, Mass.). *Antiquities of the Jews; Jewish War; Life.*

Josephus, Slavonic, Appendix to *Josephus*, Vol. iii, Loeb Classical Library.

Jubilees, Book of, translated by R. H. Charles, S.P.C.K. (London, 1917).

Julius Africanus, *Letter to Aristides*, quoted by Eusebius, *Ecclesiastical History*, Bk. I. ch. vii.

Justin Martyr, *First Apology* and *Dialogue with Trypho* (Ante-Nicene Christian Library, Vol. ii), T. & T. Clark (Edinburgh, 1867).

Kennard, J. Spencer, Jr., 'The Burial of Jesus' in *Journal of Biblical Literature*, Vol. lxxiv (Philadelphia, 1955).

Lake, Kirsopp, in *The Expositor*, Vol. VII, vii.

Letter of Claudius to the Alexandrians, translated by H. Idris Bell, *Jews and Christians in Egypt*, published by the British Museum.

Maase Abraham, quoted by M. Gaster in *The Chronicles of Jerahmeel* (London, 1899).

Mead, G. R. S., *The Gnostic John the Baptiser*, John M. Watkins (London, 1924).

Memoirs of Hegesippus, quoted by Eusebius in *Ecclesiastical History*, Bk. II. ch. xxiii, Bk. III. ch. xx.

Midrash Tehillim, edition Buber (Vilna, 1891).

Papias, translated by J. B. Lightfoot in *The Apostolic Fathers*, Macmillan & Co. (London and New York, 1891).

Philostratus, *Life of Apollonius of Tyana*, in Loeb Classical Library.

Pirke Aboth (Sayings of the Fathers) in the *Authorised Jewish Prayer Book*, Eyre & Spottiswoode (London, 1916).

Pliny the Elder, *Natural History*, in the Loeb Classical Library, Heinemann and Harvard University Press.

Pliny the Younger, *Letter to the Emperor Trajan* concerning the Christians, in the Loeb Classical Library, Heinemann and Harvard University Press.

Plutarch, *Lives of Great Men*, in the Loeb Classical Library.

Prayer Book, Authorised Jewish, Eyre & Spottiswoode (London, 1916).

Preaching of Peter, in M. R. James, *The Apocryphal New Testament*, Clarendon Press (Oxford, 1926).

Psalms of Solomon, H. E. Ryle and M. R. James, Cambridge University Press (1891).

Resurrection, Book of the, translated by E. A. Wallis Budge from British Museum, Oriental MSS. No. 6804.

Rhythm Against the Jews, Sermon delivered on Palm Sunday by Ephraim the Syrian, fourth century, quoted by Stather Hunt in *Primitive Gospel Sources*, James Clarke & Co. Ltd. (London, 1951).

Robinson, John A. T., Bishop of Woolwich, *Honest to God*, S.C.M. Press (London, 1963).

Schoeps, H. J., *Theologie und Geschichte des Judenchristentums* (Tübingen, 1949).

Schonfield, Hugh J., *The Authentic New Testament* (a modern translation), Dobson Books (London, 1956); *The Jew of Tarsus*, Macdonald & Co. Ltd. (London, 1946); *The Lost Book of the Nativity of John*. T. & T. Clark (Edinburgh, 1929); *Saints Against Caesar*,

Macdonald & Co. Ltd. (London, 1948); *Secrets of the Dead Sea Scrolls*, Valentine, Mitchell (London, 1957); *According to the Hebrews*, Duckworth (London, 1937).

Sidra d'Yahya (Book of John), quoted from G. R. S. Mead, *The Gnostic John the Baptiser*, John M. Watkins (London, 1924).

Suetonius, *The Lives of the Twelve Caesars*, translated by Alexander Thomson and revised by T. Forester, G. Bell & Sons, Ltd. (London, 1911).

Tacitus, Cornelius, *The Annals* and *History*, translated by Arthur Murphy, Jones & Co. (London, 1830).

Talmud (Jerusalem and Babylonian), standard editions and *A Rabbinic Anthology* by C. G. Montefiore and H. Loewe, Macmillan & Co. Ltd. (London, 1938).

Targums, The Targums of Onkelos and Jonathan ben Uzziel on the Pentateuch; with the Fragments of the Jerusalem Targum (Targum of Palestine), translated by J. W. Etheridge, Longmans Green (London, 1865).

Tertullian, *De Spectaculis*, translated by T. R. Glover, Loeb Classical Library, Heinemann and Harvard University Press (1953).

Testaments of the XII Patriarchs, translated by R. H. Charles, Adam and Charles Black (London, 1908).

Thomas, the so-called *Gospel of*, translated by William R. Schoedel, in Grant and Freedman, *The Secret Sayings of Jesus*, Collins (Fontana Books) (London, 1960).

Vermes, G., *The Dead Sea Scrolls in English*, Penguin Books (1962).

Williams, A. Lukyn, *Adversos Judaeos*, Cambridge University Press (1935).

Wisdom of Solomon, in *The Apocrypha of the Old Testament* (Revised Standard Version), Thomas Nelson & Sons Ltd. (1957).

Index